ABORTION

Books by Lawrence Lader

MARGARET SANGER AND THE FIGHT FOR BIRTH CONTROL
1955

THE BOLD BRAHMINS: NEW ENGLAND'S WAR AGAINST SLAVERY, 1831-63
1961

ABORTION
1966

ABORTION

by Lawrence Lader

Beacon Press
BOSTON

FOR MY WIFE
Joan Summers Lader

Contents

I: *The System* 1

II: *A Farce in Phoenix* 10

III: *How Safe Is Hospital Abortion?* 17

IV: *Hospital Abortion: A System of Fear and Privilege* 24

V: *The Doctor's Dilemma* 32

VI: *The Skilled Abortionist* 42

VII: *Methods of Reaching the Skilled Abortionist* 52

VIII: *The Underworld of Abortion* 64

IX: *The Origins of Abortion Chaos* 75

X: *Probing the U.S. Legal Maze* 85

XI: *The Religious Position on Abortion* 94

XII: *Britain's Bourne Case: The Struggle for Reform* 103

XIII: *Storm over New Hampshire* 111

XIV: *The Lessons from European Abortion* 117

XV: *The Lesson of Japan: Abortion and the
Population Crisis* 132

XVI: *A Blueprint for Changing U.S. Abortion Laws* 144

XVII: *The Century of the Wanted Child* 155

XVIII: *Legalized Abortion: The Final Freedom* 167

Notes and Special References 176

Bibliography and Sources 196

Bibliography of Legal Cases 203

Acknowledgments 204

Index 207

ABORTION

I

The System

Abortion is the dread secret of our society. It has been relegated for so long to the darkest corners of fear and mythology that an unwritten compact virtually requires that it remain untouched and undiscussed. As early as 1866, Dr. Horatio R. Storer, author of the first American treatment of the subject, *Criminal Abortion in America,* complained: "So far as this writer is aware, there exists in this or any other language no paper upon the subject at all commensurate with its importance." And yet, a hundred years later, the silence has hardly been dented. In 1962 Mrs. Sherri Finkbine, of Phoenix, Arizona, mother of four children and a prominent television performer, sought a hospital abortion after she had inadvertently taken thalidomide and faced the possibility of a deformed infant. Although there was a universal chorus of horror against the drug itself, hardly a newspaper or pulpit in the country attacked the hypocrisy of the system that denied this mother the right to protect herself and her family, and eventually forced her to seek an abortion in Sweden.

Only a handful of lawmakers have dared to force the problem on public attention. One legislator, a woman, was so vilified that she went into seclusion for months.

In its official organization the medical profession, with few exceptions, has ignored the problem although it is most intimately concerned. A few doctors have occasionally spoken out on their own. But medical critics have mainly confined their opinions to professional journals and conferences, rarely ruffling the conspiracy of silence that has enveloped the subject of abortion in public.

Although abortion remains one of the crucial philosophic, religious, and medical dilemmas of our time, it has become almost too dangerous to grapple with. It touches our most sensitive nerves. For, abortion involves the ultimate control by woman over her own procreativity. In a larger sense, each woman who decides whether or not a fetus shall become a child affects the population charts—a process strikingly evident in Japan, where legalized abortion has cut the birth rate in half.

In addition, abortion forces us to face absolutes that intrude on religious dogma. The Roman Catholic Church, for example, holds the human soul inviolate from the moment of conception. For many other faiths, it involves the sanctity of life to varying degrees. All these issues are intertwined. Religious dogma becomes political where it has the power to make its votes felt. Medical practice depends on law. The entire issue is wrapped in such fundamental controversy that society has adopted a typical attitude: it ignores it.

The impact of abortion, however, has become far too pressing to be evaded any longer. In 1957 a conference of experts sponsored by the Planned Parenthood Federation estimated that U.S. abortions could run from 200,000 to 1,200,000 annually. Dr. Christopher Tietze, of the National Committee on Maternal Health, who headed this statistical panel, considers 1,200,000 the most accurate figure today. Dr. Harold Rosen, of the Johns Hopkins University Hospital, editor of an authoritative study, *Therapeutic Abortion,* recently raised the estimate to 1,500,000.

Such estimates, of course, are complicated by the wall of secrecy that has been so carefully maintained. Still, an earlier birth-control-clinic study revealed a ratio of 1 abortion to 3.6 live births. Although dated and based on urban population, this ratio nearly describes the figure reached by the Planned Parenthood conference: 1,123,611 abortions in 1964.[1]

Further corroboration comes from the 1958 study of the late Dr. Alfred C. Kinsey and his associates at Indiana University's Institute of Sex Research. In the segment of the population represented by the Kinsey sample of urban, white, educated women, between one fifth and one fourth of all pregnancies are terminated by abortion.

Among wives in the sixteen- to twenty-year-old age group, the Kinsey sample shows that 28 per cent of all conceptions end in abortion. With separated, divorced, and widowed women of all ages, the abortion rate soars to 79 per cent.[2]

When so great a number of women each year are forced into the hands of private abortionists, the result is a shocking toll in injuries and fatalities. One recent study at the University of California's School of Public Health estimated 5,000 to 10,000 abortion deaths annually. Dr. Tietze places the figure nearer 1,000. Yet almost half of all childbearing deaths in New York City are attributed to abortion alone.[3]

No study, moreover, could begin to measure the physical and psychological injury inflicted on women by quack abortionists, often virtual butchers. Nor could it encompass the damage women inflict on themselves in attempts at self-abortion.

Into the emergency rooms of our city hospitals flow the grim products of this system:

A thirty-four-year-old mother of four, admitted eleven days after she had paid an abortionist $70 for injection of a soap solution—dead seventeen days later.

A twenty-nine-year-old mother of three, admitted four days after she had injected herself with a detergent solution—dead on the ninth day.

One Boston city hospital admits an average of 600 such cases annually; a New York hospital in Harlem about 300. One study of seventy-seven cases of "soap intoxication," as doctors call the medical effect of these abortions, revealed forty-three fatalities.

At the root of this tragic system lies the inflexibility of our state laws. Abortion can be divided into two categories: legal and illegal. Forty-two states consider abortion legal on only one ground: to save the life of the mother. These are known in the medical profession as "therapeutic abortions," but the name is misleading, since many abortions performed outside the law are equally therapeutic. "Hospital abortions" would therefore seem more accurate.*

The unfortunate result of these laws is that only about 8,000 women a year qualify for legal, hospital abortions. (The figure may be slightly higher in 1964, owing to the German measles epidemic.) As the doctor or hospital board must decide what factors endanger a mother's life, and as they are influenced by religious and political

---

* Alabama, Oregon, and Washington, D.C., allow abortion to preserve life or health; Colorado and New Mexico to prevent serious or permanent bodily injury; Maryland to secure safety. Massachusetts, New Jersey, and Pennsylvania prohibit "unlawful" abortions, with no further clarification.

pressures, hospital status-seeking, and a complexity of other issues including fear, their decisions generally favor the least controversial cases.[4]

A hospital abortion is as safe and simple as any other operation, requiring fifteen or twenty minutes of surgery and rarely keeping a patient hospitalized more than overnight. Yet a million or more women each year, automatically excluded from the realm of legality, are forced to seek out a private abortionist, to attempt abortion on themselves, or, if they are unmarried, to bear the child illegitimately. They may well wonder what bitter twist of medical logic, legal hair-splitting, or legislative inhumanity denied them the right to a safe and sacrosanct hospital abortion.

"The whole underground movement of abortion with its butchering quacks, midwives and incompetent doctors is the result of these statutes now in force," concluded *Southern Medicine and Surgery* more than two decades ago.

No state law, for example, allows abortion for what would seem the most justifiable reason by any standard of medicine, morality, or social need: the victim of rape.

In a noted Colorado case in 1955, Mrs. Margie Anson, a twenty-seven-year-old mother, returned to her Denver home after visiting her husband at the hospital. Their two-year-old daughter was staying with friends. Hearing footsteps outside her door, Mrs. Anson tried to close the snap lock, but an intruder, later identified as a 220-pound guard from a nearby Air Force base, had already forced his way into the room. He gagged her, tied her hands, and, despite her violent struggles, attacked her and fled.

Finally attracting a neighbor's attention, Mrs. Anson was taken to the hospital, where physicians verified the rape and treated her. Her own doctor subsequently cared for her injuries, and made tests which confirmed pregnancy.

Captured soon afterward, the attacker confessed the rape of two other women in addition to Mrs. Anson and attempts on three more. In January 1956 he was sentenced to between forty and eighty years at hard labor in the state penitentiary.

The Ansons knew they could never give a child of violence the same love and care as they had their own daughter. The only solution seemed to be abortion. Although Colorado law, broader than that of forty-two other states, allows abortion to "prevent serious or permanent bodily injury," which Mrs. Anson's ordeal might well have caused, she could find no hospital to help her. Appealing to the district attorney, she was told: "You can't cover up one crime with another."

Friends urged her to find a secret abortionist. But the Ansons, both deeply religious, instinctively rejected an alternative which seemed to them to magnify the brutality of the law. They decided instead to bring the child to term and offer it for adoption. "It's inhuman to expect a woman to suffer through such an ordeal," Mrs. Anson concluded.

The victim of incest, often a mere child, becomes part of an even more repellant tragedy. Not only may her emotional and physical health suffer from being forced to carry the pregnancy to term; an incestuous offspring may be considered unfit for adoption by welfare agencies. Yet no state law allows abortion on the basis of incest.

When Dr. Alan Guttmacher, now president of the Planned Parenthood Federation, was in charge of the obstetrical outpatient department at Johns Hopkins years back, the Children's Aid Society brought him a fourteen-year-old girl. She had been impregnated by her father, who had already been convicted for the crime. The Society asked that she be saved further suffering and be given an abortion.

Guttmacher, strongly in favor of it, asked permission of the Chief of Obstetrics. He was sympathetic but afraid that the law could not be stretched enough to cover the case. Guttmacher argued that even if the mother's safety was not immediately imperiled, she could suffer either emotionally or physically years hence. The Chief finally agreed to the operation if the Baltimore district attorney would sign such a legal interpretation.

At the courthouse, this official told Guttmacher: "Mine is an elective office, and I would be insane to state in writing that I authorize the Hopkins to break a state law." But he assured Guttmacher that if the abortion was performed, he would simply ignore it.

This evasion failed to satisfy Guttmacher's superior, and the abortion was rejected. Six months later the girl bore her father's child.

When a committee of the California State Assembly was considering a new abortion bill, a woman wrote: "I was raped by two men that forced my car over to the side of the road in 1960. I had to have the baby because no doctor would help me with an abortion. *Please* help other unfortunate women that this might happen to." Such pleas have been fruitless. Neither California nor any other state considering abortion reform has altered its laws to provide for rape or incest.

To complicate matters further, hospitals carry sick and diseased women to term without halting their pregnancies.

"It's like a nightmarish game of chance," protests a thirty-four-year-old mother of three who has been a cardiac patient for two years. "My last pregnancy was a mistake. My husband and I knew that another child would strain me to the limit. My doctor said I was a clear case for hospital abortion. But the hospital board turned me down, telling my doctor, 'She's got two servants to take care of her family, and a comfortable apartment. Another child will not directly imperil her life as the law provides.' What do I have to do to prove my point, drop dead a week after the child is born? Isn't it enough that another child could threaten my life a year or two from now?"

Even women afflicted with leukemia, lung cancer, tumors, or crippling paralysis may be greeted with the rationalization that another pregnancy will not adversely affect the course of their disease. Such interpretations of the law have led physicians like Dr. Guttmacher to plead for "the type of care which views the patient as a total human organism rather than a brood sow."

The absurdity of the system undoubtedly reached its peak during the 1963–64 epidemic of German measles. This disease, when contracted in early pregnancy, frequently causes fetal damage, resulting in a severely deformed child. Few mothers care to risk odds running as high as 50 per cent, and most conscientious physicians recommend a hospital abortion. "So many applications were coming in during the epidemic that hospitals began to question letters of authorization from the patient's physician," reports Dr. Carl Goldmark, Jr., president of the New York County Medical Society. "It wasn't enough that the doctor verified the disease. Many hospitals went to the extreme of requiring that an inspector from the Board of Health rush over to the patient's home to witness a measles rash that often disappears in a day."

With hospital abortions denied to such medical cases, applications based on social and economic factors are virtually ignored. "A woman well into her forties, with several children well along in school, makes an appointment," recalls Reverend Peter S. Raible, minister of the University Unitarian Church of Seattle. "She tells me that her marriage has been rocky for years, but lately she has turned to a career of her own, and for the first time in many years feels happy and sees hope in her marriage. Inadvertently, she is pregnant. Neither she nor her husband wants the child; it will end her career for some years; it will end her marriage."

A London mother writes: "I'm a woman of forty-nine years of age, nearly fifty. My husband has accidentally made me pregnant . . . and I feel like committing suicide. We can't afford to bring up another child at our time of life, and I feel too tired to go through with it. . . . I feel like a rat that's caught in a trap and there's no escape."

The law is equally ruthless to the single girl, who, contrary to what is popularly believed, forms only a small segment of abortion applicants compared with married women. But it is a particularly bedeviled segment. "Our society says to her, 'If you have the abortion, you'll go to hell,'" observes Dr. Sophia Kleegman, director of Bellevue Hospital's Infertility Clinic in New York. "On the other hand, 'If you have the baby, we'll make it hellish for both of you.'"

In many cases, abortion involves a frightening struggle between a woman's desire to create and her opposition to this specific pregnancy. Once she has decided on abortion, however, almost nothing can block her, neither obstacles of law, medical rejection, cost, physical pain, even the chance of injury or death. "So powerful and universal is the instinct for motherhood, it is evidence of the desperate state of mind of these women that they so willingly face self-destruction in their efforts to terminate a pregnancy," declares Dr. Frederick J. Taussig, author of the first authoritative study of abortion in 1936.

Not even the rigid dogma of the Roman Catholic Church, which forbids even hospital abortions, with one small exception to be discussed later, can deter its communicants. Four studies show that Catholics comprise over 20 per cent of all abortion patients, almost equal to the Catholic ratio of about 25 per cent in the total U.S. population.[5]

The search for a secret abortionist has become a common and sordid American phenomenon. Consider the case of Sally S., who became pregnant just before her husband deserted her, and had to hold on to her job to support two children:

> "During the two years my marriage had been breaking up, I consulted a psychiatrist when I could afford it, and now sought his help on abortion. He told me that his hospital demanded that a psychiatric abortion must have had previous hospitalized treatment there, but that he might be able to get me into a small

hospital if I was a severe suicide risk. I told him another child would be a terrible emotional blow even if my husband was located and accepted some responsibility. Further, I'd be virtually penniless without my job. But I loved my children too much to consider suicide seriously. Sympathetically, he admitted he could do nothing."

Then Sally began the tortured search.

"I was pushed into an underworld I never imagined. I had to crawl through the filth of a system society had forced on me. For weeks I called doctors, nurses, friends—anyone who could offer the slightest clue to an abortionist, and got on my knees to beg for help. Finally I was given a phone number in a Long Island suburb, and made an evening appointment. It was a decrepit, decaying house. An old man opened the door. His shirt was stained. He spoke almost incoherently. Everything about him and his house disgusted me. 'You'll stay and rest overnight after the operation,' he explained, starting to paw my arm. I knew I couldn't stand it another second. I turned and ran."

The grim search, the phone calls, the referrals from friends to friends of friends, all began again. Two weeks later she got another clue: a young Spanish-speaking doctor in general practice on Manhattan's upper West side. He wanted $650, and it took another week to borrow it in bits and pieces.

"This time I was luckier. His office was in an old apartment, but reasonably clean. He was nervous, admitting later he thought I was a policewoman, and broke two appointments before doing the operation. It's unbelievable that laws can turn women into outcasts and put them through such agony. No one could ever convince me I should bear a fatherless child I couldn't take care of and might have to give for adoption. There can't be any justice in exposing women to such degradation and danger."

It is clear that such a system represents the most perverted form of morality. For that small group granted hospital abortions—an elite generally composed of private patients, educated, fairly wealthy, and backed by influential doctors—it creates what amounts to a "law for the rich." Moreover, it produces open disdain for the law among large segments of society, including some legal authorities and police who protect abortionists. Abortion laws, as a result, are among the most broken laws on the books.

In light of these facts, it seems incredible that women have accepted the system so long, and that so few have cried out against the intrusion of the state into the most intimate and crucial medical decision of a woman's life. "For a state to force a woman to bear a child against her will is outrageous," observes Dorothy Kenyon, former municipal-court judge of New York.

One of the few religious leaders to attack the crux of the problem, Rabbi Israel Margolies, of New York's Beth Am Temple, demands: "Is it not time that we matured sufficiently as people to assert once and for all that the sexual relations of human beings and their reproductive consequences are not the business of the state, but rather free decisions to be made by free people?"

A Farce in Phoenix

In July 1962 Mrs. Sherri Finkbine made an agonizing decision: to abort a two-month-old fetus that might be deformed as a result of the thalidomide drug. Both her doctor and the medical board of her Phoenix hospital ruled the abortion a medical necessity within Arizona law. It was scheduled to be performed in two days. Then a fluke of publicity suddenly turned a medical diagnosis into a public carnival of prejudice and hysteria.

The Finkbine case was undoubtedly the first hospital-approved abortion ever subjected to national debate. The results could not have been more dismal. Mrs. Finkbine, whose agony was minutely detailed by the communications media, suffered no more than the medical profession, which had evaded its responsibility when put to open test. What should have been a medical decision became, in essence, the plaything of pressure groups.

Sherri Finkbine started her ordeal by accident. Thirty years old, the mother of four children, she was then conducting a nursery-school program on a Phoenix television station. Her husband, Bob, taught history in the suburban school system. "I think he'd like twenty children of his own," she once quipped.

Early in her pregnancy that May, she suddenly developed pains in her chest. Her doctor, attributing them to nervous tension, prescribed tranquillizers. When the bottle ran out, she remembered her husband's pills. The previous summer, while guiding a tour of sixty teen-agers in Europe, he had suffered from exhaustion, and a London doctor had ordered tranquillizers. Needing only a few pills, he had tucked the extra bottles in his bag and brought them back to Phoenix. Sherri, unfortunately, found them in the medicine chest, and took thirty or forty pills through June and July.

It was not until mid-July that she began to worry. The Arizona *Republic* carried a news item on the dangers of taking thalidomide, first referring to the drug as a sleeping pill and, in a subsequent edition, as a tranquillizer. Promptly Sherri phoned her doctor and brought him the bottle. He cabled the London drug store, and thereby ascertained that she had been taking pure thalidomide.

The drug had already produced the greatest "prescription" disaster in medical annals, and left a trail of horror across Europe. Taken in early months of pregnancy, it damaged the embryo and caused a malformation called phocomelia. Infants born with this perversion of nature almost always had flaps instead of arms, or no arms at all. Often they were born with shortened thigh bones and twisted legs. Sometimes an ear was missing, the nose flattened, the face permanently paralyzed.

In West Germany, where 15,000,000 thalidomide tablets had been consumed each month, 4,000 to 6,000 deformed infants were traced to the drug. At least 1,000 other cases appeared in Britain and on the Continent.

Fortunately, owing to the persistence of Dr. Frances Kelsey, of the U.S. Food and Drug Administration, thalidomide was not manufactured here, and only a handful of test samples from abroad were distributed. Still, one New York mother who took them gave birth to a deformed baby, which died forty-one minutes later, ironically on the same day the Finkbine case reached its crisis.

Few parents could have faced a more terrifying decision than the Finkbines. "The thought of an abortion left me limp with fear," Sherri stated. "Yet what if we had the baby and he was born without arms or legs, or, as some in Europe, with *neither* arms nor legs—a human vegetable? His life—or hers—would be a living death. Did we have a right to condemn a human being to that kind of existence? Already I had to fight for self-control. I looked ahead to nearly seven months more of pregnancy, of worrying and fearing, of knowing and yet not knowing, and then finally giving birth to—what? It was like standing at the edge of a great black pit."

They went to their doctor's office and he quietly explained the odds: a fifty per cent chance of giving birth to a deformed baby. "When you know you can have normal, healthy children, it's ridiculous to play around with such odds," the doctor insisted. "If you were my own wife, Sherri, my recommendation would be the same."

He showed them pictures of thalidomide babies from medical journals—most with only tiny flaps of flesh instead of limbs, one with only a head and a torso. "When I saw those pictures, all doubt was instantly and forever swept from my mind," she recalls.

The doctor asked them to write a formal letter of application for a legal abortion to Good Samaritan Hospital. On Monday the abortion board, consisting of three doctors, approved the application. Sherri was to enter the hospital on Wednesday and have the operation the next day.

Like that of forty-two other states, Arizona law allows hospital abortion in only one instance: to save the life of the mother. Although hospital boards maintain strict secrecy regarding their decisions, it is obvious that approval was granted Sherri on psychiatric grounds. In the case of a mother faced with a deformed fetus no matter what the cause, physicians must judge the impact of such deformity on the mother's life. In the event that it may lead to a complete mental and physical breakdown, the usual decision is for abortion.

Similar cases were already common in Phoenix. "All hospitals in Arizona except Roman Catholic perform therapeutic abortions routinely," reports the administrator of one Arizona hospital, "and psychological factors are considered sufficient for a consultation that justifies abortion." Like 8,000 or more hospital abortions annually in the country, Sherri Finkbine's would have passed unnoticed but for an impulsive phone call.

On Sunday morning Sherri telephoned an acquaintance, the managing editor of the Arizona *Republic,* and, finding him out, told his wife about her case. Later the medical editor called her back. She did not want her story used, only the fact that a Phoenix woman had become a victim of thalidomide, only enough to warn other women. She insisted on anonymity, and the editor agreed.

On Monday the *Republic* carried a front-page feature story: DRUG CAUSING DEFORMED INFANTS MAY COST WOMAN HER BABY HERE— "Perhaps others who may not have read that story and who have some of these European tranquillizers available will read my story and throw the drugs away." Although Mrs. Finkbine's case was given more prominence than she had wanted, her identity was thoroughly cloaked.

Neither the Finkbines nor the editors, however, realized the sen-

sational impact of the story. Fear of thalidomide had already stirred
the world. Now, in the context of a mother's decision to have an abortion, the case was tailor-made for heart-rending exploitation. Similar
headlines began to appear in other Arizona papers, and then the wire
services and radio and television networks moved in on Phoenix and
began transmitting the story across the nation and overseas.

In Phoenix itself, the impending abortion aroused the indignation
of the Roman Catholic and Fundamentalist clergy. "So you're blind in
one eye," a Catholic spokesman was quoted by a reporter. "Does that
give anybody the right to kill you?" Letters started pouring in to the
Phoenix papers—"most of them from religious nuts," an editor stated.

Supporting the abortion, the late Right Reverend Arthur Kinsolving, Bishop of the Episcopal Church in Arizona, called it "proper
under these circumstances." Pastor Lewi Pethrus, a prominent Baptist, approved it because of the threat of thalidomide to the child.
Rabbi Albert Plotkin, a local Jewish leader, considered the abortion
"a merciful act of justice." In New York, Rabbi Margolies announced:
"There is no greater sin than to condemn a helpless infant to the
twilight world of living death."

The furor was now compounded by a legal obstacle. The *Republic* interviewed County Attorney Charles N. Ronan, "active in Roman
Catholic circles," as the paper described him, and father of nine
children. "Ronan said his office would have to prosecute if a complaint were filed in the case of the Phoenix woman," the *Republic*
stated. "There were just enough fanatics in town to make sure a complaint would be filed," a local reporter concluded privately.

Faced with the threat of defending the abortion's legality in
court, the hospital's executive board called an emergency meeting.
Owing to the "controversy and emotionalism involved" and the "prec-
edent-setting" nature of the case, the board decided to postpone the
operation.

Ironically, it was Sherri's own phone call that had triggered both
the publicity outburst and, finally, legal complications. Some critics
would later brand her as a publicity-seeker.

Admittedly, her phone call lacked caution and foresight. Still,
not only was her motive blameless; it is hard to imagine that she
would purposely seek publicity when it might ruin her chances for the
operation and even jeopardize her job. As she insisted afterward: "Is
publicity about an abortion best calculated to advance the career of
a woman conducting a TV nursery-school show for children?" The

publicity, in fact, caused her eventual removal from the show as well as blocking the abortion in Phoenix.

Perhaps the underlying significance of Sherri's phone call was that it led to a chain of events exposing the hypocrisy of the abortion system.

Since, under law, the medical profession must decide what factors threaten a mother's life, only physicians or a hospital board can make this decision. And as a medical decision, religious or political pressure must never influence it. Nor must public debate. An abortion which is deemed medically essential on Monday should carry the same medical necessity on Tuesday, no matter what legal or other threats have arisen. By postponing the Finkbine operation, therefore, the hospital was virtually admitting that a medical decision made in privacy could become a different medical case only a day later in the glare of publicity.

Then the hospital showed an even stranger evasion of responsibility when it filed suit in Superior Court, naming as defendants the State of Arizona, the State Attorney General, and the County Attorney. What the hospital's lawyers hoped to gain was a declaratory judgment, making the court decide whether the abortion was legal.

Thus, in the course of this event, Sherri's name was publicly revealed for the first time, intensifying pressure on an already distraught household. Headlines now read: ABORTION CASE MOTHER TV STAR HERE. "Reporters and photographers swarmed down upon us, and the telephone kept up a ceaseless clamor," she recalls. "Newsmen called us from all over the country; and when they couldn't get through on our phone, they called our neighbors." When Sherri finally felt "as if I'd blow apart," her doctor and lawyers hid her away in a private hospital room, cut off from telephones and visitors.

At a court hearing jammed by reporters, the County Attorney argued that since there was no justifiable controversy between the hospital and Mrs. Finkbine, and the State, the case should be dismissed. The judge agreed, stating: "Defendants have avowed in open court that if the facts are as stated by the plaintiffs, then there is no controversy whatever, and that Mrs. Finkbine should proceed with her operation. . . ."

The hospital, thus failing to shift its responsibility to the court, held a final meeting of its board and its lawyers, at which it was decided to cancel the operation.

Actually, the main stumbling block, as far as can be learned, came from the doctors themselves. No individual obstetrician wanted to incur the blast of publicity that might seriously damage his career if he performed the abortion.

While such caution is understandable in an individual doctor, it hardly explains the failure of the hospital as a corporate body to stand up to its responsibility. The original decision having been made by an anonymous abortion board, the operation could very well have been performed for the record by the obstetrical staff, and the hospital could have supported it unflinchingly. If the case had come to court, the hospital and its staff would have borne collective responsibility.

In fact, the hospital's timidity is all the more indefensible when examined against the practical risk. Despite the number of hospital abortions in recent decades—a figure approximating 200,000—legal researchers have never uncovered a single case of a reputable doctor in a reputable hospital convicted of breaking the abortion law.

Thus, the likelihood of a court's declaring the decision of a skilled hospital board illegal was infinitely remote.

With time running out (abortion being considered safest when performed in the first three months of pregnancy), the Finkbines despaired of finding another hospital, even in another state, where doctors could come to a quick and favorable decision. The logical step was to seek an abortion in a foreign country whose laws clearly included the medical indications of Sherri's case.

Hurriedly the Finkbines boarded a plane to Los Angeles, Sherri disguised in wig and dark glasses to avoid the inescapable pack of reporters. At Los Angeles they rushed to the Japanese consulate, but an official, possibly fearing notoriety for his country, refused to issue a visa until Tokyo approved. It could take a week; even then the visa could be rejected. "Suddenly I felt caught in a frenzy of frustration, impatience, and mounting terror," Sherri recalls.

They immediately booked seats on a transpolar airline to Sweden, which required no visa and where legal abortion was granted for a wide range of medical and humane causes. Approval, however, was far from automatic. Sherri had to go through the standard series of interviews and tests with gynecologists, psychiatrists, social workers, and a radiologist, a process taking almost two weeks.

"Now a seeming eternity of waiting stretched before us," Bob Finkbine wrote later. "The phone looked nine feet tall. It hung there in the corner, conveying a feeling of a bomb about to explode. It rang.

I didn't move. I tried to wish the ring away. It rang a second time and suddenly the doctor was telling me the news: the board had given its approval. We were to have Sherri at Karolinksa Hospital within two hours."

When she came out of anesthesia, Bob was standing by her bed. "Did you hear what the doctor said?" he asked. "The baby was deformed." He repeated it over and over again to make sure that she understood.

"It was not a baby," the doctor told her. "You must think of it as an abnormal growth within you."

The most disturbing outcome of the case was that religious and political passions became inextricably entwined with the practice of medicine. The case took place in an election year, and Phoenix has a sizable bloc of Catholic voters, particularly of Latin descent. Political exploitation helped stir religious prejudices. Not only the hospital but also the Finkbines personally were subjected to a barrage of threats. Organized groups attempted to remove both Sherri and Bob from their jobs. A few students at Bob's school indulged in jibes and insults; pressure was applied even to the principal. The Finkbines' mail was filled with accusations of "murder." In Indiana twenty-six people signed a telegram to the King of Sweden, demanding he prohibit the abortion. In Rome, after the operation, the Vatican radio announced: "A crime has been committed."

By surrendering to legal threats and failing to perform the abortion, Good Samaritan Hospital acknowledged the power of religious and political pressure. By choosing to avoid a court trial, it not only weakened physicians' rights under the law, but also lost the opportunity to test the law before judge and jury. Such a test has long been needed in the United States. When a similar test was made in England in 1938, it produced a key court decision that significantly broadened British abortion law. Instead of progress in America, however, the Finkbine case produced only flight and refuge in another land.

At least the case would end on two bright notes. Although Sherri lost her nursery-school show, the television station loyally kept her on the staff, assigned to another program. And a little over two years later, in February 1965, Sherri gave birth to her fifth child, a healthy girl.

III

How Safe Is Hospital Abortion?

Abortion has developed an unfortunate mythology of fear. Since the public rarely differentiates between hospital abortion and underworld abortion, injuries and deaths ascribed to hack abortionists have obscured the phenomenal safety record achieved by the medical profession. Actually, hospital abortion has become one of the simplest and safest of all operations in recent decades.

Abortion deaths, used as the first measurement of safety, are virtually unknown today in U.S. hospitals. However, as only about 8,000 hospital abortions are performed annually in this country, the sample is hardly large enough to reflect this safety record. The best statistical evidence comes from Eastern Europe, where, despite the large number of legal abortions, fatalities have practically been eliminated.

In Czechoslovakia, for example, not a single death was reported in 140,000 legal abortions (1963–64); in Hungary, only two deaths in 358,000 abortions (1963–64); in Yugoslavia, less than five per 100,000 (1961).[1]

The fatality rate for legal abortions in Scandinavia is slightly higher because a slow system of committee approval and permissive laws push many abortions past the three-month .limit imposed in Eastern Europe.[2]

Such safety records are all the more impressive when compared with that of a routine operation like tonsillectomy, which claims seventeen deaths per 100,000 in the United States. Further, as Dr. Tietze points out, the risks of abortion are "only one-sixth to one-tenth as dangerous" as those attending pregnancy and childbirth. In other words, it is safer to have a hospital abortion than to have a baby.

Abortion, in medical terms, is the induced termination of pregnancy before the normal fetus has attained viability, or the capacity for life outside the womb. The word applies only to *intentional* termination as opposed to *spontaneous* abortion, which occurs when fetal growth is impaired, and is frequently referred to as *miscarriage*.[3]

The standard technique of hospital abortion is known as dilatation and curettage, or a "D and C." The patient, anesthetized to eliminate all pain, is protected against infection by antibiotics and rarely kept in the hospital more than one night.

First, the cervix is dilated or stretched to permit the use of a curette. This is done by passing a series of increasingly larger dilators into the mouth of the womb.

With his curette, a tiny metal instrument shaped like a rake, the surgeon then removes the embryo, alternating curette and forceps until the uterus is clean.

In the rare cases when the cervix cannot be stretched sufficiently by dilators, the uterine cavity is packed with thin strips of gauze, which cause contractions and dilate the cervix in about twelve hours. Surgery is then performed in the usual manner.

If an abortion has to be performed after three months of pregnancy, the standard technique is a hysterotomy, or miniature cesarian, requiring a small, longitudinal incision in the lower abdomen. However, a new technique has proved so efficient and safe when performed by skilled obstetricians, it may soon replace hysterotomy.

After the skin is anesthetized to eliminate pain, some amniotic fluid, the fluid around the embryo, is withdrawn by needle and replaced with the same amount of concentrated salt solution. Contractions and the onset of labor usually begin in about twenty or twenty-five hours. Shortly afterward, the fetus is expelled.[4]

The cost of a D and C is usually $100 to $200—$300 to $500 for wealthier private patients in major cities. A hysterotomy averages about $200, and up to $500 for wealthier patients. The salt-solution technique is the same price as a D and C.

An even newer method of abortion, developed in the Soviet Union and Eastern Europe, is a simple apparatus which performs dilatation by electro-vibration and empties the uterus by negative-pressure vacuum. Of 600 cases reported from Russia in 1963, almost 97 per cent were successful, with only minor complications in about

3 per cent. The great advantage of this method is that it reduces risk and injury to a minimum, checks blood loss, and can be performed in less than two minutes. Dr. Tietze, who observed the vacuum method at a clinic that had already used it in 1,700 abortions, calls it "particularly impressive."

In addition to the low death rate, the safety of hospital abortion must be judged by a second criterion—the incidence of physical complications after the operation. Although the medical profession has long been uncertain about the extent of such complications, five major studies in the last decade now prove that a woman's physical health, fertility, and related factors are rarely affected.

In Sweden, Dr. Jan Lindahl followed 1,013 cases with complete medical check-ups over a period of one to five years after abortion. Only one death could be associated with the operation. Immediate serious complications were found in only 3.6 per cent of all cases. Impaired function of the Fallopian tubes, for example, appeared in less than 1.6 per cent of all cases. As to a disposition to spontaneous abortion or premature delivery, Lindahl found that the operation "had not demonstrably resulted in any increased disposition." Even these figures, and all studies cited, must be considered higher than the average, since they include many women with impaired health prior to the operation.[5]

In Norway, Dr. Per Kolstad made an intensive investigation of 712 cases after abortion. Not one death resulted from the operation. Although 10.3 per cent showed some post-operative complications, only 2.7 per cent could be considered serious.

Kolstad concluded that the frequency and degree of all complications were no more than those after childbirth. Menstrual disorders and frigidity, for example, appeared in less than 1 per cent of the women. "Induced abortion is a comparatively harmless operation during the first twelve weeks of pregnancy," he stated.[6]

In Czechoslovakia in 1963, Dr. Anton Černoch found inflammatory complications in only about 2 per cent of all cases, and post-operative injuries in less than 1 per cent.

The only comparable American study was made by the Kinsey group at Indiana University's Institute of Sex Research. Although their sample was small—about 440 cases—the results were strikingly similar to those in Scandinavia. Only 6.6 per cent had severe, 6.8 per cent moderate, and 3.2 per cent mild complications.

The Kinsey group extended their research to the possible complications arising from abortion before marriage. "Again it would seem that a premarital induced abortion," concluded the report, "did not affect adversely the sexual adjustment in marriage as measured by the rate of orgasm in the first year of marital intercourse."

Of all the physical complications that may attend abortion, none demands more careful analysis than the possible impairment of fertility or the ability to produce live births.

Lindahl, finding only one case of impaired fertility out of 1,013, was led to conclude that abortion presented "little risk of persistent impairment of fertility." As to future births: "It could not be shown that the operation had caused an increased disposition to complications. . . ."

In Sweden, Dr. Per Arén reported 1.5 to 2.6 per cent showing a tendency to premature birth and sterility; in Norway, Kolstad found 3.4 per cent indicating possible sterility.[7]

Examining 2,000 women five years after abortion, Dr. K.–H. Mehlan, of the University of Rostock, found sterility in only 2 per cent. "While many physicians cling to the belief that induced abortion, even under the most favorable conditions, often produces sterility, this outcome, in fact, is comparatively rare," he states.

According to the Kinsey study, women with abortions had a live birth rate of 15.6 per thousand, just a shade lower than the 16.8 for those without abortions. "I can report that our data do not indicate that induced abortions lead to an undue percentage of sterility," Dr. Kinsey announced.[8]

Summing up the expert opinion on physical complications of abortion, Dr. Guttmacher, long a prominent gynecologist before becoming president of Planned Parenthood, states: "We feel that if the operation is properly performed so that no infection or laceration of the cervix results, it will have no effect on either the health of the woman or her reproductive future."

The safety of hospital abortion must also be judged by a third standard—the incidence of psychiatric after-effects. Medical literature has long been filled with warnings of the emotional scars, depressions, and psychoses that can be caused by the operation. One psychiatrist has insisted that women are "traumatized by the act"; another, that "abortion inevitably arouses an unconscious sense of guilt"; a third, that women at menopause suffer "torment over an abortion performed years before."[9]

The most puzzling aspect of this traditional belief in psychiatric damage is that it centers around a limited number of cases, passed down through the literature. The tradition, moreover, stems from no exhaustive studies, and "there has been no statistical documentation of such sequelae," stresses Dr. Jerome M. Kummer, associate clinical professor of psychiatry at the University of California. Kummer's views on the subject appear in his paper "Post-Abortion Psychiatric Illness—A Myth?"[1]

An increasing number of prominent American psychiatrists now dispute the past emphasis on psychic damage resulting from abortion. "We have seen in our clinic a number of patients who admitted to as many as 15 or 20 self-induced abortions without any evidence of guilt or serious depression consequent to these acts," states Dr. Arthur Mandy, of the Henry Phipps Psychiatric Clinic at Johns Hopkins.

"I have never encountered an instance of emotional disturbance following a therapeutic interruption of pregnancy in the 100 to 150 cases in which I have participated," adds Dr. Robert W. Laidlaw, chief of psychiatry at New York's Roosevelt Hospital. "I believe that when a patient is properly prepared through unhurried and repeated discussions, she can be made to feel that the problem is a medical one and that the decision has been taken out of her hands."

With thousands of cases of hospital abortion processed through government boards in the last decade, Scandinavian and Eastern European countries are the first to present extensive statistical evidence on psychiatric after-effects. Four major studies prove that the dangers have not only been exaggerated, but are statistically insignificant.

The most exhaustive research project was conducted in Sweden by Dr. Martin Ekblad, who interviewed and examined 479 women at least twenty-two to thirty months after abortion. Ekblad concluded:

75 per cent had no self-reproach
14 per cent had mild self-reproach
11 per cent had serious self-reproach

Only 1 per cent were psychiatrically handicapped in their ability to work. Few had to seek medical help afterward. The majority were "satisfied with and grateful for the operation, and had not had any depression or demonstrable impairment of their psychic health through the abortion," Ekblad emphasizes.

This statistical evidence becomes all the more impressive in light of the fact that many of the women had already suffered deep anxieties *before* abortion. In what Ekblad calls the "normal" group, 6 per cent experienced serious self-reproach, compared to 11 per cent of the total group. Many psychic problems, therefore, cannot be attributed to abortion alone. Or, as Ekblad puts it: "The greater the psychiatric indications for a legal abortion are, the greater is also the risk of unfavorable psychic sequelae after the operation."

Ekblad's study contains these additional remarks:

1. No connection exists between the age of the woman at abortion and incidence of self-reproach.

2. No connection exists between intellectual level and incidence of self-reproach.

3. There is no statistical difference in self-reproach between a childless woman and a woman with a child before abortion.

4. The woman who has not made the decision for abortion completely on her own, or has been deserted at the time of abortion by her male partner, faces the greatest risk of self-reproach.[2]

Kolstad's study shows even less psychic damage than Ekblad's. Of 134 cases examined after abortion:

82.8 per cent were glad without reserve

9.8 per cent were satisfied but doubtful

3.7 per cent were not happy but knew abortion necessary

3.7 per cent were repentant

In his study of 243 East German cases, Mehlan found that only 10 per cent expressed regret over their abortions.[3]

In a study of thirty-four women, statistically representative of over 400 who had undergone abortion at an Oslo clinic, only two showed what Dr. Bard Brekke called "very slight reaction": "just a feeling of distress and embarrassment that lasted for a few weeks and then disappeared."[4]

Kummer adds one further report from Denmark: "*No* psychiatric after-effects of the degree in question among approximately 30,000 legal abortions performed over the past fifteen years," the chief psychiatrist of the Copenhagen Mothers' Aid Society told Dr. Kummer in an interview.

In contrast to this weight of evidence against psychic damage, one small Swedish study, conducted by a social worker in 1951, reports 10 cases of impaired mental health out of 84 women undergoing abortion. (But 8 of the 10 were aborted for psychiatric indications.)[5]

As the first major American research study, the Kinsey report found that less than 10 per cent of all women admitting abortions suffered any psychological harm.

In another U.S. study, Kummer interviewed 32 psychiatrists, all but 4 associated with the University of California, Los Angeles School of Medicine. His results: "75 per cent of the psychiatrists had never encountered any moderate to severe psychiatric sequelae of abortion. The remaining 25 per cent encountered such sequelae only rarely."

From such conclusive evidence, it seems obvious that psychic damage from abortion is mainly the product of myth. In fact, a few experts are beginning to realize that much of the harm that can be substantiated is less the result of internal trauma than of guilt imposed on the women by society. Even hospital abortions in the United States are cloaked with secrecy and taboos. Few women would dare to admit socially that their physician had prescribed an abortion, for the very act, no matter how medically essential, seems to breed prejudice and ostracism. The incidence of emotional disturbance is thus intimately bound up with the beliefs of the society in which the woman lives.

By way of contrast, anthropological studies of primitive cultures show that abortion is so commonplace that "exceptions to the practice are noteworthy phenomena" and guilt and psychic damage virtually unknown. The Mataco, for example, a South American Indian tribe, supposedly abort the first fetus to make subsequent childbirth easier. Among American Indians, the Crow and the Assiniboine favor abortion in cases of desertion. In New Britain, abortion is considered essential for a pregnancy in the first year of marriage.

At the other end of the scale, in highly civilized cultures, abortion without guilt has become the social norm. Witness Japan, where abortion is granted on request, needing no official approval, and meeting no moral objections from the Shinto religion. In Poland as well, where abortion is also performed on request, medical reports show no significant psychic problems, despite a soaring abortion rate.

"Society can make the experience a traumatic one or a psychologically negligible one," concludes Dr. Garrett Hardin, professor of biology at the University of California at Santa Barbara. "If society thoroughly approves of induced abortion, the reasons for trauma virtually disappear."

IV

Hospital Abortion: A System of Fear and Privilege

Only the lucky few today receive the safety and care of hospital abortion, doled out frugally like a rare prize. The irony is that the lucky few are getting fewer. Twenty-five years ago, at least 30,000 hospital abortions were performed annually. Now the figure has been cut to 8,000 or so, a drastic reduction resulting from one of the greatest cases of jitters ever to afflict the medical profession.

Formerly, two reputable doctors could present letters of approval to their hospital and generally have an abortion performed without question. But in recent years many hospitals have established a peculiar obstacle: the abortion committee. "Abortion committees and their regulations have made it increasingly complex," states Dr. Robert Laidlaw. "At some hospitals, an abortion is practically impossible to obtain on psychiatric grounds."

Under the old system, physicians maintained medical control over their cases. The pregnant woman with a heart condition who might need abortion was studied by cardiologists. The woman who lapsed into acute depression was treated by psychiatrists. Each decision for abortion rested in the hands of two specialists, known and respected at their hospital, and each decision received almost automatic approval from the chief of obstetrics.

Obviously, no reputable hospital approved abortions recommended by physicians it neither knew nor trusted. Further, the great majority of state laws do not require two letters of medical approval. Most of them do not even require that the operation be performed in a hospital.

With the advent of the abortion committee, however, both doctors and patients suddenly became embroiled in a vast hospital bureaucracy. In addition to approval by two specialists, a case must go before a committee, generally consisting of five senior staff members and headed by the chief of obstetrics. The prejudices of each member now raise a whole new set of hurdles.

Inconceivable as it might seem, considering the Catholic Church's opposition even to hospital abortion, many non-Catholic hospitals have Catholics as chairmen or members of their committees. In a large East Coast county hospital, for example, the chief of obstetrics openly boasted that no abortion had been performed in twenty years. And this is a public hospital, not a church institution!

In a survey conducted by Dr. William Ober and the author, a Chicago physician explained the sharp curtailment of abortions at his hospital: "More Catholic doctors on committee." A Manhasset, N.Y., doctor blames his "tough and bigoted committee." A Hackensack, N.J., obstetrician cites "arbitrary decisions by members of committee." The obstetrical staff of one of New York City's most prominent voluntary hospitals, financed mainly by Protestants and Jews, faces the frequent veto of its committee chairman, a Catholic.[1]

Such prejudices may also be aimed at specific types of abortion. A professor of obstetrics at an eastern university hospital stated proudly: "We have not done a therapeutic abortion for psychiatric reasons at our hospital in the past ten years. I could say, in fact, that we do not recognize psychiatric indications." Asked whether a psychiatric abortion was more difficult today at his hospital, a Chicago psychiatrist replied, "Almost impossible."[2]

Further, many abortion committees have conjured up a labyrinth of regulations that reach the point of absurdity. Some hospitals today will accept a case of psychiatric abortion only if the woman has a past record of acute illness, and actually been treated in that hospital. Few New York women, as a result, could qualify at their own psychiatrist's hospital. And if an out-of-town woman was being treated by a New York psychiatrist, she would be forced to return home to a local hospital no matter how crucial the reasons for abortion.

"The situation has gotten worse and worse," observed the late Dr. Lena Levine, a leading New York psychiatrist and associate director of the Margaret Sanger Research Bureau. "One patient, whom I had treated for years, had the most urgent psychiatric grounds for abortion, approved by a second psychiatrist. When the hospital committee turned down her case, I had to send her to Puerto Rico for abortion."

The most disturbing aspect of the abortion-committee system is that no state law requires it, nor even mentions it. Since forty-two states allow legal abortion only to save the life of the mother—or, in some statutes, her health—and since no law defines "life" or "health," only the physician can make this decision. It is a grave responsibility, but so are most decisions for surgery. To counter the threat of being charged with an illegal operation, doctors long ago developed the defense of a second letter of approval. It has always worked well. In fact, in one of the few recent changes in state law, Oregon adopted this medical practice, and requires that a record of consultation by two physicians be kept for three years in their office or hospital.

The threat of harassment under the law is actually no more than a phantom. The possibility of a district attorney's convincing a jury that two medical specialists prescribed abortion in defiance of accepted medical standards is infinitely remote. As we stated earlier, to our knowledge, no reputable physician has ever been convicted for performing an abortion in a reputable hospital.

Still, by 1955 many hospitals had barricaded themselves behind a second line of defense, the abortion committee. Almost all big-city hospitals use the system today. "The medical profession has backed itself farther and farther into a corner," states Dr. Carl Goldmark, Jr., a leading obstetrician and 1965 president of the New York County Medical Society. "The abortion committee is just something for a hospital to hide behind. It's our greatest mistake."

If the purpose of these committees is to limit the freedom of the individual doctor and to cut the hospital's abortion rate, it has succeeded brilliantly. New York's Sloane Hospital for Women averaged 1 abortion for every 69 live births from 1950 to 1955, at which time it established an abortion committee. In the next five years its rate dropped to 1 abortion for every 225 live births—a two-thirds cut. In the last twenty years the hospital abortion rate throughout New York City has dropped to about one-third.[3]

New York's Bellevue Hospital, which averaged 1 abortion for every 76 live births from 1935 to 1945, today claims 1 for every 362 live births. The reduction at Los Angeles County Hospital has been even more drastic: 1 per 106 in 1931, only 1 per 8,383 by 1952.[4]

This pattern has been repeated throughout the country. University of Virginia Hospital averaged 1 abortion for every 120 live births (1941–52); University of California Hospital, 1 per 88 (1942–48); New York Hospital, 1 per 135 (1941–44). Today, their rates have been cut at least a third, often a half.[5]

Asked in the Ober-Lader survey whether abortion had become more difficult to secure in the last ten years at their hospitals, 70 per cent of gynecologists answering in New York City and close suburbs said yes. Asked if it had become more difficult on psychiatric grounds, 80 per cent said yes.

At many hospitals now practicing abortion by statistics, the patient is no longer a medical case but a number balanced against a quota. If she arrives after the monthly quota has been filled, she may well be rejected despite the urgency of her medical needs.

"If, by arbitrary action, a patient's dignity as a human being is reduced to that of a mere statistic—of being, perhaps, case No. 4 when, unfortunately for the patient, only three are permitted each month—does not such a policy of maintaining illusory safeguards, at the real expense of increased human tragedy, actually represent a denial of the hospital's primary responsibility?" demands Dr. Arthur J. Mandy.

This recent worship of "respectable quotas" represents a disastrous retreat by the medical profession. "The quotas and the abortion committees are simply the product of fear," states Dr. Goldmark.

Three staff doctors at the University of Pennsylvania School of Medicine admitted that the hospital had established its abortion committee in response to "the increased incidence" of abortion. The chief of obstetrics at a New York hospital stated that he had set up his committee because he did not want his department to become an "abortion mill." Indeed, this fear has become so pervasive that many hospitals now consider a minimum abortion rate a status symbol. "The fewer abortions, the better we look," a Philadelphia doctor put it.[6]

Many hospitals seek to rationalize their timidity with a virtually meaningless phrase—"collective responsibility." Instead of two specialists, the abortion committee, representing the hospital itself, now stands behind each operation. What is actually gained by this device? No other medical procedure, including a lobotomy, the sensitive brain operation that can alter and warp the whole personality of the patient, demands the sanctity of committee approval. If two specialists cannot be trusted with an abortion decision, why are five committee members more dependable? Why not carry consultation to the extreme of a vote of all staff doctors? Obviously, what passes for collective responsibility is simply a protective gimmick, the result of administrative fear.

What are hospitals so afraid of that makes them cut their abortion rates to a minimum? When a prominent obstetrician was told that his colleague's hospital feared being labeled an abortion mill, he observed: "This hospital has such a high standing that no one would think of questioning its abortion rate. No reputable hospital should be scared of doing 'too many' abortions when decisions are based on solid evidence."

Yet it seems evident that the fear of religious and political pressure has forced abortion committees and quotas on the hospitals. Asked in the Ober-Lader survey what pressures had led to curtailment of abortions, 70 per cent of the obstetricians answering said: "Roman Catholic Church or [other] religious pressure."

In San Francisco, a doctor cited the "Catholic influence in this city"; in Dubuque, Iowa, another said: "Very few have been done in this predominantly Catholic community"; in Fall River, Mass., a third blamed "the largely Catholic population."

While such pressure may have a certain basis in fact, particularly among municipal hospitals, it seems inconceivable that nonsectarian, voluntary hospitals should knuckle under to religious and political groups, and sacrifice their responsibility to their patients. In one of the few recorded cases of pressure, the district attorney in 1953 demanded the books of Dr. Louis M. Hellman, professor of obstetrics and gynecology at State University of New York Downstate Medical Center. Dr. Hellman had previously told a public meeting that half of the cases listed at his hospital as "incomplete abortions"—meaning that doctors could not tell whether they were spontaneous or induced—were probably induced by abortionists or the women themselves. When he refused to invade the privacy of patients by surrendering his books, the case went to court, and Hellman's position was upheld.

Even where such religious pressure exists, many Catholic doctors oppose it. One California doctor stated in the Ober-Lader survey: "The indications for abortion should be much more liberal, and coming from a conservative, Republican Catholic—that's progress!"

The obvious weakness of the abortion-committee system is the resulting chaos. Lacking uniform standards, some committees make their decisions by unanimous vote, others by majority. The size of committees and the requirements for membership vary from hospital to hospital. Worst of all, decisions on the same types of cases are so disparate that one hospital will approve an abortion that its neighbor a few blocks away rejects. Hospital administrations will certainly not shake off their fear of outside pressure until this internal anarchy is abolished.

The most disastrous result of the abortion-committee system has been economic and social discrimination against one group—the ward patients. In large cities the poor, particularly Negroes and Puerto Ricans, are virtually denied the same medical care as the privileged few.

Of hospital abortions performed in New York City during 1960–62 only 7 per cent were non-whites, as compared with 93 per cent whites.

In this same period, 16 ward patients in municipal hospitals, 66 in voluntary hospitals were granted abortions, compared with 792 private patients. Under pressure of the German measles epidemic in 1964, ward patients received a little better share of abortions: 32 in municipal, 64 in voluntary hospitals, as against 483 private patients.[7]

In a survey of 60 leading hospitals across the country, the rate of abortions for private patients proved to be almost four times greater than for ward patients:

University of Iowa Hospital (1960–62), 1 abortion per 1,535 live births; 1 per 219 private patients.

University of Mississippi Medical Center (1957–62), 1 per 4,339 live births; 1 per 147 among private patients.

New York Hospital (1961–63), 1 per 1,219 live births on the wards; 1 per 465 among private patients.

The disparity between ward and private patients is even greater in the case of psychiatric abortions. At Sloane Hospital for Women, for example, private patients receiving psychiatric abortions outnumbered ward patients more than 10 to 1.[8]

Many municipal hospitals, which carry the majority of poor patients, have virtually eliminated abortions. New York's Metropolitan Hospital performed only 1 in 13,000 live births between 1959 and 1961; Los Angeles' Harbor General Hospital, only 1 per 3,474 live births between 1955 and 1960.[9]

Although some municipal hospitals claim that such low rates stem from the fact that poorer patients rarely seek obstetrical aid until the fourth or fifth month of pregnancy, past the abortion safety-limit, and are not even aware of indications like German measles, these circumstances could hardly account for the huge discrepancy between ward and private patient rates.

Such discrimination seems far more likely to be the result of a system that interprets the law one way for the rich, another for the poor. As rigid quotas continue to lower the abortion rate, an increasing percentage of approvals is going to wealthy, influential women who can afford private rooms, and who can enlist the aid of specialists to help pass their cases through abortion committees.

Another danger of abortion committees is that they promote a "punishment syndrome" among medical men sitting as a high court of justice, having no contact with or understanding of the patient other than through her records. Removed from the control of her own physician, the patient becomes the pawn in a bureaucracy often more intent on protecting hospital status than meeting critical human needs. After approving an abortion, one committee reversed itself on discovering the woman was unmarried. Another committee member expressed his antipathy by snapping: "Now that she has had her fun, she wants us to launder her dirty underwear." Dr. Mandy describes "such obvious hostility" as "clearly irrational."

The most frequent punitive measure is the insistence that sterilization be combined with abortion in a single package. Many committees demand this "deal" as a guarantee that the patient will not return to seek another abortion. With the exception of German measles cases, committees may bargain for a patient's right to future motherhood against the immediate medical necessity of terminating a pregnancy.

Such a trade is not only cruel but medically senseless. "Sterilization presents one set of problems; therapeutic abortion another," states Dr. Harold Rosen, of Johns Hopkins University School of Medicine. The two are unrelated, yet suddenly yoked together to expiate the committee's own guilt over approving abortion. The patient requiring abortion on psychiatric grounds, for example, must suffer permanent punishment because of an immediate crisis. "The enforced and permanent renunciation of motherhood, imposed as the penalty when a specific pregnancy is to be interrupted, even though for good and valid therapeutic reasons, seems much too heavy a price for any patient to be compelled to pay merely because she happens to be emotionally ill," adds Rosen.

While sterilization is often justified for a mother whose health would be jeopardized by future childbearing, or who voluntarily decides to limit her family, tying it up in a neat little package with abortion is a reprehensible product of the committee system. And the growth of this practice in recent years represents the ultimate renunciation by hospital bureaucracies of their responsibility to the patient.

For two decades the senseless jitters of the medical profession have backed it into a corner of fear. Under the guise of eliminating the alleged abuses of the old two-letter system, the profession has built up a host of more dangerous abuses and become the patron of the privileged few. First and last, abortion will always be a medical problem between the patient and her physician. By allowing this relationship to be violated by various committees, as well as by political and religious pressure groups, the profession has dealt harshly with both itself and the public.

V

The Doctor's Dilemma

The restrictions imposed by abortion committees and quotas have gravely intensified the physician's basic problem: deciding what cases qualify for hospital abortion. Since forty-two state laws offer no guideline but a threat to the mother's life, the physician must differentiate between a risk to health and that to life—"often a rather nebulous" distinction, experts point out. "It is sometimes difficult to assess properly the seriousness of a disease, and especially difficult to state with reasonable certainty that allowing pregnancy to run its natural course will result in the death of the mother." No decision is more difficult than in cases of psychiatric abortion.[1]

To determine how neighboring hospitals would diagnose the same set of indications, two Stanford University researchers polled twenty-six California hospitals on a typical psychiatric-abortion case. The woman, thirty-six years old, had given birth to six children within ten years. After each of the last three births, she had suffered from acute depression, and was now pregnant for the seventh time. Should she be given hospital abortion? Ten of the hospitals answering approved the case, twelve rejected it.[2]

Such divergence of opinion has led many hospitals and abortion committees to consider psychiatric abortion on only one ground: acute risk of suicide. But suicide itself, as Dr. Iago Galdston, formerly of the New York Academy of Medicine, stresses, "is one of the most difficult things to forecast in any patient."

To appreciate the complexities of forecasting, consider the case of a man who telephoned Dr. Harold Rosen for an emergency consultation. He and his wife had been separated for a year, but obstacles would delay their divorce another nine months. A week before, he had learned that the woman he had been seeing since his separation was pregnant. He held an important job supervising a large technical staff. She held an equally responsible position. Although they were deeply in love and wanted to marry, she refused to bring scandal on either of their families by bearing the child before marriage. If the pregnancy became known, the sensitive nature of their relationship would lead to blackmail or dismissal for both of them. Now she was considering suicide.

Dr. Rosen suggested that the woman come for consultation, which she did three days later. She insisted she could not ruin her lover's life. Doubting the possibility of legal abortion, she could see no other solution but suicide. When Dr. Rosen suggested she take a vacation and bear the child for adoption, she bluntly rejected this alternative. She had worked out the suicide so that it would appear unintentional. She had already purchased the ticket for a sea trip, and would simply disappear over the side of the ship. It was the only way out of an impasse that would destroy her lover and their families.

A week later, the couple arrived together. Crying throughout most of the session, she repeated her original plan for suicide, and her partner now implied he would follow her in the act. When Rosen suggested further sessions, she refused. He then urged her to get in touch with her hometown physician, which she did. Rosen wrote this doctor: "I cannot state that she actually will kill herself, but the possibility exists. Since she has already decided upon the means, in my opinion this risk must be run unless the pregnancy be interrupted."

Her hometown physician sent her to a second psychiatrist, who decided the suicide threats were dangerous enough to warrant abortion. On the basis of these two letters, the operation was performed.[3]

Since no psychiatrist could predict this suicide with certainty, the risk could be calculated only by past experience and intuitive knowledge. "All you can do is rely upon your judgment," one physician told a New Hampshire legislative hearing, "and your judgment comes from your experience and your convictions and you people who depend upon us in our judgment." Even statistics tell little. In two Swedish studies, one revealed that 5 per cent, the other 3.7 per cent, of female suicides were pregnant. Without knowing whether the pregnancy caused the suicide, however, we can be certain only that the risk exists. The severity of the risk is one of the most puzzling intangibles in medicine.

Dr. Rosen's case, which occurred a decade ago, might never have been granted legal abortion today in the face of increasingly stringent quotas and hospital regulations. Psychiatric abortions, as we have seen, have been cut back sharply. While they made up about 50 per cent of all hospital abortions in New York City in 1955, they have been shaved 19 per cent in the last decade or so.[4]

In fact, one group of physicians claims that most suicide threats are only bluff, and that psychiatrists—the "unwitting accomplice," Dr. Sidney Bolter, himself a psychiatrist, calls them—are too easily swayed into supporting abortions by hysterics. "Certainly it is the consensus that these pregnant women rarely carry out the threat," he insists.

This same group has tried to discount almost all other mental illnesses that have long been considered qualified reasons for hospital abortion. For example: "Schizophrenia may be treated with insulin, while the mother carries the child, without harm to mother or child," one psychiatrist explains.[5]

Many hospitals and abortion committees today are almost obsessed with cutting abortions for mental illness to a minimum. The dangers are obvious. "What must I do to prove how desperately ill I am?" one patient demanded of Dr. Mandy. "Must I attempt or actually commit suicide or finally be committed to a mental hospital to prove it to them?"

The second danger is the lack of concern with the mother after childbirth. Although a State University of Iowa medical report and many other researchers have emphasized that "with the more severe type of neuroses" a continuation of pregnancy "might seriously jeopardize" the mother's future mental health, they have been met with indifference. The conservative viewpoint expects the mother to struggle along on her own—with psychiatric help if she can afford it!

And what of the child born to an emotionally sick mother? What are his chances if his mother remains a psychotic during his youth, or if she must be hospitalized? "It is not enough to be concerned with saving the life of an embryo," insists Dr. Richard L. Jenkins, professor of child psychiatry at the University of Iowa, "if no constructive opportunity is provided for that life to be developed."

One recent case pinpoints both these dangers. A woman mental patient at New York's Manhattan State Hospital was raped by another inmate who managed to escape from his security quarters. The hospital refused to perform an abortion, and the woman carried the child to term. The infant turned out to be normal, but since both parents are psychotics who may be confined for the rest of their lives, his care depends upon the only close relatives, two aged and indigent grandparents. From any point of view, the hospital's rejection of abortion in this instance seems abysmal cruelty.

Finally, psychiatrists themselves are being shunted into the background by committees and quotas. The very nature of emotional illness demands highly individual care and judgment, and a decision on abortion can best be made by the psychiatrist and his consultant, who have attended a case over a long period. Yet increasingly today, the hospital accepts only the preliminary report of these specialists and turns the decision over to its abortion committee.

A woman who had suffered an initial attack of ulcerative colitis during her first pregnancy finally recovered after prolonged hospitalization and psychotherapy. But on the day she learned she was pregnant a second time, she experienced another violent attack and was admitted to the hospital in critical condition. Obviously, the psychiatrist who had treated her during both illnesses—not a bureaucracy of committees and regulations—possessed the detailed, intimate knowledge to make the abortion decision with a trusted consultant. Such decisions are complex enough. The frantic determination of hospitals to standardize policy and work through committees not only compounds the problem, but restricts and demeans the judgment of the psychiatric profession.

"The need to decide each case on an individual basis makes for difficulties when attempts are made to standardize policy," concludes Dr. Theodore Lidz, "whether such policy concerns a hospital which is attempting to establish rules or a society rewriting its laws."

The liberal viewpoint in psychiatry, therefore, still considers schizophrenic and manic-depressive psychoses justifiable grounds for abortion. Granted that some psychiatrists in the past may have abused the two-letter system of approval and favored borderline cases, such presumed abuses are far less harmful in the long run than the present paralysis of hospital policies. The drive to handcuff psychiatrists in dealing with abortion, to label an important part of the profession "unwitting accomplices," presents one of the most ominous trends in medicine.[6]

In deciding what physical illnesses qualify for hospital abortion, doctors have the advantage of clearer medical guidelines but the disadvantage of a crazy-quilt of contradictions in interpretation. When the Stanford University survey submitted eleven typical cases of abortion to twenty-six California hospitals, not one achieved anything close to unanimous approval.

Ironically, the case most strongly supported was that of a fifteen-year-old girl who had been raped by a mental defective. Fifteen hospitals which answered approved the abortion; seven turned it down. Yet neither California law nor any other state law allows abortion on the grounds of rape!

What has evolved from the chaos of the abortion system, therefore, is that many hospitals stretch the law, so to speak, by their own interpretation. Although many refuse to do an abortion for rape, as we have seen in the Colorado and Manhattan State Hospital cases, others consider rape a threat to life because of its traumatic impact on the woman. Such decisions obviously are influenced by ethical as well as medical factors, and a fifteen-year-old girl generally stands a better chance of approval than a thirty-year-old woman. The doctor's dilemma in a rape case he considers essential for abortion is that one hospital may reject it while a neighboring one a few blocks away approves it, or he may even have to search for approval in another city or state.

A further dilemma has arisen as a result of advances in medical knowledge. Illnesses like diabetes and pernicious vomiting, once considered severe threats to the pregnant woman, can now be so medically controlled that they rarely qualify as grounds for abortion. On the other hand, new threats have arisen, the most prominent being rubella, or German measles, whose dangers have long been recognized but fully grasped only in the last year.

This seemingly harmless infection, producing two or three days of minor rash, fever, and discomfort, has turned out to be a cruel attacker of the fetus. In 1941, researchers discovered that a woman exposed to rubella in the first three months of pregnancy was vulnerable to a virus whose impact on the fetus causes heart disease, blindness, mental retardation, and even early death in the infant. No one knows exactly how the virus destroys. The most accepted theory is that it invades the protective lining of the uterus and damages blood vessels and heart-muscle tissue.

Australian researchers estimate the risk of fetal damage as high as 60 per cent if the virus is contracted in the first month of pregnancy. Most U.S. physicians place it at 50 per cent, based on a 1960

British study of limited cases. A 1964 British study, however, showed that the risk in the second month of pregnancy may even be higher than in the first.

Just a year later, these estimates sound frighteningly conservative. In the last available report of May 1965, Dr. Gilbert M. Schiff and his associates tested the first 300 babies of 1,549 born at the University of Cincinnati Hospital since the recent rubella epidemic. Of these 300, 276 had one or more defects, major or minor, associated with rubella. This staggeringly high percentage of defects forecasts "a major tragedy," warns Dr. Richard L. Masland, of the National Institute of Neurological Diseases and Blindness.

The rubella menace has been sharply intensified by the epidemic of 1963–64. In New York City alone, the incidence of the disease increased tenfold. In the country as a whole, almost 2,000,000 women of childbearing age contracted the virus, according to a National Foundation–March of Dimes report. Of these, an estimated 82,000 were in the critical first three months of pregnancy, and an estimated 15,000 to 20,000 infants were born defective or malformed.

Disturbing enough already, these figures may have to be revised upward as a result of recent discoveries. In Dr. Schiff's study, 90 per cent of the mothers with defective babies were not even aware they had contracted rubella. The possibility of undetected infection can lead to grave consequences. "If this rate of unrecognized maternal rubella is widespread," states Dr. Virginia Apgar, of the National Foundation, "it means thousands of rubella babies could be born with hidden defects and with no reason for doctors to suspect and look for trouble." Since defects like mental retardation may not be discernible even at the age of one year, the full impact of a rubella epidemic cannot be assessed until long afterward.

Further, researchers in post mortem examinations have found the rubella virus in brains, lungs, kidney, and liver, and now fear that diseases like hepatitis and bone damage, normally unconnected, may result from rubella.

Even more disturbing is the recent discovery that babies affected by rubella before birth can still retain and spread the virus for long periods without showing any signs of infection. This "shedding" action exposes countless women—nurses, doctors' wives, or friends of the contagious infant's family—who, perhaps unknowingly, may be in the early stages of pregnancy.

In regard to the U.S. annual rate of 250,000 infants suffering defects, Dr. Apgar concludes: "German measles may be responsible for far more of them than anyone suspected." In other words, the last estimate of 15,000 to 20,000 defective rubella babies may be highly conservative. Dr. John L. Sever, of the National Institutes of Health, recently predicted that 30,000 defective children will be born as a result of the 1964–65 epidemic.

In the face of a new rubella epidemic throughout the West Coast, Hawaii, and Puerto Rico in 1965, medical science has yet to develop a strong defense system. The virus itself was not isolated until 1961. In the next few years, two tests to detect the infection were introduced, both, however, extremely complicated and taking as long as two weeks for results. Not until April 1965 did researchers discover a simple test that can be completed in a day. Taken in a series, the three tests offer reasonably accurate proof that a mother has or has not contracted rubella; the problem is that the tests are available only at the best-equipped hospitals.

The crucial break-through, of course, will come in the form of a vaccine for immunizing girls before childbearing age. Despite obstacles so far in cultivating the virus and finding a model animal that satisfactorily carries a clinical infection, research sponsored by the National Foundation may hopefully reach this goal before the next epidemic cycle, predicted for 1969 or 1970.[7]

In the meantime, the medical profession is confronted with a dilemma so vast that it might rightfully come within the realm of government health policy. An estimated 82,000 women in the first three months of pregnancy were affected by rubella in the last epidemic; with reason to believe there may be a sharp increase of this figure in the next year, how many must be forced to bear infants— possibly half of them born defective—as a result of chaotic and cruel abortion laws? If the three-test series proves that a woman has contracted rubella, does she not have the right to demand an abortion from her hospital?

Hospital policy has been as conflicting on these questions as on every other aspect of abortion. In the Stanford University study of 1959, only ten California hospitals approved an abortion for rubella; twelve rejected it. Even during the emergency of the 1964 epidemic, some New York hospitals, as we have seen, carried their timidity to the absurd extreme of demanding that a City Health Department inspector witness a patient's rash before approving abortion. At least two prominent non-sectarian voluntary hospitals in New York and Long Island added the further requirement that a patient must have previously delivered a child on their premises.

The optimistic side, however, is that New York hospitals as a group almost doubled their abortion rate during the epidemic and greatly expanded approvals for rubella. Contrasted with 300 abortions annually in previous years, 579 were performed in 1964. Also, whereas rubella abortions made up only 4 to 7 per cent of all abortions from 1959 to 1963, they rose to almost 57 per cent in 1964.

But even this liberalized trend hardly meets the enormity of the challenge. If the present 8,000 hospital abortions throughout the country for *all* causes were suddenly doubled, would the demands of the epidemic be sufficiently met?

When as eminent an authority as Dr. Allan Barnes, of the Johns Hopkins School of Medicine, states that a 50 per cent risk of a defective rubella baby is "a risk few people should take," it seems probable that the demand for abortion by women infected in early pregnancy would be overwhelming. The brunt of the challenge falls particularly on public hospitals, municipal and county. For it is these hospitals that have virtually shunned abortions of any type. A trickle of twenty-three rubella abortions performed by New York City municipal hospitals in 1964, even when supplemented by twenty-three in the wards of private hospitals, would hardly meet the demands of non-private patients during an epidemic. The scope of the crisis in the next five years requires an awakening of public responsibility. Not just the medical profession, but city and county governments will have to discard their old timidities and prejudices if the nation is to stave off a flood of defective babies.[8]

With the exception of rubella, the physical indications for abortion have diminished in the last decade. In this shrinking list, the majority of the medical profession still recognizes:

> *Cancer of the cervix*
> *Severe cardiac disease*
> *Severe hypertension*
> *Nephritis or kidney disease*
> *Breast cancer*

The disagreement arises over such indications as pulmonary tuberculosis, which many experts feel is so well controlled that pregnancy does not have to be deferred; and over such eugenic indications as conflicting Rh factors between parents, where the risk of an infant's becoming a lasting invalid is often discounted.

The real conflict in the profession, and a most difficult problem for the individual physician, begins when a case goes beyond the immediate limits of medicine into the socio-economic realm. Often a mother's life is not threatened that week or that month by pregnancy. A woman with two or three children who is severely crippled by multiple sclerosis may not die as a result of another birth; nor may a woman bedridden with polio; nor a cardiac case on the edge of poverty and forced to walk the stairs to a fourth-floor tenement.

Nevertheless, under the physical and emotional strain of bearing a child against their will, they may very well be pushed to the breaking point. Where economic hardship is added to the burden of illness or disease, it may not cause the immediate death of the patient, but it can certainly hasten it.

"Socio-economic factors in the background of a prospective mother," state Drs. Edmund Overstreet and Herbert F. Traut, of the University of California Medical School at San Francisco, "may well make the difference between a pattern of life which will permit her to carry the pregnancy with only moderate risk and one which may well put her life in jeopardy as a result of its added burden."

Nevertheless, most hospitals fervently avoid a case with socio-economic factors. The Stanford University study submitted the case of a thirty-seven-year-old mother of five, deeply in debt and supporting her family on a menial job. Since her forty-two-year-old tubercular husband was fit only for occasional employment, she would obviously be physically and emotionally swamped by the burden of another child. Yet one California hospital approved abortion; twenty rejected it.

As far as the individual physician is concerned, although he may personally favor abortion under such tragic circumstances, he is intimidated by the rigidity of the law. "I am not opposed either emotionally or intellectually to socio-economic indications for abortion," Dr. Guttmacher stated when he was at Mt. Sinai Hospital, "but as long as I am chief of an obstetrical service, I am strongly against them as the sole indication while the present New York statute stands unmodified."

The question, however, is whether physicians have not bent over backward to stay within the law, when court decisions have already given them more leeway than they seem willing to use. As far back as 1928, an appeals court ruled in an Iowa abortion case: "In order to justify the act of Dr. W., it was not essential that peril to life should be imminent. It was enough that it be potentially present though its full development might be delayed, to a greater or less extent." (*State v. Dunklebarger*)

Similarly, in a noted California case in 1959, the appeals court not only cited this Iowa case, but went on to say: "Surely the abortion statute does not mean . . . that the peril to life be imminent." (*People v. Ballard*)

What the medical profession has failed to answer in its own conscience is whether socio-economic factors can be separated from the patient's prognosis, or whether the patient's life must be examined in entirety. "Our patients do not live in a vacuum," Dr. Laidlaw insists. "Therefore, we are thinking as psychiatrists, 'Will the carrying through of another pregnancy and long periods of infant care tip the scales and make the burden something too heavy for this personality makeup to endure?'"

If the answer is yes, if the physician is convinced that the burden has become too heavy to endure, it would seem high time that physicians and hospitals cease being cowed by conservative interpretations of the law. Their responsibility to their profession and their community is care of the *total* patient. When socio-economic factors affect her very existence, they must be included with everything else in a decision concerning abortion. Many hospitals have already accepted such broad indications as rape and rubella. Now they must accept the same responsibility in the socio-economic area.

VI

The Skilled Abortionist

When some years ago Dr. G. Loutrell Timanus, of Baltimore, sent a bouquet of flowers to a renowned gynecologist who had referred him patients, the gynecologist wrote Timanus: "I have a feeling that you think you are under obligation to me. As a matter of fact, I believe the reverse to be true. . . . I feel that we doctors who are too spineless to risk the odium of such work owe you the thanks. I have the highest regard for you, and there is no need for you to express any obligation to me."

Beyond an exchange of professional pleasantries, the letter marks a medical phenomenon. For Timanus was no ordinary practitioner. In Baltimore, and virtually along the whole East Coast, he had built an impressive reputation over twenty-five years as a skilled abortionist. Professionals have called his work extremely competent. At Johns Hopkins Medical School, classes in dilatation and curettage, based on some of his techniques, were unofficially known as "Timanus Day." Perhaps the final stamp of approval was the source of his referrals. His patients were accepted only with a referring letter from one of a list of 353 of the most prominent doctors in Maryland, Washington, D.C., and surrounding areas. Moreover, when the medical profession itself needed an abortionist, it generally turned to Timanus. According to his records, at least ten per cent of his cases were women doctors, wives or sweethearts of doctors, nurses, or related members of the profession.

Obviously Dr. Timanus presents a startling contrast to the stereotype abortionist created by crime reporters, the sensational

42

press, and most police officials—a faceless phantom, reached at a secret telephone number after the patient has identified herself by coded word or phrase. Usually, in such portrayals, the patient is transported in an intermediary's car and taken blindfolded to a well-camouflaged office, changed frequently to elude the police. The abortionist may even be masked so that the patient can never identify him.

Actually, many skilled abortionists are proud of practicing openly. Timanus' nameplate was always on the door at 1307 Maryland Avenue, his number in the telephone book. Born in this building, which had been owned by his father, he kept his office here from 1916 until his retirement in 1951.

Timanus freely expresses his views on abortion even socially, debating the subject violently with friends, and has always proclaimed his profession openly at the highly fashionable clubs on Maryland's eastern shore and at Miami Beach to which he and his wife belong. He sends a constant stream of letters to newspapers, attacking abortion laws. "I'm an incorrigible crusader against the hypocrisy and inhumanity of our system," he announces in booming tones.

This enthusiasm, he admits, often unnerves his children, whose social and professional status could be damaged. His son is a leading lawyer, a former Bar Association president, in a southwestern city; his daughter is married to a prominent doctor in the same city. "Why, hell, they're big enough to stand on their own accomplishments and stop worrying about what their father's doing," he insists.

A distant cry from the stereotype abortionist who hustles his patients into the street five minutes after the operation in fear of the police, Timanus treated his cases with intricate care. The operation was divided into two parts, usually on separate days. After surgery, his patients rested in bed at his nurse's home at least six hours. He checked their recovery by phone the next few days. His files are crowded with letters of appreciation, one woman praising his "great work and very human kindness"; another stating: "There are no words I know powerful enough to tell you how grateful I am."

While Timanus never presumed to be a philanthropist, his fees averaged less than the $1,000 and $1,500 that many underworld abortionists in major cities were demanding in 1950. When he first retired in 1946, he was charging about $200. When he returned to practice part-time in the next four years, his prices rose to $400 and

$500. For hardship patients he charged virtually nothing. In a few cases involving the very rich, he received $2,000 and $3,000.

"I never made more from abortion than any skilled doctor would make from his specialty," Timanus states. He claims never to have split a fee with referring doctors except in one case. Above all, in contrast to underworld abortionists, paying no taxes on unreported income, Timanus has stated in writing that he filed tax returns on all medical receipts.

Now seventy-three, tall, strapping, with thick white hair, ruddy skin, and squinting blue eyes that mark his Swedish ancestry, Timanus lived for years like a country gentleman. At Queenstown, Maryland, he built "Sportsman's Hall," a redbrick mansion with white columns, replete with horses and dogs. Today, he has replaced it with a smaller but still commodious home at Rehoboth Beach, Delaware, and a winter apartment at Miami Beach. These luxuries, he insists, came not from abortion income but from Florida and Maryland real estate, in which one sale alone brought him $300,000 and in which he still holds considerable property.

Since Dr. Timanus' retirement, the most prominent example of a skilled abortionist—particularly notable for his philosophic and humanitarian motives—is Dr. S. In his quaint, sprawling office on Main Street in a small town three hours' drive west of New York, he has performed 28,658 operations. The startling feature is their cost. For almost thirty years he charged $10. A decade or so ago, the price rose to $50 and reached $100 only recently when the expenses of a law suit and antibiotics sharply increased his overhead.

Since Dr. S. is the leading family doctor in town (still practicing, he prefers anonymity), his office may be filled with as many tonsillectomies and hardening arteries as abortion cases. "He could pack his schedule day and night with regular patients," states the local newspaper editor. "He does abortions because he darn well believes in them."

Frail and puckish at seventy-five, Dr. S. has white tufts of hair fringing his head and neck, and often sports a black Viscount Montgomery beret that proclaims his Scottish ancestry. He has long been a legend in his state. When he walks down the street, he is greeted with smiles and handshakes. "I'd say I've done abortions for half the families in the county, including the police," he observes. Although his cases come mainly from the East Coast, particularly from New York and New England, he has treated women from as far away as Laos, Finland, and Hong Kong.

Having lived in town since boyhood (his father, ironically, was district attorney of a neighboring county), Dr. S. is an intimate friend of the mayor, the police chief, and almost every official. His home, a simple seven-room frame house, indistinguishable from dozens of others on an unimpressive street, reflects the modest scale of his prices for abortions and other medical services. Neither his home furnishings nor his clothes indicate great wealth. His one luxury is a Cadillac, with which he and his wife indulge their hobby of travel. As one of the most popular members of the Rotary Club, he is always in demand for lectures and for showing colored slides of his trips, events that turn out brother Rotarians in full force.

Dr. S. is as much a radical philosopher as he is an unorthodox physician. Both his home library and his office study, hidden away on the floor above his operating room, are crammed with books on economics, political science, and population problems. His desk holds a statue of Thomas Paine. His walls are crowded with pictures ranging from Lincoln and Franklin (under whose great-great-grand-son he studied) to Joseph Lewis, president of the Free Thinkers of America. In his soft, gentle voice, Dr. S. constantly denounces to friends and patients the injustices of abortion laws. His favorite propaganda weapon is to distribute fountain pens inscribed: "Energy is the most important thing in the Universe. . . . Electricity and God are One."

Dr. S. maintains close ties with his abortion patients, many of whom continue to send him Christmas gifts and cards years after treatment. He frequently houses women overnight in one of the small rest rooms in his office if they cannot afford a local hotel. He is particularly sensitive to the needs of Catholic patients, carefully examining their religious attitudes toward abortion. If a woman shows any doubts, he makes her return the next day and often refuses to treat a hesitant patient. His files are filled with letters of appreciation, one Catholic calling him "one of the most beautiful humans that ever lived."

"I am again eternally grateful for *everything*, and only wish there was something I could do for *you* other than financial payment which seems in passing from me to you, so absolutely insignificant," another woman wrote. "Whatever talents, abilities and energies I may have are yours at any time you may need them."

The most striking characteristics of skilled abortionists like Dr. Timanus and Dr. S. are the standards of their medical training and surgical techniques. Born in Baltimore in 1892, Dr. Timanus comes from noted ancestors. His paternal grandfather was a judge of the Orphan's Court, his maternal grandfather a college professor. Dr. Timanus graduated from the University of Maryland Medical School in 1914, and interned at Baltimore's Presbyterian Eye, Ear, Nose, and Throat Hospital. For ten years he served as medical supervisor of Baltimore's Playground Athletic League, during which time he cared for the health of thousands of youngsters, and was confronted with the harsh reality of desperate women.

"I learned to face mothers from the industrial areas with seven and eight children who probably would have broken under another child," he recalls. "Schoolteachers sought me out, pleading pitifully for girls who would be banished from school and home if they produced an illegitimate birth."

Moved by these human needs, Timanus was also imbued with a rebellious spirit, molded by his grandfather, the professor. "He questioned everything," Timanus recalls. "He made me examine the absurdities of conventions and laws that shackled society." When, later, Timanus went to Europe in 1928 to study abortion techniques in Paris, Vienna, Berlin, and London, he was appalled by their crudity.

His rebellious nature probably would have led him in unorthodox directions no matter what his profession, but as a doctor with social insight, he turned his protest against medical hypocrisy. Once, in addressing a medical conference, he declared: "I believe the fault lies with the medical profession. Girls seek the advice of family physicians and are given no help; they are almost pushed from the door."

By 1928, Timanus had decided to master one area of medicine, and so developed a special forceps and new designs and sizes of curettes that increased the efficiency of abortive techniques. "If I was going to perform abortions," he concluded, "I intended to be the best in my profession."

Dr. S.'s medical training began at the University of Pennsylvania Medical School, with internships at Pottstown Hospital and Philadelphia General Hospital, and research studies at New York's Rockefeller Institute. After medical-corps service in World War I, he became chief pathologist at a large state hospital for five years and pioneered in the early use of bronchoscopy.

In 1925 he opened his own office in his hometown. One of his first cases was a pregnant mother with severe liver damage; she already had eight children. "I told her husband she might never survive without an abortion," Dr. S. recalls. "The next day he returned with his priest and flatly forbade the abortion. The woman had the child and died shortly after."

"There was nothing dramatic about my decision on abortion," he concludes. "I just started taking a few of the most pressing cases with my regular practice. It certainly wasn't a matter of money. It was simply a matter of helping people who needed me badly."

For utmost protection of their patients, both Dr. Timanus and Dr. S. performed abortions in two steps. At the woman's first visit to his office, Timanus packed the cervix with surgical gauze soaked in weak Lysol solution. The packing dilates the cervix, helps detach the placenta, and sterilizes the vagina. Then the woman returned to her home or hotel with directions to walk or be as active as she wanted.

Timanus did the actual curettage the next day, with the patient under sedation at the home of one of his nurses. The gauze would be removed, the woman douched. He then removed the uterine contents with placental forceps and scraped the uterus clean by curette, a process taking about fifteen minutes. A skilled abortionist works with an amazing sensitivity to feel and sound. With the last curettes, he can tell whether the uterine walls are clean. "A uterus speaks to you," Timanus says. Finally he would swab the patient with septic solution and order her to stay in bed at his nurse's home.

Instead of packing with gauze, Dr. S. used his own adaptation of a soft soap paste. Inserted only in small amounts and never under pressure, its purpose is to dilate the cervix and soften the tissues. Kept in place overnight, the packing causes little discomfort. The next day, Dr. S. performed the curettage, using sedatives to prevent pain and antibiotics against infection.

The safety standards of skilled abortionists are strikingly high. In 5,210 cases recorded by Dr. Timanus, there were only two deaths. "Whether these two deaths were attributable to my negligence or whether they were incidental, I would find it hard to say," Timanus told a medical conference.

In 28,658 cases treated by Dr. S., there was only one death. The woman was bleeding when she arrived at Dr. S.'s, and died on the table. Although an indictment was brought against him, the jury could not agree on the cause of death and voted against conviction.

What makes the careers of such skilled abortionists a political as well as medical phenomenon is that Dr. Timanus and Dr. S. remained virtually untouched by the police. Both insist they never paid police protection. Both frequently treated the families of police officers. Timanus, in fact, co-operated with the police when a blackmailer attempted to extort money from him, and his testimony led to the blackmailer's conviction.

In an even longer career of almost forty years, Dr. S. has had only one brush with the police, in addition to the indictment already noted. A woman with five children charged him with having injured her during an abortion. The case blew up, however, when her lawyer tried to pressure Dr. S. into an out-of-court settlement bordering on blackmail. After the woman gave birth to another child before the trial, casting doubt on any abortion injury, the jury voted for acquittal.

Considering this absence of police interference, it is obvious that the skilled abortionist may be not only tolerated but actually ignored by officials. Some observers make an even more affirmative judgment. "I would say that Dr. S. has always been ranked as one of our leading citizens," concludes the local newspaper editor. "The community values his work deeply."

Dr. Timanus' arrest and trial, therefore, after his practicing openly for almost twenty-five years, still remains an enigma. It was in May 1950 that he suddenly realized he was under observation. His secretary noticed mysterious cars parked across the street whose occupants seemed to be watching visitors to the office and taking notes of license plates of cars pulling up to the door. Timanus also suspected that his phones were being tapped, but he refused to take the easiest course and close his office for a year or move elsewhere. Whether motivated by stubbornness or a conviction of his own legality, he felt secure that his letters of referral from the medical profession met the requirements of the law.

On August 21 a dozen policemen raided the office, breaking into the examining room while a patient was on the table. They gathered up all records, including names and histories of patients, and took Timanus, his staff, and his patients in the waiting room to the station house.

There is some question as to the validity of the search warrant itself. Asked on the stand if the warrant had been shown by the police on entry, Timanus' secretary replied, "No, I am sure they did not produce anything. . . ." She recalled only seeing the warrant in the police car, and although it had her name but not her home address, it was still used to search her house.

Timanus stated that the judge who signed the warrant could not possibly have read it. When a police sergeant was asked on the stand how long he had been in the judge's chambers with the warrant, he said four or five minutes. Yet the warrant ran over 20 typewritten pages.

The raid was based on two complaints: one made by the sister of the blackmailer previously mentioned—a strange coincidence, since Timanus' testimony had helped to convict him; the other by the nurse of a retired Baltimore abortionist, sentenced for practicing abortion herself. The fact that she had been recently released makes for an even stranger coincidence.

The trial might have proved a unique test case. Timanus, as far as can be determined, was the first skilled abortionist in open practice who could base his defense on medical referrals under a fairly liberal state law. Maryland law allows abortion "by a regular practitioner of medicine when, after consulting with one or more respectable physicians, he shall be satisfied . . . that no other method will secure the safety of the mother." The crucial word is obviously *safety*. It is a reasonably broad word, implying mental and emotional as well as physical safety, and could have been the key to the trial.

Among the patients summoned by the prosecution, for example, Mrs. A. stated, "I wasn't in very good mental state of mind." Would you say you were desperate? asked the defense. "Yes, sir."

B., who had been divorced just before the abortion, said, "I had a miscarriage two months before and I didn't think I was physically able to carry it through. . . . I was very upset from losing my husband."

C. called her mental condition "bad." Was it desperate? "Desperate, definitely."

D., whose mother had just died, said, "I was under a very nervous strain at the time. . . . I was on the verge of a nervous breakdown."

Although these patients were obviously threatened by severe emotional disturbances, the defense never summoned psychiatric experts whose testimony might support the psychiatric basis of abortion, or marshaled previous court cases settled on such grounds. The famous Bourne decision in Britain, for example, had already established that mental damage could be equally essential to physical damage as a basis for abortion, and a battery of star medical witnesses had supported this contention. Since the decision was now part of English common law, it could rightfully have been introduced under U.S. common law. There were additional U.S. cases that justified abortion when mental as well as physical health was threatened *(Commonwealth v. Wheeler);* yet the defense failed to apply such cases.

Further, Timanus refused to exploit his medical letters of referral, an essential defense weapon, since the law demands consultation with one or more physicians. One doctor, for example, had written: "On account of A.'s physical condition, I recommend a dilatation and curettage"; another: "Please examine B. and if necessary do a diagnostic dilatation and curettage. Thank you for past kindness to my patients, thank you."

Unfortunately for Timanus, one physician called by the prosecution denied that he had ever sent Timanus patients, even when their pictures were shown him. "He had referred many cases," Timanus stated later, "but I could not find his letters until long after the trial."

The crux of the district attorney's case was that Timanus had performed abortions not necessary to "secure the safety of the mother." The state's expert medical witness testified that legal abortions should be performed only for specific indications like heart disease. "Since the prosecution contended my cases had no heart, kidney or lung disease, it was actually the medical profession that convicted me although each doctor had called his case a medical necessity in his referral letter," Timanus stated later.

The overwhelming weakness of Timanus' case was that he refused to subpoena a single physician of the hundreds who had referred him patients. Admittedly, some might have denied the referrals. But if only a few had supported their recommendations for abortion, such testimony might have been crucial for Timanus' claim that he was practicing within the law.

Instead, Timanus insisted on protecting the medical profession. His hope was that many referring doctors would appear in court voluntarily, and he sent the same letter to each of the 353 doctors on his list: "I do feel that having done this work legitimately, referred by doctors to me, that all doctors should take this case that is now pending against me as casting a reflection on their good judgment and their ability to decide which of their patients should have what treatment."

Not one doctor appeared in court or even answered his letter!

"I tried to be ethical even in that situation, and I did not take the stand or incriminate any of these doctors," he told a medical conference later. "Why did those 353 doctors refer those patients if no need for abortion existed, and why were they not willing to stand back of their action?"

Timanus, of course, was striking at the Great American Hypocrisy: the fact that most of the medical profession prefers to keep the skilled abortionist in practice but refuses to take any responsibility for him. If just one or two prominent physicians had testified for Timanus, the trial might have been altered. Instead of a routine abortion case, there might have been a significant interpretation of Maryland law based on the profession's right to call on a doctor in open practice for abortions it considered essential.

With all the flaws in Timanus' defense, including his own refusal to summon medical witnesses, his conviction on November 7, 1951, was hardly a surprise. He was fined $5,000 and sentenced to six months in jail, later reduced to four and a half months. He has never returned to practice.

The real mystery is why the police raided his office in the first place. Perhaps the political and religious hierarchy, a close-knit structure in Baltimore, had changed their policy after twenty-five years and decided to close down all abortionists. Although this policy reversal cannot be proved, a police officer later admitted he had been instructed to "get Timanus." And when Timanus was discussing his case with a retired judge toward the end of the trial, and raised the possibility of naming referring doctors, he was curtly warned, "Keep your mouth shut!"

VII

Methods of Reaching the Skilled Abortionist

The skilled abortionist defies generalization. Like Dr. S., some practice openly, ignored by the police. In a major northwestern city, a prominent woman physician, recently retired, practiced abortion during her whole career, and was considered an exceptional surgeon by the medical profession in the area. Her place has been taken by four other abortionists, who have offices in the same building in the heart of the business district, known to most residents and unmolested by the police. They charge only $250 to $350.

By contrast, most big-city abortionists, particularly in areas of Catholic influence, are forced into secrecy. "When a friend of mine with three children became pregnant accidentally, she and her husband asked their obstetrician about an abortionist," a Chicago lawyer reports. "After he refused to discuss the subject, she contacted a neighbor who had undergone abortion, was given a telephone number, and told to come to an apartment at a fashionable address. She didn't see the doctor until she was on the operating table. Although she was drowsy from anesthesia, and the doctor's face was covered by cap and mask, she still recognized him. It was her own obstetrician!"

While practicing openly in other branches of medicine many physicians perform a few abortions a week. One hospital director in a wealthy New York suburb has been doing abortions on the side for thirty years. A general practitioner on New York's West Side takes four or five cases a week after hours and charges about $600; but in the plushier offices of Park Avenue and Central Park West, the rate runs as high as $1,000 to $2,000.

The skilled abortionist in open practice is more typical of rural than urban areas. In a small Illinois town, for example, a general practitioner charges a modest fee of $125. Born and raised there, he has been friends with the mayor and other officials since boyhood, and his operations have never been harassed by the police.

In Grove, Oklahoma, with a population of 1,000, Dr. J. Bryan Henrie performed abortions at his clinic for thirty years. He helped found the public library, served as a city councilman, and was chosen Father of the Year by the PTA in 1960. "If you couldn't pay, he never said a word," one resident reports. In 1962, the death of a patient at a Tulsa hospital was presumably linked to an abortion at Dr. Henrie's clinic. When he was tried and sentenced to prison, the whole town turned out for a farewell party, many women weeping.

The search for a skilled abortionist may be the most desperate period in a woman's life, involving at least three critical pressures. First, her time is limited, for almost no abortionist will perform the operation after three months of pregnancy. Second, the abortionist's location may require a long trip to another part of the country, an obvious obstacle if the woman has children at home or a job. Third, she may have difficulty finding a doctor she can afford. Accompanying these pressures is the psychological strain of being forced into secrecy for an operation she considers her right.

One obvious starting point in the search is a friend who has already used an abortionist, or a nurse, a hospital official, or anyone with close medical contacts. A far more logical yet highly limited source is the woman's own family physician or obstetrician. Unless she has enjoyed a long and trusted relationship with this doctor, however, her chances of help are negligible. Fear of being implicated in a court abortion case restrains many physicians from referring patients.

This timidity of the medical profession is strikingly evident in the Ober-Lader survey of obstetricians and gynecologists throughout the country. Of 338 answering the question, about 10 per cent admitted they referred patients to abortionists. Of these, the greatest number resided in California, Florida, New York, and Washington— all states with a sizable complement of skilled abortionists. One Seattle doctor sent thirty to forty patients a year; a California doctor, twenty; a Florida doctor, ten to twenty. Most, however, averaged four or five referrals annually.

Asked in the same survey what percentage of their medical friends and associates sent patients to abortionists (perhaps a more psychologically accurate estimate of the truth), this same group of obstetricians stated 15 per cent. Some of the individual estimates, however, were significantly higher. A Tulsa physician said that 100 per cent of his medical associates referred patients; a Beverly Hills, California, doctor, 75 to 90 per cent; a Miami doctor, 80 per cent.

From this survey, and supplementary interviews with lawyers, sociologists, and journalists, the location of skilled abortionists in 1964 has been charted.

Chart 1: Location of Skilled Abortionists

Alabama:	At least two in Birmingham.
California:	A major center, not only in San Francisco and Los Angeles (including Beverly Hills and Pasadena), but in smaller cities, like Fresno, and numerous towns which cannot be identified.
Colorado:	One or two.
District of Columbia:	Major center for surrounding states.
Florida:	At least two skilled practitioners in both Miami and Jacksonville. Some capable Cuban abortionists have moved to Miami and take referrals from same U.S. doctors who sent patients to Havana.
Georgia:	At least two in Atlanta, but standards unverified.
Idaho:	One near Boise.
Illinois:	At least one in Chicago, five in rest of state.
Indiana:	One in Evansville, one in smaller town.
Kansas:	One in Topeka.
Maryland:	At least five near Washington, D.C., and in rural areas.
Michigan:	As many as ten in Detroit.
Massachusetts:	One "gynecologist of repute" in Boston, a few in rest of state.

Missouri:	One in St. Louis.
Montana:	One.
New Jersey:	Many in Jersey City and urban complex near New York.
New York:	A key center with dozens of experts, not only in New York City, but in Westchester and Long Island suburbs.
North Carolina:	At least one in major cities, but ability unverified.
Ohio:	Two or more in Cleveland and Akron.
Oklahoma:	At least one in Tulsa, three or more in rest of state.
Oregon:	At least two in Portland, a few in rest of state.
Pennsylvania:	At least one in Philadelphia, some in rural areas.
Rhode Island:	Two in Providence, four in rest of state.
South Carolina:	A few in major cities, competence univerified.
Tennessee:	One in Nashville.
Texas:	At least two in Houston, others in Austin and other cities.
Utah:	One in Salt Lake City, one in smaller town.
Virginia:	One in Washington, D.C., suburbs, one in rural area.
Washington:	Four or more in Seattle, a major center; others in smaller cities.
Wisconsin:	One in Milwaukee.

If a woman cannot find a skilled abortionist near home, or afford his price, her search may take her across the U.S. border or overseas. The minimal cost of an auto trip to Mexico, and the moderate price charged by skilled abortionists there, make this alternative advantageous for residents of the West Coast or Southwest. Even the plane fare from New York plus the fee of a Puerto Rican abortionist add up to less than the cost of most Park Avenue abortions.

Significantly, many physicians will make referrals only overseas, as the risk of being involved in court action is negligible. However, just as often, their reason is that of trust in a particular doctor. One

New York psychiatrist who sends patients only to a Tokyo doctor insists, "I have known this surgeon since his training at a leading New York hospital, and trust his work implicitly. Despite the travel cost to Japan, I emphasize to patients that an emergency demands the financial sacrifice."

Women from New York, Boston, and other East Coast cities usually arrive alone at Puerto Rico's San Juan airport, carrying only enough clothes for three or four days. They come mainly on Fridays to have a long weekend of rest. They have been coming in such increasing numbers that their mission is now labeled the "San Juan weekend," and the letters in the model number of their jet plane, DC-8, are often jocularly translated as Dilatation and Curettage.

Although local experts estimate that 10,000 women from the States visit Puerto Rico for abortions, this figure is probably high. Still, Dr. Carlos E. Bertran, 1963 president of the Puerto Rican Medical Association, has described it as a "fantastic traffic." And a prominent New York obstetrician was recently told by a leading Puerto Rican abortion clinic: "Please don't send more patients for months. We just can't handle them."

The foresighted woman obviously arrives with the name of a San Juan clinic and an appointment already made by her physician. Only three or four clinics of superior medical standing perform abortions in San Juan; many of their staff surgeons are Cubans who once practiced in Havana and still get referrals from the same East Coast doctors.

Those patients who take the riskier course of reaching San Juan without the name of a clinic try to get it from a taxi driver or a druggist, or simply consult the phone book and call physicians at random. One former Medical Association president complains that women have arrived at the doorstep of his home before breakfast.

The best San Juan clinics charge about $500, and include an overnight room and nursing care. With the increased demand for abortion, however, unlicensed practitioners in smaller cities now lure patients with a price of $150. Midwives, patronized almost solely by Puerto Ricans, charge even less.

The Puerto Rican Medical Association, whose key members are devout Catholics, bitterly attacks the tolerance of legal officials toward abortion. Although Puerto Rican law is reasonably restrictive, police action has always been perfunctory. In the only noteworthy recent indictment, a retired U.S. Army medical officer was charged with illegal abortion on a Boston college student, but the jury voted 10 to 2 against conviction. With airlines, hotels, drugstores, and other elements of the economy having a sizable stake in thousands of abortion tourists, Puerto Rican authorities are not likely to alter their tolerance.

The U.S. abortion center for the West Coast, comparable to Puerto Rico in the east, is Tijuana, Mexico. Largely patronized by residents of San Diego, California, since it's only a short drive away, it also draws a constant flow of patients from Los Angeles and even more distant cities. Almost as important as a center for the Southwest is Nogales, Mexico, convenient to Arizona, New Mexico, and other nearby states.

Both Tijuana and Nogales have two or three excellent clinics each, charging from $300 to $350. One California obstetrician whose patients have used the Tijuana clinics reports: "I have *seen* many postoperatively and to date no bad results." Another California physician says: "I see them afterwards, and the recent cases, apparently dilatation and curettage, were done under favorable conditions with no complications."

Although Mexico, like Puerto Rico, is predominantly Catholic and its law severely restrictive, police interference is almost unknown. The danger, however, is that an influx of patients has produced a rash of unskilled practitioners, who even employ "steerers" to roam the streets. With their bargain prices, they are patronized by less affluent Americans, and clinics in San Diego and Los Angeles have noted a surge of infections from bungled operations.

The fastest growing abortion center is Tokyo, where Japanese law permits abortion on demand. However, as many cases, particularly foreign, go unreported by doctors anxious to avoid taxes, no accurate statistic on the number of U.S. patients is available. The best estimate is 1,000 annually.

Despite the cost of the trip, the surgical fee averages a low $15. And as the competition for this practice is vigorous among clinics and doctors, Americans are rarely charged more than the Japanese.

The great advantage of Japanese abortion is the high degree of surgical skill in the chief Tokyo clinics. The government requires a special license for abortion, and the law provides for periodic inspections of approved clinics.

A further advantage is the absence of red tape. The American woman, arriving in Tokyo, simply visits the clinic where her appointment has been made, or, having no appointment, easily secures the names of the best clinics from a Japanese acquaintance or the telephone book. There are no examination boards, no papers to fill out: abortion here is as routine as contraception.

Although Scandinavian abortion laws are more liberal than any in the United States, they contrast sharply with those in Japan. Each case must go through intensive investigation by committees. Even for Scandinavian citizens, approval is far from automatic. In Sweden, for example, over a quarter of the applicants are rejected, and the total number of legal abortions has been virtually halved in the last decade.

The hurdles are even more complex for foreigners, and the Swedish embassy recently warned that few non-resident Americans have a chance of approval. Of fifty-six recent U.S. cases, all with documented proof of medical necessity, only eight passed the board, five of whom were married.[1]

Still, a Scandinavian abortion offers unexcelled medical care, and the price averages $75 for surgery and hospitalization.

Abortion is equally controlled in West Germany, Switzerland, and Israel, but regulations are interpreted liberally. In the Protestant cantons of Switzerland, for example, under what one local gynecologist calls "our reasonably lenient law," a commission meets twice weekly to examine foreign applicants. Just as some U.S. doctors send patients only to trusted Tokyo clinics, others have long associations with skilled Swiss surgeons.

For foreign patients, abortion in the Soviet Union and Eastern Europe remains an enigma. Although all members of the Soviet bloc (except East Germany) grant abortion on demand, or virtually on demand, only those few Americans with close political contacts there have secured approval.

The primary exception is Poland. With routine clearance needed from only one doctor or state hospital, Poland just about equals Japan as the freest abortion nation in the world. State hospitals charge less than $10, private doctors about $40. The government so far has placed no limitations on treatment of any foreigner with a tourist visa. "We have never been instructed to turn down anyone, including American women," concludes a staff gynecologist at a Warsaw maternity center.

Although few definitive studies have been made on the type of American woman using the skilled abortionist, it has been established that the majority are married, and that abortion has become a prime technique of family planning when contraception fails. Even if comparisons between the United States and Eastern Europe are not fully valid, it is enlightening to consider those reports from Russia, Hungary, and Czechoslovakia, where statistics are officially compiled.

Analyzing a recent Russian survey, Dr. David M. Heer, of the Harvard University School of Public Health, concludes that "in this sample less than 10 per cent of the women seeking a legal abortion were without spouse."

In Hungary in 1963, 85 per cent receiving legal abortions were married. In Czechoslovakia the same year, 82 per cent were married, the majority having two or three children.[2]

Although based on a limited group—educated, white, and in the upper 20 per cent of the socio-economic scale—the Kinsey report offers the only competent profile of U.S. abortion. The rate among married women, as in Eastern Europe, is significantly high. In fact, among young wives the rate is as high as 28 per cent, declining after age twenty, rising sharply again at age thirty-six, and reaching its peak after forty, when most women have determined to end childbearing.

The Kinsey report shows abortion to be an equally crucial technique for the American wife who has already borne a large family. Among women who had ever been married regardless of marital status at time of interview, those aged thirty-six and older who had conceived five times aborted 19 per cent of their pregnancies. Those who had conceived six times aborted 34 per cent.

For the single American woman, our profile is less illuminating. Taking Kinsey's total sample of single women, 8 per cent have premarital pregnancies. Of this 8 per cent, 6.4 per cent have abortions, 1.2 per cent marry while pregnant, and about four tenths of 1 per cent give birth out of wedlock. But this profile must be adjusted to the fact that many girls who conceived while single married shortly afterward and thus were not included in the Kinsey analysis as unmarried females. In fact, the younger the girl, the larger proportion of pregnancies carried into marriage. Girls who married by twenty carried 51 per cent of pregnancies into marriage; those married after twenty-five carried only 7 per cent.

While only 58,000 babies were born out of wedlock in 1938, the number has soared to 268,000 by 1964—a 24 per cent increase in the last four years alone! Surprisingly, the greatest increase in illegitimacy has taken place in the twenty-five- to thirty-four-year-old age group, not among teen-agers, as often assumed.

Even accounting for the increase in legitimate births, these mounting figures primarily mark a shift from abortion toward unmarried motherhood. A primary cause is the religious emphasis, particularly in the Catholic Church, on bearing the child rather than terminating the pregnancy. According to one Los Angeles study of illegitimacy: "The high percentage of Catholic mothers is accounted for in part by the belief of Catholic people relative to the immoral nature of any abortion, which would tend to make most Catholic women who found themselves illegitimately pregnant carry through to term."

Second (and a cause unreflected in the Kinsey report, with its high urban concentration), many pregnant girls from smaller cities and towns lack the knowledge, contacts, and experience to deal with abortion. "Few unmarried mothers we know," observes the director of a New York adoption service, "even considered abortion. They wouldn't have known where to turn."

Finally, abortion is eliminated for another group of single women—those determined to bear a child out of psychological necessity. The neurotic characteristic of this group is an inability to face the reality of pregnancy until the time for abortion has passed. "I've seen hundreds of cases, often well-educated college women, who won't admit they're close to motherhood until the sixth or seventh month of pregnancy," reports Dr. William Rashbaum, a New York obstetrician who made a survey of extra-marital pregnancies at Mt. Sinai Hospital.

"We've had many girls who were fired by their employers before they'd accept the fact of pregnancy," adds Charlotte Andress, director of New York's Inwood House, an agency for unwed mothers.

For this group, the bearing of a child represents a complex range of psychological drives: a form of self-punishment, a tangible expression of guilt, a mark of expiation. "A drive for a baby at any cost," Leontine Young calls it in her study *Out of Wedlock*. "The baby is not desired for himself but as a symbol, as a means to an end. . . . Almost without exception, they placed their babies for adoption and then, as if they had really completed a necessary phase of their lives, went ahead to do new and different things which they had not felt free to tackle before."

By far the most tragic, if unspoken, factor in the increase of unwed motherhood is the selfish interest of society. As long as the demand for adoptable babies remains greater than the supply, society adjusts its morality toward a preference for illegitimate birth over abortion.

Unfortunately, the balance has altered recently, and "for the first time within memory, there are more babies available for adoption than there are parents wanting to adopt," says Pearl Buck, the noted author and authority on adoption. While the demand for white babies still exceeds the supply in many areas, the critical problem is that in New York and many cities with minority populations, the balance has not only altered but altered radically; the excess of infants for adoption are mainly Negro and Puerto Rican.

Since there is almost no demand for these babies, only 3 to 5 per cent are adopted. In New York City alone, in 1964 over 20,000 illegitimate births were recorded, the great majority being Negro or Puerto Rican. In that year 537 mentally and physically healthy babies had to be kept in municipal hospitals because they had been abandoned by their mothers and no homes could be found for them. The others, if they are lucky, find a home in the tenements of Harlem, cared for more often by relatives than by the unmarried mother. The rest end up in municipal orphanages or shunted from one foster home to another in the no-man's land of unwanted children.

Although a few agencies have made determined efforts to place these babies for adoption (one placing eighty Negro children over recent years compared with a high of twenty previously), their successes are obviously a miniscule part of the total, desperate need.

It is easy enough for religious moralists to extoll the advantages of unwed motherhood over abortion while ignoring the cost of this pitiful increase in unwanted children. In dollars, if tragedy can be measured monetarily, the cost is steep, on both a federal and a local level. Of 3,000,000 dependent children receiving federal and state aid, the U.S. Social Security Administration estimates that 20 per cent of the families are headed by unmarried mothers. When the support of approximately 600,000 illegitimate children is added to local welfare costs at hospitals, orphanages, and private institutions, the figures mount drastically. In New York City alone, the Welfare Department pays up to $30 a day to support over 500 abandoned babies.

A dollar price-tag, of course, is an almost irrelevant aspect of the problem. The true havoc is human and immeasurable. "It is the child who bears alone the total burden of his illegitimate birth," Pearl Buck stresses. It is nearly impossible to measure this burden—the guilt, the stigma, the psychic damage that a child, even when happily adopted, may carry with him for the rest of his life.

For the unwanted, unadopted child, the penalty is even more critical. Pediatricians and psychiatrists have consistently stressed the high mortality rate among infants in orphanages and institutions, who literally wither away from lack of love and care; one nurse, no matter how devoted, can spare little time for a single case among the dozens under her charge. Even those children kept in the family by grandmothers or aunts while the mother works, too often become the flotsam of our depressed neighborhoods. Left to shift for themselves, they become prime candidates for juvenile delinquency, perversion, and often jail.

Answering the accusatory label of "sin" so blithely pinned to abortion, Rabbi Israel Margolies pointedly retorted, "The civilized mind would be hard put to devise a greater sin than to condemn a helpless infant to the twilight world of the slum or the orphanage, which is where most of the unwanted and illegitimate children end up. If there is to be any talk of sin, then by Heaven, here is where it may be found!"

Further, a society that forces a single girl to bear a child against her will, and then makes it even more painful to keep the child, cares little about the traumatic impact of yielding the child. The only comprehensive study, as far as is known, comes from Dr. Hans Binder, of Basel, Switzerland. Analyzing 350 unmarried mothers in 1941, he found that a third of the women had been psychologically damaged, 7 per cent of them severely. In light of this evidence, Dr. Binder considered these women "so severely and permanently injured by the experience that an abortion might have been justified."

It is clear that the damage to both mother and child, by any psychiatric, social, or humane standard, makes unwed motherhood a questionable alternative. Where choice is possible, the pregnant girl may consult a physician (or, if possible, her parents) and find abortion preferable despite its drawbacks.

"My daughter fell in love with a college classmate and became pregnant after they had known each other only four months," a Boston executive stated recently. "Fortunately, she had the sense to talk it over with her mother and me. They were only kids with two more years of college, and she wasn't even sure they were really in love or ready for marriage. The boy would have married her immediately, but she didn't want a 'shot-gun' wedding, nor the risk of an early divorce and consequent harm to the child. The boy was a brilliant engineering student, and a hasty marriage could have wrecked his career as well. When she decided to postpone a decision until graduation, I was able to find her a skilled abortionist in another state. It may not have been a pleasant solution, but it was the only responsible one."

VIII

The Underworld of Abortion

It was the last Christmas Eve for Jacqueline Smith, a twenty-year-old fashion designer who had been living in New York with a twenty-four-year-old salesman. When her family in Pennsylvania reported her disappearance, detectives searched for her for two weeks. They never located a body. Miss Smith had been taken to a cut-rate abortionist—a Brooklyn hospital attendant with no medical training, who offered a bargain price of $100. When she died on the operating table on December 24, 1955, the attendant and his helper dismembered her body and disposed of the wrapped pieces in trash cans along Broadway. Both eventually received long prison sentences.

Untrained and often thoroughly incompetent abortionists are surely the most terrifying product of the underworld which feeds on the abortion system. Whereas the skilled abortionist can be studied through his close ties to the medical profession, the underworld of abortion remains virtually unknown. Its practitioners, preying mainly on poor and ignorant women, rarely have a medical degree. In an analysis of 111 consecutive convictions in New York county, less than a third were physicians. The remaining two-thirds boasted such non-medical occupations as clerks, barbers, and salesmen.

In a New York indictment of an abortion team, as reported by *The New York Times,* one member was a dressmaker, Mrs. Mary Poggioreale, who had been performing operations for four years; the other, a New Jersey boatyard worker, Frederick Leonardis, who had been imprisoned for abortion as far back as 1942.

When a Los Angeles girl, sixteen-year-old Brenda B., was

brought by her mother to an abortionist, a real-estate salesman by oc-
cupation, the girl died on the table from almost four times the correct dose of anesthesia. A New York abortionist, reputed to have
grossed at least $250,000 a year, turned out to be a former hospital
interne who had studied medicine abroad but never secured his
license. Two women indicted a few years ago in Brooklyn combined
prostitution with their abortion trade.

Even those underworld abortionists with medical degrees often
represent the lowest depths of physical and mental disintegration.
In their study of New York convictions, Jerome E. Bates and Edward
Zawadzki report one abortionist diagnosed as a schizophrenic, and
another who would treat patients at half-price if they catered to his
perversions. Still another abortionist, arrested recently after two patients died on his table, had been charged twice with indecent exposure.

Alcoholism is common among this group. One patient described
an abortionist approaching her with a curette while drinking half a
glass of whisky "to steady his hands." Bates reports a physician "so
drunk that he . . . perforated the vagina entering the peritoneal cavity
and tearing loops of bowel with the curette. His practical nurse was
so sickened that she, along with the girl's boy-friend, volunteered
testimony against him. Alcohol had so robbed this man of his skills
that he degenerated to the practice of criminal abortion and even
this he could not perform with any greater skill than the most ignorant midwife."

Another typical underworld abortionist described in the Bates
study started drinking heavily as a result of an unhappy marriage
and was confined temporarily to a New York state hospital for alcoholism. As his marriage disintegrated and he plunged into heavier
drinking bouts, he began to forget appointments with patients or receive them while intoxicated. He was plagued with visual and
auditory hallucinations and complained of seeing rats and snakes.
Finally he gave up regular medical practice and joined a group of
abortionists, performing hundreds of operations before his arrest.
During another alcoholic splurge while his trial was pending, he was
confined to a state hospital with a diagnosis of dementia praecox and
alcoholism, and spent almost three years under treatment.[1]

The most disgraceful aspect of underworld abortion is that these
sick, incompetent, and often dangerous practitioners are concentrated in depressed urban areas. Since their prices are almost always

lower than those of skilled abortionists, they draw clients primarily from the poor and unsuspecting. The alcoholic mentioned above, for example, was arrested when he bungled an operation on a waitress, and she had to seek help at a local hospital. Such cases, generally listed on hospital records as "incomplete abortions," offer one barometer of the tragic growth of underworld butchery. A total of 10,000 "incompletes" were admitted to New York City municipal hospitals in 1964. At Bellevue Hospital alone, 21 per cent were febrile or infected—a reasonable clue to crudely mishandled operations.

The second barometer of this underworld trade is that deaths from abortion have doubled in New York City in the last decade. The principal victims are the deprived minority groups.

As far back as 1948, Dr. Christopher Tietze attacked the "shockingly high mortality rates recorded for the colored population." The rates have climbed steadily. Today, almost 80 per cent of all abortion deaths occur among non-white (including both Puerto Rican and Negro) women.[2]

Thus, minority groups are punished doubly by the viciousness of the system. Not only are they granted a pitifully small number of legal abortions; at the same time, they are forced into the underworld of abortion, into the grasp of hacks and butchers. The result has been an abnormally high percentage of abortion deaths.

In tenement areas, crowded with immigrants unfamiliar with the language, unfortunate victims are exploited by quack "doctors" who decorate their offices with forged or counterfeit "diplomas." Their favorite trappings are a conglomeration of electrically operated devices—shock machines, massage instruments, even elaborate cabinets with switches and flashing lights. The victim not only is defrauded of any legitimate treatment but is even charged extra for these flamboyant touches.

The wealthier patient can also be trapped in the underworld of abortion when desperation and haste eliminate caution. A few years ago, the twenty-two-year-old daughter of a noted Philadelphia executive eloped with a policeman, but they separated soon afterward. When she discovered that she was pregnant, she went to her mother, who, afraid the child would interfere with divorce proceedings, took the girl to the first abortionists she could locate—a couple whose chief occupations were those of bartender and hairdresser. They dosed the girl with a dangerous abortion compound that went to her bloodstream and lungs, killing her almost immediately.

A booming trade has led the underworld to develop a vast machinery of "rings," a complex business organization, each with its own "feeders," managers, and often police protection. Such a ring, operating in the Bronx for many years, was headed by Hugo F., an unlicensed doctor; managed by Mrs. C., in whose home the operations were performed; and fed by referrals from the owner of a surgical supply company. The ring charged as much as $500 for each operation and probably grossed over $200,000 annually. It was finally broken up by the police when a patient died on the table.

Generally, the feeders are druggists, taxi drivers, and hotel bellhops who receive a percentage of each referral. The business manager takes care of these disbursements, as well as payments to landlords, police protection, the touchy business of running a secluded office, and the moving of the office at regular intervals.

Secrecy is the foundation of these underworld rings. Potential clients are rarely given more than a telephone number, which is changed frequently. They are often required to meet a contact at a parking lot or hotel lobby, and then be driven blindfolded to the office, where an alarm system and hidden escape doors offer protection against police raids.

Once on the operating table, the patient can rarely identify the abortionist, who is fully covered by surgical mask and cap. The patient's head may even be isolated by a screen.

Here, in this environment, there is little regard for even minimal safety standards. Although some rings may use antibiotics, filthy offices and surgical equipment intensify the risk of infection. Although rest for at least six hours after the operation is essential, patients are hustled out thirty minutes later as a precaution against the police. Anesthesia is rarely used, since it would delay the patient's departure. Particularly on Fridays and Saturdays, when as many as fifty women may be handled, an abortion ring virtually resembles an assembly line.

At the bottom level of this tragic underworld is self-abortion, the frantic attempts by women too poor to afford even a hack abortionist. Into the emergency room of a New York municipal hospital recently came a woman with a piece of catheter—a rubber tube used to dislodge the fetus—still protruding from her cervix. In her clumsy probing, she had pierced her uterus, and despite surgery, she died six hours later.

The catheter, or "bougie," is supposedly sold by drugstores to draw off urine, but in neighborhoods of poverty, almost all purchases are for abortion. Dr. Alan Guttmacher describes the steps through which women are led by pharmacists from menstrual pills to bougies. "She pays him a couple of dollars, which probably means the family eats less for a week, and takes the pills as directed on the box. They are legitimately sold as menstrual regulators, I must add. But four or five days later the woman comes back and says reprovingly, 'Those pills weren't no good.' The pharmacist then says: 'You're hard to bring around. I think you'd better take this,' and gives her a bougie. She says, 'What do you do with this?' He counters, 'I sold one to Mrs. Jones, and she lives near you, doesn't she? She'll show you how to use it.' Over a cup of tea in the kitchen, the campaign to evacuate Mrs. X's uterus is planned and later executed."

The hazardous implements for self-abortion range from wire coat hangers, umbrella ribs and knitting needles to such rustic improvisations as a goose quill dipped in turpentine. All are dangerous. Few are effective except in the hands of experts. Slippery elm sticks, which swell with moisture when inserted in the cervix, and celery stalks, employed similarly in South America, have the inherent peril of easy infection.

An even more lethal technique is the injection of soap solution. A mother with three children was admitted to Boston's Massachusetts General Hospital with severe abdominal pain, vaginal bleeding, and a temperature of 105 after douching herself with a soap and bleach solution by syringe. "She was alert and asking to go home and care for her children although she was gray and appeared about to die at any minute," the attending physician reported. Despite blood transfusion and every emergency measure, she died twenty-six hours later.

Another woman, admitted to Boston City Hospital, had used a douche of green soap and glycerine. Her uterus was distended far beyond its normal size for the period of gestation. A third case used a strong detergent as a douche. The common denominator in all these fatal or near-fatal cases is some form of soap which goes direct to the uterine veins and brings collapse and death in minutes or hours. Often an air bubble blocks a blood vessel and produces an air embolism. Other times, a deadly infection known as gas gangrene leads quickly to massive destruction of the blood. The same disastrous consequences can be caused by Lysol, vinegar, silver salts, lye, and other chemicals that women frequently inject under pressure through douche nozzle or syringe.

Equally perilous is a uterine paste, generally made of soft soap, iodine potassium iodide, and aromatic substances. Again soap is the potential killer. In the cases studied by Dr. Frank Dutra and his associates, a twenty-five-year-old woman brought to the hospital in a coma died nine hours later from blood-vessel blockage. Paste also can cause acute peritonitis, and Dutra calls the fatality rate "fairly high."[3]

The use of soap pastes and similar chemicals for abortion has been parlayed into a huge business by underworld manufacturers and unscrupulous drugstores, particularly in depressed urban areas. The leading paste for many years, known as "Metro Vac," was manufactured by "Dr." Charles Faiman for a few cents a tube and sold for $10 and up. On his profits, he lived in splendor in a Dallas mansion until the U.S. Food and Drug Administration caught him shipping his products across the Texas state line and jailed him.

A similar paste, "Ultra Jel," made of soap, castor oil, iodine, and a few other ingredients, was responsible for three sudden deaths before it was banned from the market. Tablets of potassium permanganate, used as an abortifacient by insertion into the vagina, proved so dangerous that the Food and Drug Administration prohibited its sale except by doctor's prescription. This caustic, tissue-destroying agent damages the vagina walls and can cause massive hemorrhaging, ulcers, and infection. Still, despite government controls, women manage to procure it and continue endangering their lives.

The Food and Drug Administration is locked in a constant struggle to unearth new abortifacients and ban them with "cease and desist" orders—a sometimes futile task. The underworld manufacturer makes a slight change in the composition of his product, disappears behind the blind of another post-office-box number, and keeps peddling it through shoddy drugstores and direct-mail advertisements. Generally billed as "An Aid to Delayed Menstruation," these nostrums are considered of little value by the medical profession except in rare cases where a woman tends to miscarry easily. Yet all too often women use them, find them effective (especially those women who were probably not even pregnant to begin with), praise them to their friends, and the cycle of ignorance and danger builds.

In fact, through the centuries a vast range of folklore has given

rise to a myth of effectiveness about dozens of presumed abortifacients. As early as 1933, Dr. William J. Robinson stated: "The tons of
tansy, pennyroyal, savin, quinine, colocynth, calomel, wormwood, etc.,
which the poor women are taking, endangering their lives and
ruining their health, sometimes irretrievably, are in my opinion an
additional indictment of our anti-abortion laws."

The favored remedies also include ergot, Spanish fly, apiole,
lead salts, kerosene, mercury salts, oil of wintergreen, nitrobenzine,
castor oil, croton oil, rue, and a seemingly endless list of purga-
tives and irritants. Rarely of any value, all involve varying degrees of
danger.

Although many U.S. police departments, like those of Los Angeles and New York, maintain special abortion squads, curtailment
of underworld abortion remains perfunctory at best. The bulk of
police effort is concentrated on abortion deaths: one New York abortionist a few years ago was tracked all the way to the tiny principality
of Andorra, on the French-Spanish border, after a girl died on his
operating table. When obstetricians in the Ober-Lader survey were
asked if police in their area curtailed abortionists, they frequently
replied, "Only if fatalities." A New York suburban doctor, for example, stated that abortionists "flourish until there is an accident."

Otherwise, responses were varied throughout the country. A
doctor in Phoenix, Arizona, said his city was closely curtailed. Berkeley, California, reported very rigid curtailment. A Cleveland doctor
called the police diligent. By contrast, a major Texas city reported no
restrictions. In a large Oklahoma city, abortionists practice reasonably freely. An Ohio physician stated: "Competent abortionists not
investigated too strongly." In key Washington cities, abortionists
practice without arrest.

Surprisingly few abortionists over the years have been indicted,
and even fewer convicted. In Chicago during a ten-year period, there
were thirty-eight prosecutions and nine convictions. Minnesota, in a
six-year study, averaged nineteen convictions a year; Connecticut,
about eight convictions annually from 1938 to 1954. In a five-year period the New York county district attorney indicted ninety-six abortionists and won seventy-three convictions—a record that has since
been exceeded as a result of investigations by the Police Women's
Bureau.[4]

The chief problem confronting investigators is getting evidence
that will stand up in court. Although the police occasionally receive

tips from embittered husbands or boy-friends who feel that the patient has been overcharged, or injured, women must by necessity be the key witnesses, and they are generally reluctant to testify. Further, abortion investigation demands a highly trained team of experts, and many police departments consider the manpower and time too great an expenditure for the results.

Since the quickest source of testimony are those "incomplete" abortions at local hospitals, detectives often pressure women on admission in the hope of getting a lead. "More is to be gained by questioning the woman when she feels the worst," a police officer told a conference in San Francisco.

To avoid this harassment, staff doctors often make a practice of listing abortion patients under "miscarriage," a category generally reserved for spontaneous abortions and seldom bothered by the police. "My first responsibility is to save the patient's life," states a resident surgeon at a Harlem hospital, "not to help detectives track down an abortionist."

Still, the police have other methods of applying pressure. They can threaten to charge the patient as an accomplice in abortion, although few state laws make the woman criminally liable—a fact little known, and rarely considered by women during interrogation. More effective is a threat to drag her name through the courts and newspapers unless she co-operates in giving testimony against the abortionist. As many police departments have a working arrangement with local editors whereby the woman's anonymity is guaranteed, she may well sign a complaint.

The most unsavory obstacle to abortion investigation lies within the police department itself· regular payments to the cop on the beat as well as to higher officials, which safeguard the underworld ring from raids. In contrast to the skilled abortionist, who may do only a handful of operations a week among hundreds of regular patients visiting his office, a ring is highly vulnerable. Even if it moves its office frequently, the steady flow of patients, often at odd hours, can arouse the suspicions of apartment superintendents, elevator boys, delivery men, and, above all, patrolmen.

Although no one knows the extent of abortion payoffs, a Long Island gynecologist, questioned about a flourishing ring in his suburb, insisted, "Somebody must get ice." An assistant district attorney was convicted in Brooklyn in 1939 of protecting a prominent abortionist and taking bribes for tipping him off when his office was about to be raided. A year later another assistant district attorney was disbarred for taking $8,000 in bribes from two abortionists.[5]

Then there is police extortion—a variant form of protection. A detective who suspects the existence of an abortion office may ask a trusted woman friend to make an appointment and go through the routine process of examination. As soon as she is on the operating table, the detective raids the premises. Instead of making an immediate arrest, he hints that a suitable payment will wipe the incident from the record, and the abortionist quickly becomes embroiled in series of payoffs.

When a major ring was raided in the Bronx in 1954, the first person summoned for assistance by the ring was a detective who had arrested the abortionist a few years before. Both the detective, a member of the force for twenty-eight years, and his detective son were subsequently dismissed by the police department for "associating" with abortionists. It is probable that the pair had been protecting the ring since the first arrest.

The most flagrant and bizarre of all extortion plots began to unfold on June 30, 1965, when three New York City policemen allegedly raided a North Bergen, N.J., apartment with drawn guns. Two were crack detectives; all boasted a long list of medals and citations. In his apartment, Dr. Luis Bulas (or Dulas) Barquet had supposedly just completed an abortion operation, and the three policemen demanded $50,000 for dropping the arrest.

This may only have been the final chapter in a long series of shakedowns. Barquet had left Cuba in 1959, where he is said to have operated an abortion clinic catering mainly to Americans. Arriving in Florida, he reportedly continued his abortion practice there until he finally moved to New York, where he opened an office on East Forty-third Street. One report contends that he had been paying New York police $3,500 a month for protection. Possibly to escape this endless drain, he moved his office to New Jersey in June 1965.

Whether the first police extortionists tracked him across the river, or whether the big raid on June 30 was carried out by another group has never been determined. According to police-department charges, three policemen accompanied Barquet to New York, although one newspaper claimed that he was kidnapped. They registered at an Upper West Side hotel, where Barquet was told to phone his wife in Florida and arrange for her to meet him at Kennedy International Airport with the money.

One version of the story is that Mrs. Barquet called a Westchester lawyer, who instructed her to put shredded newspapers in the package instead of cash. Another version is that the lawyer called police headquarters, which then initiated the trap. Supposedly, police investigators were waiting at the airfield when Barquet arrived with one of the extortionists. The investigators seized this man before the package was actually transferred, possibly because they thought he was getting suspicious. Whatever happened, Barquet and his wife somehow disappeared, and a nationwide alarm was sent out for their apprehension.

Meanwhile, the police department demoted the three officers accused of extortion. But the plot was still so tangled that on July 14 the New York *World Telegram and Sun* stated:

"No one at police headquarters is ready to explain:
"Why two key witnesses, the doctor and his wife, were allowed to slip out of police hands.
"Why no criminal charges have been filed against the three officers although they face departmental trials for assertedly conspiring to conceal an illegal abortion for $50,000."

A month later, although the three officers had been dismissed from the force, there was still no one at police headquarters ready to explain what had happened to Dr. Barquet and his wife.

"It may be safely said that if there were no moneys paid by abortionists for protection from persecution, this factor alone would materially diminish the volume of the trade," concluded a Supreme Court Grand Jury investigation.

The number of women trapped in underworld abortion can never be accurately tabulated, but the Kinsey report at least gives us an estimate of part of the tragedy—the percentage of self-abortions. Of all abortions among white, non-prison females, 8 to 10 per cent induced the abortion themselves. Even this is a minimum estimate, since the Kinsey sample covered only the higher socio-economic groups. Far closer to the true figure is the Kinsey study of Negro women, and white and Negro prison women, where about 30 per cent of the abortions were self-induced.

This figure is supported by an earlier study by Dr. Marie E. Kopp, which covered a broad range of social and economic backgrounds. Of 10,000 study cases, 7,667 had illegal abortions, of which 1,863—almost 25 per cent—were self-induced.

The deepest horror of the system is that many women submit

to abortion when they are not even pregnant. Terrified by a delayed period, they resort to catheters and hack abortionists at the risk of a perforated uterus, and often death. "I remember particularly a sandy-haired menopausal woman with a large household of children whom we vainly tried to save," recalls Dr. Guttmacher, "and at autopsy, incontrovertible evidence was found that there had been no recent pregnancy, much to the staff's astonishment. It seemed such a cruel, unnecessary death."

In a study of 500 cases when the late Dr. Hannah M. Stone was medical director of the Margaret Sanger Research Bureau, over half the women who thought they were pregnant were not.

Since the hack abortionist rarely turns down a customer even if an operation is unnecessary, the ignorant woman with neither time, money, nor facilities for an accurate pregnancy test may be exposed to the cruelest of deceits. The least society can do is to guarantee free tests in every welfare clinic in every depressed area. The agony of abortion injury and death is shocking enough. Without cause, it is intolerable.

IX

The Origins of Abortion Chaos

Since abortion laws are often treated as if they were as permanent a part of the social fabric as the Ten Commandments, it seems startling to realize that both our civil laws and the canon law of the Roman Catholic Church in its present form are a comparatively recent innovation.

Abortion was hardly an issue in Britain until 1803; and in most of the United States, not until shortly before the Civil War. In fact, under common law before that time, abortion was not even punishable as a crime when performed in early pregnancy, or before "quickening," as it was called. Since terminations generally occurred before quickening, the problem was virtually academic and largely ignored.

The prohibitions against abortion are essentially a product of Christian philosophy, for most societies before the Catholic Church included abortion in their basic framework of government and morality. The earliest known record of an abortive technique goes back almost 3,000 years before Christ, in the royal archives of China. An Egyptian medical papyrus of 1550 B.C. mentions another technique, one that resembles both contraceptive and abortifacient. Although the code of Hammurabi, Babylonian king in 1728 B.C., and the Jews during their Egyptian exodus established penalties against abortion, these were strictly limited to the payment of compensation when an assault on a pregnant wife resulted in miscarriage. The eminent historian William Lecky has stated: "The practice of abortion was one to which few persons in antiquity attached any deep feelings of condemnation," and describes it as "almost universal."[1]

The Greek city states and ancient Rome, the foundations of Western civilization, made abortion the basis of a well-ordered population policy. Plato (427–347 B.C.) insisted on abortion for every woman after forty. Aristotle (384–322 B.C.) preached all forms of population control and urged: "When couples have children in excess and there is an aversion to exposure of offspring, let abortion be procured before life and sense have begun."

The Greeks, Romans, and Egyptians all developed an extensive literature on abortive techniques, ranging from the insertion of papyrus and dry sponges to the irritation of the uterus by laurel and peppers. Soranus of Ephesus, a Greek who became the most renowned physician in Rome (A.D. 98–138), described in detail such necessary indications for abortion as a contracted pelvis, and swellings and fissures of the cervix interfering with delivery. Yet he opposed abortion by surgery, as did all medical texts of the period, despite the fact that gynecological instruments were already highly developed, and vaginal instruments found in the ruins of Pompeii.[2]

Although the Hippocratic oath is the only significant work in early Greek sources to condemn abortion, Hippocrates himself is supposed to have advised a musical entertainer, requesting abortion, to leap vigorously into the air seven times, thereby producing a miscarriage. The incident is highly questionable, however, since even most of the texts so long attributed to Hippocrates (ca. 460–370 B.C.) have been cast into doubt by recent scholarship. The most accepted theory today is that the anti-abortion section was written into the oath by Hippocratic disciples—that small, austere Pythagorean sect which preached that the soul was infused into the body at the moment of conception.

Neither Roman law nor morality opposed abortion, since the basic legal principle was that the fetus was not a human being but *pars viscerum matris*. This principle probably stemmed from the Stoic philosophy, which, in contrast to Pythagorean belief, considered the soul created only at birth. Abortion, therefore, was not punishable by criminal penalty or social stigma.[3]

The only control was exerted by the husband, whose rule over the family as *pater familias* was absolute. On one hand, he could order an abortion; on the other, he could punish his wife or divorce her if she terminated a pregnancy without his consent.

By 200 B.C., however, Roman women were demanding emancipation and using abortion, not only for family limitation, but also for personal vanity and social ambition. The incidence of abortion was at its peak during Caesar's reign. The *Lex Julia et Papia* (18 B.C. and A.D. 19) sought to stem the increase through tax benefits and political preferment for additional children. Septimius Severus (A.D. 193–211) even attempted to exile wives for abortion, but the penalty seems to have been rarely applied, and probably only when the father had refused consent to the operation. The laws and tradition of abortion had become too ingrained for over 700 years to be shaken by these peripheral impediments. Even when Christianity achieved official toleration throughout the Roman empire in 313, the old abortion laws remained unchanged.[4]

Christian dogma, however, came into immediate and bitter conflict with Roman custom. The first known Christian writings—*The Didache*, for example (A.D. 65–80)—excoriated abortion. Tertullian (155–222) branded it "murder by way of advance" and pronounced: "To prohibit birth is to accelerate homicide. . . ." The canons of St. Basil condemned abortion at any point in fetal development, and the Council of Ancyra in 314 laid down ten years' penance for the act.

Despite universal agreement within the Church that abortion was murder, the exact moment at which a fetus was infused with a rational soul (and "murder" was applicable) remained through modern times one of the thorniest dilemmas of Christian dogma. A few extremists, St. Basil among them, condemned all abortion. The overwhelming majority of theologians, however, followed Aristotle's view, that the soul developed in three stages. The vegetable soul at conception was followed by a higher stage of animal soul, and finally by a rational soul. In accordance with this theory, the Church generally punished abortion as murder only if performed after the soul became rational, or "animated." This point, again probably drawn from Aristotle, was set at forty days after conception for a male child, and eighty or ninety days for a female. No one ever explained how fetal sex was to be determined.

The decision to punish abortion before animation only lightly seemed an eminently practical solution for a young religion seeking to convert an empire that had lived so long under tolerant civil law. Nor did Christianity exert any undue pressure for change on Roman civil law. As late as the sixth century the famed Justinian code exempted abortions before forty days from penalty.

Although a few Catholic theologians attempted to eliminate the Church's forty- and eighty-day concession, it was reinforced constantly through the centuries. About 1140, Gratian compiled all previous Roman laws and canonical decrees in his *Decretum.* Summing up Gratian's position, Reverend Roger J. Huser, an eminent modern Catholic scholar on abortion, states, "If the fetus is not yet animated, murder is not involved." In canon 20, *Sicut ex,* a letter from Pope Innocent III (1198–1216) to a monk who had caused his mistress to abort, the Pope held that the monk was "not irregular," as Professor John T. Noonan, Jr., of Notre Dame Law School describes it, if the fetus was not "vivefied" or animated. This crucial distinction was adopted into an official collection of ecclesiastical law in the Decretals of Pope Gregory IX (1227–1241), with the old forty- and eighty-day theory generally accepted as the dividing line.[5]

With the publication of *The Laws and Customs of England,* by Henry de Bracton (d. 1268), English common law, the basis of early American law, becomes entwined with Church dogma. The Anglo-Saxons seem to have regarded abortion solely as an ecclesiastical offense, but Bracton for the first time places abortion under civil law in the event that the fetus has already been formed and animated.[6]

Soon the practical English jurists were replacing the theological theory of animation with another demarcation line for the beginning of fetal life, known as quickening. This concept probably was adopted from Thomas Aquinas, who added motion as a principle of life to Aristotle's three-stage soul. Henceforth, common law would punish abortion only if performed after the mother felt the child jump in her womb. It was a tolerant approach to the problem, for only a woman or her husband could testify in court as to the exact moment of quickening.

Further, neither in England nor later in the United States did common law attempt to define this moment. The closest approach by recent medico-legal experts is that post-mortem examination showing the fetus in the fifth month of growth is evidence of quickening.

Even for abortion *after* quickening, Sir Edward Coke (1552–1634) in his monumental summation of English law, the *Third Institute,* called the punishment simply "great misprision." Sir William Blackstone (1723–80), whose *Commentaries* had vast influence on early U.S. law, advocated Coke's position when he stated: "Life begins in contemplation of law as soon as the infant is able to stir in the mother's womb."

Strangely enough, this lenient attitude toward abortion may

never have been enforced. Some legal scholars doubt that, after England's break with the Catholic Church, abortion was even prosecuted under common law. And English ecclesiastical courts seem to have lost all interest in the problem after 1527: the preamble to the first British legislation on abortion in 1803 states that "no adequate means have been hitherto provided for the prevention and punishment of such offenses." Under common law for hundreds of years before 1803, abortion before quickening was probably practiced with minor interference.[7]

Meanwhile, after long adherence to the concept of animation, the Catholic Church suddenly came under the most stringent sanctions ever imposed. In 1588, Pope Sixtus V issued the bull *Effraenatum*, which wiped out the old forty- and eighty-day rule and declared all abortions murder at any period of fetal development. The punishment was excommunication, and only the Pope could remove it.

The explanation of this startling shift lies in the personality of Sixtus V, who set out vehemently to cleanse the Renaissance Church, even making adultery in Rome a hanging offense. "An extremist in the pursuit of virtue," explains Professor Noonan, "he displayed towards sins connected with sexual intercourse a severity which would have done credit to a New England Puritan."

Not only did leading theologians of the period dispute the wisdom of this drastic act; most Catholics seemed to ignore it. Less than three years after its passage, a new Pope, Gregory XIV, announced that it had not produced "the hoped-for fruit" but had led to constant sacrilege. Those Catholics affected, in brief, had simply overlooked their excommunicated status. In 1591, therefore, Gregory revoked all the penalties applied by Sixtus except those for an abortion after forty days. The old system was back in effect.[8]

It would last until 1869. After almost eighteen centuries of agonized debate within the Church, Pope Pius IX returned to the sanctions of Sixtus V and eliminated the distinction between a non-animated and animated fetus. All abortion would be punished as murder. Although a few theologians still consider the old forty- and eighty-day rule applicable for canonical penalties, the majority view today is that punishment is based on abortion from the moment of conception.[9]

The importance of this seemingly endless debate is its impact on our civil laws. The Catholic hierarchy, in its violent opposition to any change in the present system, has constantly resorted to the argument that all abortion is against "the precept of God" or "the law of nature." In the encyclical *Casti connubii* of 1930, Pope Pius XI condemns any deliberate limitation of "the generation of offspring" as an "act against nature." After the Draper report to President Eisenhower in 1959, which recommended assistance to underdeveloped nations plagued by population growth, the administrative board of the National Catholic Welfare Council attacked all solutions for population control except those "morally acceptable under the natural law of God."

Far from being natural law going back to the dawn of history, or even to early Christianity, the present Church law on abortion (discounting the three-year interlude under Sixtus V) is less than a hundred years old. Through the centuries popes have clashed with popes, theologians with theologians. When the Church itself could not reach a reasonably permanent decision until 1869, it is obviously absurd for the non-Catholic to accept such claims of "natural law."

In fact, the Church has constantly adapted itself to changing forces. To understand the 1869 decision, it is necessary to place the decree of Pius IX against two recent movements—the development of birth control, and the advances in biological knowledge of conception—for the 1869 decision followed the rapid emergence of contraceptive practice and a corresponding decrease in the birth rate of France, the largest Catholic country in Europe. The birth-control movement would soon sweep Belgium and other nations with sizable Catholic population, and, under Margaret Sanger, reach its peak of organization in the United States. The Pope's stringent position on abortion was undoubtedly linked to the growing threat of contraception. Although it would be a few decades before the Church began open warfare against birth control on a political and social level, the 1869 decision seems to mark the start of the moral offensive.

Further, the 1869 decision was undoubtedly the climax of a radical shift in Catholic theology on the ensoulment of the fetus, probably impelled by new biological research. After its long dependence on Aristotelian biology, the Church could turn to the discovery of the spermatozoon in 1677 by a Leyden medical student. Professor Noonan wisely links this discovery with the Church's new thesis that the rational soul was infused, not on the fortieth day, but at the moment of conception. The Pope's physician in 1661 was one of the first to support "instant animation," and many theologians added their support after 1736.[1]

A second link between biology and dogma could be Ferdinand Keber's discovery in 1853 that the male sperm actually enters the female ovum to produce insemination. It seems a strange coincidence that once science had finally revealed the process of conception, Pius IX defined the dogma of Mary's Immaculate Conception only a year later, speaking of her as having been preserved from all stain of original sin "from the first moment of her conception" in her mother's womb. Only sixteen years after Keber, the Pope made the final break with Aristotle's animated fetus and decreed that abortion from the moment of conception was murder.

An integral part of the theological struggle leading to the 1869 decision were two dominant Catholic attitudes concerning sex and procreation. The first holds that the act of sex is intrinsically evil. From its most guilt-ridden and impassioned expression by St. Augustine around 400, inveighing against intercourse as the greatest threat to Christian spirituality, this theme echoes through the centuries. St. Gregory, Pope from 590 to 604, decreed that if the slightest pleasure "befouled" the intercourse of married couples, a sin had been committed. St. Bernardine of Siena preached that, "of 1,000 marriages, I believe 999 are the devil's." Peter Lombard, Bishop of Paris in 1159, taught that lust, the result of original sin, transmits itself from generation to generation through intercourse. The Calvinist theology and New England Puritanism would eventually inherit and adopt this dismal obsession with sex and immorality. Significantly, the ultimate victory of the Puritan crusade, the U.S. statute of 1873—aimed at abortion as well as contraception—carries in its title the words "Obscene Literature and Articles of Immoral Use."

The second dominant attitude from Catholic theology is that the only reason for intercourse is procreation of the race. "We Christians," said St. Justin in the second century, "either marry only to produce children, or, if we refuse to marry, are completely continent." St. Bernardine calls the purpose of marriage "to fill paradise." St. Francis de Sales insists that the "primary and principal" end of marriage is "the procreation of children."

Such teachings eventually resulted in a Catholic policy of population growth. In a pastoral letter of 1913, the German bishops bluntly linked the expansion of the Church with nationalism by emphasizing that the procreative goal of marriage would "secure the continuation of the Church and the state." After the devastation of World War I, the French bishops asserted: "It is to sin seriously against nature and against the will of God to frustrate marriage of its end by an egotistic or sensual calculation. . . . It is necessary to fill the spaces made by death, if we want France to belong to Frenchmen and to be strong enough to defend herself and prosper." In *Casti connubii* in 1930, a virulent attack on contraception and abortion, Pius XI exhorted "that the people adhering to the worship of God and our Savior should daily increase."[2]

While the first British legislation on abortion was obviously influenced by such theological dogma, the 1803 statute presents a series of strange contradictions. Replacing the common law that had existed for centuries but rarely been applied, it follows Catholic dogma in seeking punishment for *all* abortion, yet still clings to the common law's dividing line of quickening.

Oddly enough, the law is aimed solely at abortion by poisoning or other noxious substances. No mention is made of abortion by surgery or other methods. Even stranger, abortion by poisoning is simply lumped together in a vast and rambling statute of seventy-nine bits and pieces, covering poisoning in general, robbery, murder, stabbing, and incendiarism. Officially known as *43 George 3, c. 58* and, more loosely, the Ellenborough act, it was a catch-all piece of legislation inspired by a fanatical chief justice who seemed determined to excoriate the British for a raft of sins that had long been overlooked or ignored.

The act was hustled through Parliament by Edward Law, the first Baron Ellenborough, who had become Lord Chief Justice the year before. The son of the Bishop of Carlisle, he had already proven himself a grim, unyielding attorney general in the sedition trials of Englishmen accused of sympathy with the French Revolution, and in his refusal to allow any mitigation of the debtor laws. In fact, he stoutly opposed any reform of criminal law, and the 1803 act gave him the dubious distinction of having added ten new capital felonies to the books. The fact that Ellenborough produced thirteen children may also provide a clue toward his attitude on British population.

Unfortunately, we may never know the exact motivation behind Parliament's action. Prior to the signing of the bill by King George III on June 24, there was no debate in either House, nor any mention of the bill in the London *Times*. The fact that poison to induce miscarriage was simply grouped together with other types of poisoning indicates that no particular concern was given abortion, and the bill passed as a routine measure to strengthen existing laws.

On the other hand, the population problem had just begun to prod the minds of Englishmen. In 1798 Thomas Malthus, the "gloomy parson," published his celebrated *Essay*, which for the first time raised the specter of mankind's multiplying in geometric steps of such vast rapidity that the demand for food and other necessities might soon overwhelm the supply. As a humane clergyman, Malthus was haunted by the poverty of the working class, and desperately groped for a method to control a population that had increased 25 per cent in the previous three decades.

It is doubtful, however, that England's rulers shared the same concern. The nation's meteoric industrialization, which would soon make it manufacturer to the world, demanded an increasing flow of workers. And if children of ten were expendable at the mills and mines, and often eliminated before adulthood by the ravages of disease which medicine had not yet learned to control, the labor supply obviously had to be accelerated beyond the recent increase in births.

Already burdened by bad harvests and the economic crisis of 1799, Britain would soon be locked in the bloody and exhausting Napoleonic campaigns. The army had long depended on mercenary troops, but the cost was high. Any diminution in the nation's manpower was obviously undesirable.

Lord Ellenborough was certainly aware of the rumble of working-class discontent against a tide of births which could bury a poor man with ten or fifteen children under inescapable poverty. Jeremy Bentham had vaguely described the use of "sponges" in 1797 as a contraceptive measure, but *coitus interruptus* and abortion were still the basic methods of family limitation.

Only a few years later a brilliant, self-educated London tailor named Francis Place, who had struggled through grinding poverty and fifteen children himself, began to harangue labor and political leaders on the disastrous consequences of large families. Place was the first open rebel against the burden of a large brood on a wage-earner who could hardly support two. In his handbills at workers' meetings, and in *Illustrations and Proofs of the Principle of Population*, he became the first campaigner for contraceptive techniques.

Ellenborough was equally aware of the impact of disease on population growth. As Professor William L. Langer, of Harvard University, has pointed out, the plague was stamped out, only to be replaced by such killers as smallpox, typhus, cholera, measles, scarlet fever, and influenza. Tuberculosis in particular was the main cause of early death in the nineteenth century. Undernourished and disease-ridden, living in squalid, bug-infested houses that were jammed even to their dank cellars, and often drinking from polluted water supplies, the masses in Britain's cities were an easy prey to every epidemic. As late as 1840 almost half the children born in Manchester died before the age of five.

Ellenborough must also have known the threat of infanticide to population growth. The custom was rampant in 1800, and even in 1845 Benjamin Disraeli claimed: "Infanticide is practiced as extensively and as legally in England as it is on the banks of the Ganges. . . ." So many unwanted infants were being abandoned or smothered in France that in 1811 Napoleon ordered foundling hospitals to be equipped with a turntable device to save parents from recognition when leaving their children. The death rate reached hideous proportions at these hospitals, however, and Langer was led to note grimly that the care provided came to little more than legalized infanticide.

All these factors undoubtedly lay behind Ellenborough's determination to end the traditional quickening provision of common law. Still, a precise interpretation is hindered by a jumble of motivations. If the Ellenborough act was intended to protect the fetus as a human being, why did it not define the beginnings of life except by the inference of lighter penalties before quickening? If, in addition, it was meant to protect the mother from injury by abortionists, why does it provide no medical circumstances for a legal, hospital operation? As a result of a conglomerate heritage of religious dogma, fetal rights, maternal protection, population policy, and national growth, and even an obsession with the suppression of sin, it is little wonder that the 1803 act, and later U.S. laws modeled on it, inflicted confusion and misery on society for at least a hundred years.

X

Probing the U.S. Legal Maze

The most notorious woman in New York by 1838 was Madame Restell, thought to have been born in England as plain Caroline Trow. Billed as a "female physician," she proclaimed her "celebrated powers for married ladies" constantly in the advertising columns of the daily press. The packets of drugs and treatments she prescribed at $10 and $20 quickly produced the fortune on which she built a sumptuous mansion at Fifty-second Street and Fifth Avenue, close to the residences of John Jacob Astor and other millionaires, and, ironically, even closer to the new St. Patrick's Cathedral.

The interior of the Restell mansion was floored in mosaic tile, the doors made of rosewood and framed by Corinthian columns, the furniture upholstered in imported satin. In the stable of her extensive gardens, she kept seven horses in stalls of mahogany, and five carriages. When she drove down Fifth Avenue, a giant mulatto footman perched high on the front seat.

Needless to say, Madame Restell had proved abortion highly profitable, and although she spent money furiously all her life, her estate came to more than half a million dollars. Such success, almost equaled by other abortionists in the city, could be attributed to only one factor: the stringent prohibitions of the first New York State law of 1828. Describing the parade of abortion advertisements in almost every paper, and the drugstore shelves crowded with nostrums, Dr. Horatio Storer concluded that abortion in the Civil War period was already "an established custom."

In the country as a whole, however, the process by which various states passed from the old common law to the prohibitions of their own legislative acts, invariably producing the present system of underworld abortion, was extremely gradual. In fact, many states retained all or part of the old quickening rule well past the Civil War and even into the twentieth century.

In two Massachusetts cases in 1812 and 1845, the court ruled that abortion with the woman's consent was not punishable at common law before quickening. Even when the Commonwealth passed its first legislation in 1845, and eliminated quickening, abortion not causing the woman's death was treated only as a misdemeanor, or misdeed. (Commonwealth v. Bangs; Com. v. Parker)

Of nine states whose courts ruled on quickening, seven held that abortion before quickening was not an offense of any kind at common law. Most of these decisions were shortly before the Civil War. But as late as 1879 a Kentucky court ruled that it "never was a punishable offense at common law to produce, with the consent of the mother, an abortion prior to the time when the mother became quick with child." (Mitchell v. Commissioner)

Although such decisions were eventually nullified by legislation, they prove how deeply common law on abortion was rooted in the American heritage, and how long the right of abortion in early pregnancy was preserved. In fact, Arkansas did not punish abortion before quickening until 1947; Mississippi not until 1956. Rhode Island had no abortion act at all until 1896.

The first abortion law in the United States came from Connecticut in 1821; yet abortion before quickening was not made an offense until 1860. Illinois in 1827 punished only the use of poisons, and did not include surgery and other means until 1867.

Although the Territorial Legislature of Iowa acted against abortion in 1839, not until 1878 did the courts decide that abortion before quickening was a crime.

Vermont had no legislation altering the common law until 1846, and even then abortion not causing the woman's death was only a misdemeanor.

New Hampshire and Virginia passed no legislation changing the common law until 1848; New Jersey not until 1849. That same year the State Supreme Court ruled that abortion before quickening "is not an indictable offense."

Nebraska today still uses language similar to that of the common law, prohibiting abortion only of "a vitalized embryo, or fetus, at any stage of utero gestation." *(State v. Cooper)*

The break with common law, therefore, fragmentary until well after the Civil War, was further softened by an entirely new concept—the legal, medical abortion. New York was the first state to write such a provision into its 1828 statute. The Revisers' Notes of the legislative committee explain that the new law "is founded upon an English statute, *43 Geo. 3, c. 58* (Britain's first abortion law of 1803); but with a qualification that is deemed just and necessary." That qualification legalized those abortions "necessary to preserve the life of such mother, or shall have been advised by two physicians to be necessary for such purpose." Here for the first time in any law, as far as is known, the medical profession was entrusted with the decision on abortion.

The same exemption in case of medical necessity was written into the Ohio law in 1834, and the Indiana and Missouri laws in 1835. Almost every state eventually followed their lead.

The enigma in the development of British legislation is that no similar medical exemption was explicitly stated. A new abortion statute in 1828 prohibited surgical instruments as well as medical agents in abortion. An 1837 amendment wiped out any lesser punishment for abortion before quickening, thus ending the common-law tradition. The final version of the law as far as parliamentary action is concerned was passed in 1861, adding such touches as punishment of abortion whether the woman was pregnant or not.[1]

Although the British medical and legal professions have for at least sixty years assumed that the law covers medical abortion, the assumption was never tested until a court case in 1938. Since the act bans "unlawful" abortions, the court ruled that the operation must be lawful under certain circumstances. Or as *Lancet,* the noted British medical journal, observed on July 9, 1938: "Parliament possibly with great sense, had left to the generations that came after 1861 to define from time to time what should be lawful."

The replacement of the common law in the United States by legislation, often giving the medical profession control over the abortion decision, must be interpreted as an integral part of the humanitarian movement of the mid-nineteenth century. Governments were playing an increasing role in the protection of the health and safety of their citizens. In England, for example, vaccination against smallpox was offered free to thousands of children after its discovery in 1798 and then made compulsory in 1853. The medical provisions of the new abortion acts were intended to provide similar protection against swarms of hack abortionists who were endangering the lives of women.

Shortly after the passage of New Jersey's first abortion legislation, the State Supreme Court sharply emphasized this purpose by ruling in 1858: "The design of the statute was not to prevent the procuring of abortions so much as to guard the health and life of the mother against the consequences of such attempts." *(State v. Murphy)*

Almost a hundred years later, the same court reaffirmed this point, maintaining the crucial word "health" when ruling that the statute protected the "life and health of the mother." *(State v. Siciliano)*

Increasingly in recent decades, other courts have stressed the medical aspects of the law in protecting the mother in preference to the fetus. Glanville Williams, eminent legal scholar of Cambridge University and president of the British Abortion Law Reform Association, concludes that the "chief evil of an abortion is no longer thought to be the loss of the unborn child, but the injury done to the mother by the unskilled abortionist."[2]

Still, among the diverse and often conflicting purposes of abortion statutes in the last century, the legislatures and courts were certainly intent on preventing destruction of the fetus as far as possible. Unlike Catholic theologians, however, they were never concerned with the infusion of the soul into the fetus. In fact, the word "soul" is never mentioned in any law or court decision.

What they were concerned with was violation of "the mysteries of nature" which would deny potential human beings to the destined expansion of America.

Consider these court decisions:

The first, from Pennsylvania in 1850, labels abortion "a flagrant crime because it interferes with and violates the mysteries of nature by which the human race is propagated and continued." *(Mills v. Commonwealth)*

The second, from Wisconsin in 1923, brands abortion "an offense against morality" because it "interferes with the normal functions of nature in the perpetuation of the race." *(Foster v. State)*

Obviously, the courts considered an expanding population a

primary objective of these statutes. Like Lord Ellenborough's England, the United States needed factory workers to fill the volcanic demands of industry after the Civil War, and agricultural hands to sow and reap the vast new frontiers in the West. With large families an economic national asset, lawmakers and judges recognized the value of abortion acts that promoted every possible birth.

While employing such arguments as the "mysteries of nature" to defend population expansion, the courts, on the other hand, carefully rejected that point of Catholic theology which equated a fetus at the moment of conception with human life. The sanctity of the fetus was judged, not by religious dogma, but on the old common law.

In 1872 the New York State Court of Appeals ruled that "the child does 'quicken,' that is, become endowed with life . . . [and] there is a period during gestation when, although there may be embryo life in the fetus, there is no living child. . . ." *(Evans v. People)*

Similarly, a Wisconsin court ruled in 1923 that "a two-month-old embryo is not a human being in the eyes of the law," and emphasized that abortion at that point was not an offense against a person, "because the law does not recognize a mere embryo as a person or human being." *(Foster v. State)*

This same attitude toward the beginning of human life is demonstrated today in the laws governing the death of a fetus before birth. Almost no political jurisdiction in the United States requires registration of fetal death before twenty weeks, and often before twenty-eight weeks, which would indicate that the state does not equate the loss of a five-month-old fetus with the loss of human life.

One final, predominant factor lay behind the design of U.S. abortion laws—the Puritanical obsession with sin. Since both abortion and contraception eliminated the visual product of immorality, they were particularly distasteful to the Calvinist mind. If an unmarried girl became pregnant, she must be punished. Her rightful punishment was to carry before the world the permanent mark of her fall. So many unwed mothers were doing away with their children that a New Hampshire act, for example, excoriated "many Lewd women that . . . do secretly Bury and Conceal the Death of their Children . . . to avoid their Shame and to escape punishment." What seemed to concern the lawmakers more than murder (since the 1791 act provided comparatively mild fines or two years' imprisonment at most) was that the woman's shame might be hidden from society.

When a Massachusetts doctor, Charles Knowlton, published the first book detailing four methods of contraception in 1832, he was sentenced to hard labor in a Cambridge jail, not because he had broken a birth-control law (non-existent then), but because he had "offended morality."

Even the early experiments in anesthesia, particularly when used in childbirth, were condemned as sinful, since mothers were deprived of the privilege of suffering.

In its long struggle to suppress sin by legislation, the Puritan mind considered abortion and birth-control laws the ultimate triumph in the use of fear—particularly fear of pregnancy among unmarried girls—to uphold morality. Few theologians today support this theory. "If sexual morality can be upheld only out of fear of pregnancy, then the buttress is flimsy indeed," insists Reverend Peter S. Raible. "Fear cannot make people moral. Morality can grow only from the inner conviction of a person."

Still, the final outburst of Puritanical fervor helped produce not only state legislation on abortion, but morality's most fanatical warrior, Anthony Comstock, the tall, grim-jawed, and bewhiskered secretary of the New York Society for the Suppression of Vice. Almost no prosecutions against obscenity had been brought in any state until after the Civil War as Comstock reached manhood. He would spend the rest of his life turning the nation into a battleground against sin. "If I could but live without sin, I should be the happiest soul living," he wrote in his diary, "but sin, that foe is ever lurking, stealing happiness from me."

Significantly, the Puritan crusade in Victorian England followed the same pattern of extending legislative prohibitions, not only over abortion, but over other forms of sexual behavior as well. Before the Reformation, for example, sodomy was punishable solely by church law. But, by 1885, all homosexual acts between men, whether in public or in private, were made a criminal offense.

Starting in New York, where Comstock made his reputation pouncing on booksellers and art dealers whose products displayed even a miniscule view of feminine anatomy, he eventually destroyed more than fifty tons of "obscene" books, almost 4,000,000 pictures, and over 28,000 tons of plates for their printing.

Comstock not only inspired the Boston Watch and Ward Society, but made the United States "one great society for the suppression of vice," as a New York assistant district attorney put it. For Comstock was no solitary crusader but the final synthesis of the Puritan movement. "Somewhere behind him an Army of Puritans was solidly massed," concluded Heywood Broun, one of his biographers.

By 1872 Comstock felt certain that Congress, too, had joined the Army. Determined that the nation must be purged of sin by federal legislation, he drafted a sweeping and rigid bill entitled "An Act for the Suppression of Trade in and Circulation of Obscene Literature and Articles of Immoral Use." The Act not only controlled the mailing of art, literature, and other media deemed obscene; it banned from the mails any drug, medicine, or article for abortion or contraceptive purpose; forbade their advertisement through the mails; and outlawed their manufacture or sale in the District of Columbia or federal territories.

Even while this bill was up for approval, Comstock prepared his crusade in his room at the YMCA in Washington, sitting up all night to write decoy letters to abortionists who had advertised in the national press. The Comstock bill passed swiftly through the House at 2:00 a.m. with not a single word of debate. In the Senate it was tabled without discussion, then reintroduced and passed three days later. The only debate centered on elimination of a section that would have allowed possession, sale, or mailing of contraceptives on the prescription of a physician in good standing.[3]

Signed by President Ulysses S. Grant on March 3, 1873, the bill gave Comstock personally, as special agent for the Post Office Department, almost unlimited authority over American vice. Empowered to open any package, letter, paper, or book going through the mails, he alone was also the judge of what was obscene or immoral.

Comstock plunged into his duties furiously. In three days in Chicago, for example, he made eleven arrests. One of his favorite targets was the celebrated Madame Restell, who had been troubled only once by police in her career of over forty years. After purchasing two sealed packets of abortifacients from her Fifty-second-Street office, Comstock arrested her on February 7, 1878. While waiting trial, she committed suicide in her gold-trimmed bathroom.

In the next few years Comstock's federal law was to become the model of most state laws against contraception, the New York law, for example, being passed in 1881. Margaret Sanger, at the start of her birth-control campaign, was indicted under the Comstock law in 1914 for mailing the first issue of her militant newspaper. But the final irony was that Comstock, who had sworn publicly to harry

Mrs. Sanger through the courts, caught a chill at the 1915 trial of William Sanger, her husband, who was included in the indictment, and a few weeks later was dead.

What we have inherited, therefore, mainly from the Victorian era, is not only a tangle of laws of frequently obscure and conflicting purpose, but laws whose basic premise has long been discarded by society.

If our legislatures a hundred years ago were mainly concerned with American expansion and the perpetuation of the race, this objective has been universally nullified. The rational control, rather than expansion, of population has become one of the crucial challenges of our time. Long recognized by local governments, which have increasingly extended birth-control services through public-health agencies, the challenge was reaffirmed in President Lyndon B. Johnson's State of the Union message in January 1965: "I will seek new ways to use our knowledge to help deal with the explosion of world population and the scarcity of resources." Two former presidents, Harry S Truman and Dwight D. Eisenhower, have become co-chairmen of the nationwide campaign of the Planned Parenthood Federation. And even the Vatican is slowly approaching a decisive reappraisal of its stand on birth control and population. Obviously, the vast preponderance of American opinion today is the diametric opposite of the population policies of expansion which helped shape our old abortion laws.

If the original objective of our abortion laws was medical and humanitarian—that is, to protect the woman from butchery by incompetent, non-medical abortionists—this objective has been equally nullified. The laws as applied today produce the reverse effect. Instead of entrusting the abortion decision to the medical profession, which has long demonstrated the safety of hospital abortion, they invariably force women to the most dangerous forms of underworld abortion. Further, conscientious physicians seeking proper treatment for their patients may expose themselves to prosecution.

"If the real aim of the law were to prevent deaths from unskilled abortionists," concludes Glanville Williams, "there would be an exemption for the medical profession; but in fact doctors are treated not only by the abstract law but in the sentencing policy of judges just as severely as the abortionists."

If the banishment of sin and sexual immorality was an essential objective of our laws, few religious groups in the last fifty years, with the exception of some Fundamentalist sects and the Catholic Church, have clung to the thesis that society can eliminate sin through legislation. Laws lose their validity, and public respect for law is gravely injured, once the majority breaks such laws openly and flagrantly. The nation learned its most bitter lesson from the Volstead Act. When the prohibition against alcoholic beverages was ignored even at the highest levels of government, its repeal became predestined.

While every faith has the right of moral suasion to turn its communicants, and the public at large, against any practice it considers sinful, no religion can use the power of law to force its beliefs on other groups. Even the Catholic hierarchy, which has vehemently supported retention of laws on adultery and divorce, as well as on abortion, long after the majority had demanded reform, seems to be softening its position. The most significant sign of change is the recent statement issued by Richard Cardinal Cushing of Boston: "Catholics do not need the support of civil law to be faithful to their religious convictions, and they do not seek to impose by law their moral views on other members of society."

Indeed, the only valid remaining purpose of our abortion laws is the protection of the fetus as a human being infused with a rational soul. Inasmuch as both common law and almost all court decisions bearing on this point have placed the beginning of life after the moment of quickening, the issue is primarily religious. Since 1869 only the Catholic Church has maintained a consistent theology of ensoulment at the moment of conception. The Protestant faiths have not only avoided a decisive stand on the beginning of life; their approach to abortion is strangely ambivalent. They want to protect the sanctity of the fetus, yet increasingly recognize the need to protect the life and health of the woman. As we shall see in the next chapter, this confusion as to when an early fetus actually becomes a human life in religious terms is the crux of the abortion dilemma.

XI

The Religious Position on Abortion

"A statute stands until public feeling gets enough momentum to change it, which may be long after a majority would repeal it if a poll were taken," Learned Hand, one of our most eminent federal judges, observed in 1936. The conflicting positions of our three major faiths on the beginnings of life, however, have long inhibited such growth of public feeling, and shrouded theological debate on abortion in a fog of obscurity.

In vast areas of the world, by contrast, such debate has never troubled either the public or the private conscience. Since the Shinto faith holds that a child becomes a human being only when it has "seen the light of day," no religious or ethical objections to abortion have ever been raised in Japan. In Mohammedan lands, the Islamic belief is that life begins in the fetus only after 150 days. Neither Buddhist nor Hindu theology contains any scriptural prohibitions against early abortion, treating it as a social rather than religious issue. In fact, the Indian government in 1965 began to investigate the legalization of all abortion, modeled on the Japanese system, as part of its policy of population control.

If U.S. abortion laws, stemming from the Christian tradition, have their primary basis in the protection of potential life, the continuance of these laws is linked inextricably with two questions: When does a fetus in religious terms become a human being, infused with a rational soul (if the concept of soul is accepted)? When does the fetus in religious terms become a human entity apart from its mother?

The Roman Catholic position: Since the Catholic Church abolished the forty- and eighty-day theory of animation in 1869 in regard to

94

censure of abortion and made the punishment excommunication, theologians have tended to brush over the problem of the exact moment when the soul enters the fetus. The generally accepted dogma is that the fetus is a human being from the time the male sperm fertilizes the female ovum. Still, with their increasing acceptance of recent embryology, many theologians admit the impossibility of pinpointing the moment.[1]

Once the infusion of the soul had been pushed back to conception, the Church faced the further problem of fetal baptism. If the fetus failed to become a living child, it could suffer eternal torture unless original sin were removed by baptism. Therefore, if a Catholic mother dies before giving birth, a viable fetus is extracted from the womb and baptized. Or, when unviable, a fetus may be administered baptism by syringe, a process still not unanimously accepted.

The implications of "immediate animation" since 1869 pose further problems for theologians. If the fetus is aborted spontaneously, canon 747 prescribes baptism for every living fetus, conditional baptism if doubtfully living. What if the mother, as often happens, is not even aware of conception or spontaneous abortion? How many early fetuses are denied salvation by such fine points of moral theology?

Another inconsistency, raised by Reverend Lester Kinsolving, Vicar of the Episcopalian Church of the Holy Spirit, Salinas, California, is that while Catholics baptize the fetus, they do not give it extreme unction or burial, which would follow logically if it were a human being. "That this microscopic and unviable entity is considered by Roman Catholic law (though not by its dogma) to be a human being is the point of controversy," he insists.

Since the Catholic Church forbids all abortion, no Catholic hospital may perform the operation even for medical necessity. Nor may Catholic doctors perform hospital abortions at non-Catholic institutions, or even refer Catholic patients who may need medical abortions to Protestant or Jewish colleagues.

The final authority for this policy was stated in *Casti connubii*, of Pope Pius XI, in 1930: "The life of each (mother and fetus) is equally sacred, and no one has the power, not even the public authority, to destroy it."

What this means in practice is that the fetus takes preference over the life of the mother, and that both, in many cases, are sacrificed. Morally, the Church contends that the natural death of mother and child is a lesser evil than the death of fetal life through abortion. "An innocent fetus an hour old may not be directly killed to save the lives of all the mothers in the world," concludes Dr. Austin O'Malley in a noted Catholic treatise on medical ethics.[2]

Certainly the most frightful dilemma that could be imposed on a Catholic couple is the knowledge that a pregnant wife might die without hospital abortion. And four studies with a patient breakdown by religious affiliation indicate that Catholics comprise 22 to 38 per cent of reported abortions (see Chap. I, *f.* 5).

The one exception to the Church's prohibition of hospital abortion is miniscule. Called the principle of "double effect," it covers those rare cases in which the operation is an innocent act whose effect is good, and the termination of pregnancy follows without direct intention.

For example, if a surgeon performs a hysterectomy on a pregnant woman for cancer of the uterus, his intention to eliminate the malignancy is considered a good effect. Should the fetus die, it is accepted as an *indirect* result of the operation and therefore allowable.

In an ectopic pregnancy, where the fetus grows abnormally in the abdominal cavity, ovary, or, most commonly, the Fallopian tube, the surgeon's direct intention is to save the woman's life by eliminating abnormal growth. Therefore, here too the indirect death of the fetus is allowable.

"In the application of the principle of double effect, 'indirect voluntary,' " concludes the most concise summary with the Imprimatur of Richard Cardinal Cushing of Boston, "there is no question of choice between saving the life of the mother and saving the life of the child, or of killing one to save the other. The physician does not directly will the death of either. Mother and child have an equal right to life."[3]

Such theological hair-splitting, implying that a surgeon can eliminate a cancer without consciously "willing" fetal death, is strained enough. But theological inconsistency further complicates application of the doctrine. In 1902 a Congregation of the Holy Office ruled against any procedure that would directly attack the ectopic fetus. In 1945 *The Homiletic and Pastoral Review* stated unofficially: "The theologians of the last century who held that it is gravely sinful to remove an unruptured tube containing a living fetus, because such a procedure is direct killing, were right in their principle, but wrong in their facts. . . . It is not direct but indirect killing."

Although the validity of this interpretation has never been established, most Catholic hospitals and physicians follow the doctrine of double effect today.

"Meanwhile, we cannot help wondering how many mothers may have died uselessly or cruelly between 1902 and 1945 while the moral theologians were sticking fast to their theocratic absolutes," concludes Reverend Joseph F. Fletcher, professor of Christian Ethics at the Episcopal Theological School, Cambridge, Mass.[4]

The position of Judaism: Although Judaism has no central authority, and its congregations are organized into three branches, Orthodox, Conservative, and Reformed, often differing in interpretation of Jewish tradition, its position on the beginnings of human life contrasts sharply with Catholic theology.

Judaism has never been concerned with the concept of soul and the moment of its infusion in the fetus; nor does it treat the fetus as a human entity apart from its mother.

"Only when a child is about to be born, and has actually begun to emerge," states Rabbi Israel Margolies, "is it termed a *nefesh*, a living soul, and only then may we not 'put aside one life for another.' Prior to actual birth, the unborn infant is not deemed truly to be a living soul, a human being. If it should die before birth, or even during the first thirty days of infancy, no funeral service is held, no Kaddish, or memorial prayer for the dead need be recited, because this infant is not considered to have lived at all.

"The fetus is part of its mother, and just as a person may choose to sacrifice a limb of his body in order to be cured of a worse malady, so may the fetus be destroyed for the sake of its mother," Margolies concludes.

The chief Talmudic source on abortion is the Mishna, a collection of early religious-legal decisions, in which it is stated: "A woman that is having difficulty in giving birth is permitted to cut up the child inside her womb and take it out limb by limb because her life takes precedence." According to Rashi, a noted Jewish scholar of the eleventh century, the reason for permission to take the life of the unborn child is that the embryo is considered a living thing only when its greatest part has emerged from the womb. Hence, taking its life cannot be called murder.

With the exception of these authorities, codified by Maimonides in 1168, the Jewish position is based on a series of opinions, or "responsa," handed down by the great rabbis and teachers through the centuries. While Orthodox rabbis in particular may reject more modern interpretations, the responsa are accepted by most Jewish communicants.

In his recent responsa, Reverend Isaac Klein, a Conservative rabbi, elaborates Maimonides' rule against the "pursuer." Since the child causing a difficult birth and threatening the woman's life "is regarded as one pursuing her and trying to kill her," states Klein, it may rightfully be aborted.

In the case of a woman spitting blood in early pregnancy and advised by physicians to take a drug producing miscarriage, Rabbi Elizer Deutsch (1850–1916) approved the act on the basis of these concepts: It was less than three months after conception. No overt act like surgery was involved. The woman herself performed the act, making it self-preservation.

Rabbi Solomon B. Freehof adds: "Solomon of Skola in Responsa (1878) says that if it is within the first forty days of the pregnancy, there is no possible objection to an abortion; but even if it is older, the danger to the mother's life and health determines if an abortion may be performed."

The late Sephardic Chief Rabbi Ben Zion Uziel extended the protection of health to the case of a woman threatened with permanent deafness if she went through with her pregnancy. "Uziel decided that since the fetus is not an independent *nefesh* but is only a part of the mother, there is no sin in destroying it for her sake," Freehof states.

Similarly, recent Jewish responsa approve the latest medical indications for abortion. In the case of German measles, "since there is strong preponderance of medical opinion that the child will be born imperfect physically, and even mentally, then for the mother's sake (i.e., her mental anguish now and in the future), she may sacrifice this part of herself," Freehof observes.

As for psychiatric abortion, according to the responsa of Rabbenu Tam, impairment of any part of the body is to be regarded as having potential fatal consequences, and a disturbed mental and emotional state can certainly be regarded as a condition of impaired health. "To the psychiatrically orientated Jewish authority of our time," says Rabbi Armond F. Cohen, "a definitely established suicidal tendency relating to pregnancy would warrant a therapeutic abortion."

In the last few years, a few Reform rabbis have preached a far more radical position. "It is a man and woman who must decide whether or not they wish their union to lead to the birth of a child, not the church or the synagogue, and certainly not the state," Margolies insists. "The parents alone have the right to determine whether the unborn fetus shall live, or be aborted in its pre-natal state."

Supporting the Margolies doctrine "that every parent should have the right of free choice in the matter of abortion," Rabbi Albert Plotkin, of Phoenix, Arizona, concludes: "I believe there should be complete abolition of all restrictive laws concerning the whole question of abortion."

Admittedly, this is a minority view. While the basic Jewish position places the life and health of the mother above that of the fetus, and raises no religious obstacles to destruction of the fetus for medical necessity, there is little support for the abolition of all abortion laws.

The Protestant position. Only one policy statement on abortion has come from the combined Protestant churches in the United States. Although stressing the sanctity of potential life, and condemning abortion as a method of birth control, the National Council of Churches of Christ in 1961 approved hospital abortion "when the health or life of the mother is at stake." The inclusion of the crucial word *health* thus sets Protestant thinking far in advance of most state laws. Medical abortions have always been performed at hospitals under Protestant control.

In addition to the National Council, a few individual denominations have released policy statements. "One of the issues often discussed is the question of priority as to saving the mother's life or the child's life," observed the General Assembly of the United Presbyterian Church in 1962. "This must be decided on the basis of the specific medical problems involved."

In 1958 the Lambeth Conference, including representatives of the American Protestant Episcopal Church as well as those of the Anglican Communion, established a policy similar to the National Council's by allowing abortion "at the dictate of strict and undeniable medical necessity," a phrase broad enough to cover health as well as life. A statement by the Episcopal Church's Department of Christian Social Relations declared that abortion "is probably decided among Episcopalians on the basis of the moral judgment of the individual, her family, the parish priest, and her physician."

The United Church of Canada declared in 1960: "If, in the judgment of reputable medical authorities, the continuation of pregnancy seriously endangers the physical or mental health of the mother, therapeutic abortion may be necessary."

By far the most radical statement yet issued by a Protestant group came from the 1963 General Assembly of the Unitarian-Universalists. Condemning our "laws which narrowly circumscribe or completely prohibit termination of pregnancy by qualified medical practitioners" as "an affront to human life and dignity," this group demanded legalized abortion if "there would be a grave impairment of the physical or mental health of the mother; the child would be born with a serious physical or mental defect; pregnancy resulted from rape or incest; there exists some compelling reason, physical, psychological, mental, spiritual or economic."

Amplifying this resolution, Reverend Donald S. Harrington, minister of New York's Community Church, stated: "Where the new life is likely to be unwelcome, and to be born into circumstances that are unfit, consideration of the preciousness of human life might well justify abortion rather than continuing development."

Reverend Raible adds: "I would allow abortions for general health reasons, including too many children, too close together. I would allow abortions for social reasons, when the child would disastrously affect the mother's life, such as in the case of the stigma placed on the unmarried mother. I would allow abortion for economic reasons, when a child would heighten poverty or be resented for the financial burden it places on the family."

Here are the most sweeping Protestant positions yet taken, coming close to the demand of a few Reform rabbis that all abortion laws be abolished. Unfortunately, they represent one of the smallest Protestant sects. Except for a handful of spokesmen of major denominations, such as Fletcher and Kinsolving, both Episcopalians, the great bulk of Protestant officials have maintained a disturbing silence. This in spite of the fact that damage to health, morality, and justice challenges every precept of Christian concern.

In the Finkbine case particularly, when the hospital board debated its earlier decision for abortion, a unanimous statement from all local Protestant and Jewish ministers might have roused the city to the ethical issues involved. Ironically, the most significant Protestant statement came from a deaconess of Sweden's State Lutheran Church: "If there is a clear indication that the life of the mother is in danger or that her health is seriously threatened, it would seem more in line with the commandment of love that the realized value of the mother's life be given priority to the potential life of the fetus."

In contrast to the silence of most Protestant theologians, a recent stirring of interest by one major denomination, the Baptists, has led to a preliminary "position paper" by Reverend William H. Genné, executive director of the Department of Family Life, National Council of Churches. "We must learn to think of therapeutic abortion as a rightful part of ethical medical services, which can be used with a high degree of safety under proper auspices," he declares.

"I feel that the present restrictions placed on abortion are at the present time too narrow and force hospitals to make the agonizing decision of either breaking the law or refusing to perform an abortion that should be performed to the best interest of all concerned," adds Elizabeth Miller, an official of the American Baptist Convention.

Even having defined the positions of the three major faiths, we are still far short of a clear-cut statement regarding the beginnings of human life. Neither Protestantism nor Judaism separates the soul from the body, nor attempts to set a precise moment at which the fetus is imbued with a soul. In fact, both consider the human being, not a body with soul added, but rather a developing unity of body, mind, and spirit.

Yet the Catholic doctrine of immediate animation, depending entirely on faith and becoming an absurdity in practical application, has maintained an inexplicable influence over Protestantism.

The Catholic, accepting ensoulment at the moment of fertilization, must grapple with the dilemma of reconciling theology with the scientific facts of natural wastage in embryonic development. Biologists now know that at least one in three of all fertilized human eggs or embryos fails to develop correctly and dies in the uterus, resulting in spontaneous abortion or reabsorption. About half this wastage occurs before the fourth or fifth week.

Further, as Catholic doctrine insists that every fertilized egg is an ensouled and human personality, it then faces the likelihood of extending fetal baptism to grotesque lengths. As a Catholic theologian explains in a critical analysis of the immediate-animation theory: "We should have to insist that a search should be made in the menstrual flow of every woman who has had sufficiently recent matrimonial intercourse to see if there were not some germ there, or, better still, we ought to pour baptismal water on this blood, taking care that the water should penetrate everywhere, and pronouncing *sub conditione* (of life) the baptismal words."[5]

The crux of the religious dilemma is that almost all Protestant denominations are trapped in the same Catholic web of animation and the impenetrable obscurities of ensoulment, though cloaked in more modern terminology. Though rejecting the theory of soul entering the fetus at a given moment, Protestantism has nevertheless developed its own mystique built on the phrase "protection of the sanctity of life." A resounding phrase! But Protestant theologians have never precisely defined its meaning. Does Protestantism sanctify as human life an inch-long piece of fetal tissue? Does such tissue suddenly lose its sanctity if the fetus is spontaneously aborted? Does it possess any more sanctity than an appendix or any other human tissue that is commonly excised when the mother's health is threatened? In sum, how large a collection of fetal cells and tissue mark the start of the human personality?

As long as Protestantism adheres to the indefinable mystique of fetal sanctity and fails to answer such questions precisely, the abortion dilemma can never be solved in religious terms. To state that the mother's life and health take precedence over the fetus in hospital abortion only avoids the real issue. Thrusting the problem at the medical profession is a weak evasion. When a girl of fourteen is forced to bear a rapist's child, when the mother of seven children, barely able to support and educate two or three, is forced to add another to an impoverished household, Protestantism must face the responsibility of deciding whether such embryos should by any standard of Christian principle be preserved as human lives.

Unless Protestantism wants to continue its unstated but inherent subservience to Catholic doctrine, it is high time the Protestant leadership announces: A piece of tissue cannot be sanctified as human life. The mother's life has far more value for what she is than fetal tissue for what it might become.

Only when all Protestant denominations have escaped from the shadow of animation can society free itself from the conflicts of the present abortion system. Only when Protestantism and Judaism together have clarified public thinking, and released a momentum of public feeling, as Judge Hand described it, can abortion reform begin to take shape.

XII

Britain's Bourne Case: The Struggle for Reform

The first decisive move for reform in either Britain or the United States originated in 1938 in the solitary courage of an eminent London surgeon, Aleck Bourne. Convinced that the right of physicians to prescribe medical abortion had to be defined by the courts, Bourne decided to force a test case by operating on a fourteen-year-old girl who had been raped by soldiers, and then notifying the police. The Bourne case, labeled by the London *Daily Express* "one of the most important in medical history," drew the support of a glittering array of British medical leaders, including Lord Horder, personal physician to King George VI. Not only was a century of silence shattered; Bourne's acquittal resulted in the first liberal guide-lines for physicians, which largely eliminated police harassment and prosecution.

Although a handful of Austrian, German, and Scandinavian feminists had advocated abortion reform at the turn of the century, the earliest British reformer to consider it a possible method of birth control, and to demand a society "in which children will be welcomed and created as achievements, not flung into life as disastrous accidents," was Stella Browne. When she argued for the legalization of abortion before the Neo-Malthusian and Birth Control Conference in London in 1922, part of her startled audience walked out of the hall.

In the trial of a woman who had performed an illegal abortion on the mother of three children in 1931, the late Mr. Justice McCardie went far beyond the accepted limits of British court procedure by insisting: "The law of abortion as it exists ought to be substantially modified. It is out of keeping with the conditions that prevail in the world around us." His concluding words provide a unique proclamation from the English bench: "I cannot think it right that a woman should be forced to bear a child against her will."

Not until 1934 was abortion reform supported by a national organization. At the Annual Congress of the Women's Co-operative Guilds, a resolution, passed by 1,340 to 20, called upon the government "to revise the abortion laws of 1861, thereby making of abortion a legal operation that can be carried out under the same conditions as any other operation." In 1936 a special committee of the British Medical Association asked the government for clarification of existing laws, a request that proved fruitless. That same year the Abortion Law Reform Association (ALRA) was organized in London, and soon enlisted the support of an impressive list of doctors and lawyers, including Lord Horder and Sir Sydney Smith, and authors and scientists, among them Lord Boothby, H. G. Wells, and Sir Julian Huxley.[1]

Two years later, the Bourne case came to court. As a Fellow of the Royal College of Surgeons, Bourne had long been distressed by the shackles placed on the medical profession by the 1861 law. Early in his career he had aborted a young girl referred to him by a distinguished colleague, and been criticized by some members of his hospital staff at St. Mary's. Now he wanted legal clarification from the courts, and the 1938 rape case, he stated later, was "a God-given opportunity as she had suffered the extremity of cruelty and horror and was, withal, an innocent child."

The girl had been watching the changing of the guards at Whitehall Palace, London. Afterward, she had been invited by two troopers to visit what they described as an amazing curiosity, "the horse with the green tail." Naïvely, she entered the stables and was dragged to a barracks room, where, held by five associates, she was assaulted by the two troopers, who were later identified and imprisoned.

When a pregnancy test proved positive, the girl was taken by her parents to local school officials, who referred the case to the Abortion Law Reform Association, and eventually to Bourne. Although British law provided a penalty as high as life imprisonment for performing illegal abortion, the fifty-one-year-old surgeon stated later that he "never felt an atom of fear." First, he admitted the girl to St. Mary's Hospital with a letter of approval from both parents, and kept her under observation for eight days to study the impact of the assault on her physical and mental health. On June 14 he performed the abortion without fee and in the presence of the resident obstetrical surgeon.

At six that evening, two police officers appeared at the hospital and warned Bourne against going ahead with the operation. He told them it had been done that morning, "as in my opinion as an obstetrical surgeon, it may be dangerous to a girl of her age to bear a full-term child." He was then committed for trial at Central Criminal Court.

The trial was held on July 18 and 19 at the Old Bailey, in a courtroom packed to the walls with noted representatives of the medical and legal professions. The importance of the case was accentuated by the appearance of the attorney general himself, as prosecuting attorney. Mr. Justice Macnaghten, who presided, emphasized to the jury that "the issue which you have to try is an issue that has never before been raised." For, unlike most U.S. state laws, which include the words "life" or "health" as a criterion for medical abortion, the British law of 1861 simply prohibits an "unlawful" abortion, and no court had ever defined what type of abortion or what indications were lawful for the medical profession.

Bourne was determined to prove that the operation could be lawfully performed by physicians, not only to save life, but to preserve health. In his most crucial testimony at the trial, he insisted: "I cannot draw a line between danger to life and danger to health. If we waited for danger to life, the woman is past assistance."

Not only the trauma of the assault on this fourteen-year-old girl, but also the danger of bearing a child at her age, he argued, "would sooner or later undermine her physical health and produce physical symptoms.

"When I am speaking of derangement of the nervous system, I know and most medical men know that it sooner or later would undermine her physical health and produce symptoms which may wreck her whole life. Ninety-nine per cent of my colleagues would be agreeable to an operation such as I performed."

A battery of star witnesses supported Bourne's argument. Lord Horder testified that "as far as I can judge . . . the facts would have led me to the same conclusion as Mr. Bourne." After citing instances of emotional shock resulting from similar cases of rape, Dr. J. B. Rees, a prominent psychiatrist, asserted that this girl "was almost certain to get some form of mental breakdown." Dr. Joan Malleson affirmed that her "mental condition might put her in grievous danger."

Justice Macnaghten's summary to the jury made two points, clearly a landmark in medico-legal history: "Life depends on health"; and, "It may be that if health is gravely impaired, death results." Furthermore, he declared, only the physician has the responsibility of deciding this danger. "The law is not that the doctor has got to wait until this unfortunate woman is in peril of immediate death and then at the last moment, if successful, snatch her from the jaws of death."

If in light of this information the jury believed that childbirth would have made this girl "a physical or mental wreck," Justice Macnaghten instructed, it could rightfully decree that Bourne had operated "for the purpose of preserving the life of the woman."

The jury took only forty minutes to decide that Bourne had operated for this purpose, and handed down a Not Guilty verdict, to the applause of the courtroom audience. Lord Dawson, writing in *Lancet*, called the decision "epoch-making." "The British medical profession believed it had won a notable victory," observed *The New York Times*. Just what did the victory mean to physicians? "The upshot seems to be that . . . 'preservation' of life may be liberally interpreted," stated the *Daily Express*. "It may be held that health, and therefore life, is menaced by nervous or mental breakdown arising from the circumstances attending the pregnancy."

The Bourne case, of course, was not an amendment to parliamentary law but an interpretation of it, called case law, which would guide but not bind other judges in future trials. In the 1948 case of *Rex v. Bergmann and Ferguson,* for example, the judge, in addressing the jury, said: "I fully adopt those words (of Justice Macnaghten's) and invite you to bear them very much in mind." The jury's verdict of acquittal thereupon upheld the "good faith" of the medical profession in prescribing an abortion. Ten years later another case, *Rex v. Newton and Stungo,* would enforce and broaden the psychiatric grounds of the Bourne decision.

Canada and other Commonwealth nations subsequently accepted the Bourne precedent in their case law. "Any doubt which may previously have existed as to whether abortion by a doctor would be justified to preserve the mental health of a patient has been removed by the decision of *Rex v. Bourne*," declared Dean G. P. R. Tallin, of the Manitoba Law School.[2]

Apparently, then, doctors could now consider mental, as well as physical, health grounds for hospital abortion. In addition, the "most important effect" of the case, states Glanville Williams, ALRA's president, was that "it made the police (who are our prosecutors) take the view that they need not prosecute a medical man for any abortion performed openly according to customary procedures, whatever the ground on which it is performed." Yet the practical application of the decision failed to equal the first flush of optimism.

A year later, an official interdepartmental committee established by the government under Sir Norman (later Lord) Birkett recommended a parliamentary amendment "to make it unmistakably clear that a medical practitioner is acting legally when in good faith he procures the abortion of a pregnant woman in circumstances which satisfy him that continuance of the pregnancy is likely to endanger her life or seriously imperil her health." But this official report was ignored for almost three decades. Government after government refused to submit an abortion bill, contending that the Bourne case had adequately defined the law.

In addition, physicians increasingly complained that their hospitals rejected abortions seemingly valid under the Bourne precedent. "Some doctors believe that the Bourne judgment may be overthrown by a higher court," one Member of Parliament told the House of Commons. "If we could give the doctors the greatest assurance of statute law, that would be of great help and would fortify them in their own judgment on these matters," urged another Member of Parliament.

The outcome after almost three decades, Glanville Williams concludes, is that "abortions are now performed openly at several hospitals under the Bourne decision." But with the majority of hospitals still plagued by fear, "the total figures are small." At London's University College Hospital, for example, probably performing more abortions than any other hospital in the country, the total is far less than a hundred a year!

The uncertainty regarding the Bourne decision and its application to statute law reached a peak during the thalidomide disaster of 1962. Although almost a thousand mothers who had taken the drug bore defective babies, few hospitals granted abortion on these grounds. The bitterness of the public, as well as of the medical profession, was reflected in a nationwide poll taken by the *Daily Mail*: 73 per cent responding favored abortion under these circumstances.

The most recent test of British attitudes, taken in 1965 by National Opinion Polls, reveals intense dissatisfaction throughout the country with the present abortion system. Over 72 per cent favored legalization of abortion when the mother's physical and mental health required it, when a child might be born deformed, and when pregnancy resulted from a sexual offense.[3]

More than ten years ago, ALRA became convinced that the Bourne decision would have to be affirmed and extended by parliamentary amendment, and launched a campaign that has proved the foremost example of harnessing public support in any Western nation. Among the organizations supporting ALRA's program are the British Humanist Association, the Progressive League, the National Council of Women, and the National Union of Townswomen's Guilds.

Among those influential public leaders serving in its offices and committees are the Dowager Viscountess Monckton of Brenchley; Baroness Gaitskell of Egremont, widow of Hugh Gaitskell, former leader of the Labor Party; Lord Chorley of Kendal, Lord in Waiting to the King, 1946–50; and Lord Willis of Chislehurst. Significantly, no spokesman for any major religious faith has joined the ALRA directorate.

ALRA has not only stirred a continuous debate in the press but also gained the backing of eminent periodicals like the *Economist*, the *Spectator*, and the *Guardian*.

A series of forums at the universities of Oxford, Cambridge, Manchester, Aberdeen, and York, and at other educational centers, has steadily crystallized opinion behind abortion reform.

After ALRA decided to campaign for a parliamentary amendment, it drew up a program of brief and limited objectives, calling for legalization of abortion at the request of a patient or her guardian:

When it is necessary for preserving the physical and mental health of the woman,

When there is a serious risk of a defective child being born,

When the pregnancy results from a sexual offense—rape, incest, or intercourse with a girl under sixteen.

The first of these objectives was incorporated into a parliamentary bill introduced into the House of Commons in 1952. Unfortunately, it faced the complex hurdles of the British legislative process. Since little time is allotted to private members' bills originating outside party sponsorship, the abortion bill was "talked out" in a few minutes and thus killed.

Continued pressure on the government to support abortion reform was invariably ignored. When the Home Secretary was asked a parliamentary question on the subject in 1957, he replied that "legislation for this purpose would be highly controversial and I have no reason to think there is any practical need for it."

In February 1961 Kenneth Robinson, M.P., introduced a bill to legalize abortion on the grounds supported by ALRA. Comparing its provisions with Sweden's moderate law, he estimated that such legislation would permit only 40 per cent of the abortions allowed in Sweden. "Surely it is infinitely better, whatever fraction of the total number of abortions this would represent, that they be performed by skilled doctors in the full light of day, preferably in hospital, with proper hygienic surroundings and as part of the National Health Service," he insisted.

This bill fared a trifle better, the debate running for two hours. But when the government's spokesman announced, "Our attitude . . . is one of neutrality," the bill was predestined to be killed once more.[4]

A third bill was introduced in June 1965 by another M.P., Mrs. Renée Short, whose speech drew frequent cries of support. "It is my belief that only a very small minority of people would oppose reform on religious grounds, but that small minority can no longer be permitted to impose its views on the majority," she told the House. "This would be a negation of democracy."

Small a minority as the Catholic population of Britain may be —about 10 per cent—it was a Catholic M.P. who leaped to his feet at the second reading of the bill a few weeks later and shouted, "Object!" Since it was too near the end of the session to permit further private members' business, the bill was killed again.

Mrs. Short, however, promptly brought a motion to force the government to grant more time for the bill, and at least 144 M.P.'s put their names to the motion. The ALRA *Newsletter* concluded: "The cause of abortion reform has advanced further this session than in any previous session of Parliament."

Late in 1965 Lord Silkin introduced a broader bill into the House of Lords, allowing abortion where indicated by social conditions.

The blunt political reality, however, is that in almost three decades since the Government Abortion Committee recommended a new statute, Parliament's progress has been painfully slow. Although every poll has shown public sentiment behind reform, the Catholic minority can continue to block legislation as long as the predominant Protestant groups, particularly the Anglican Church, fail to recognize and support the moral and humanitarian basis for new legislation.

The situation is complicated by the fact that the bill may not even solve the problem, according to many experts. "My own opinion is that even if the bill is passed, it may not make much difference to hospital practice," concludes Glanville Williams. "I think we are making a mistake in not going all out for legislation for the medical profession without a statutory list of indications." The longer this basic issue is avoided, the longer Britain—and, for that matter, any nation—will suffer the cruelty and human waste of underworld abortion.

XIII

Storm over New Hampshire

When a pregnant woman was rushed to the Hitchcock Hospital at Hanover, New Hampshire, a few years back, the staff agreed that her life was gravely endangered unless they terminated the pregnancy. It would have been a routine abortion had not one doctor, recently transferred from New York, asked whether the operation came under the scope of New Hampshire law. At first the hospital's attorney shrugged off the query, stating: "We've done similar abortions many times before."

That night, however, highly distressed, he telephoned the department of obstetrics. Having consulted the state attorney general, he discovered that the law did not cover the case. The attorney general had been sympathetic, but insisted that the doctors risked fines and prison sentences if they performed the operation. Consequently, the hospital saw no alternative but to move the patient to a nearby state where her case came within the law. The pregnancy was terminated, and the woman recovered.

At the next meeting of the Grafton County Medical Society, which includes the Hanover area, this case became the subject of vehement protests. Heretofore, no doctor had been aware of the dangerous implications of an antiquated abortion law. They were angered that a statute could imperil a patient's life, and that physicians could be subject to fines and imprisonment for carrying out the most essential care. Under the leadership of two staff members of Hitchcock Hospital, Dr. John Lyle, an obstetrician and gynecologist, and Dr. Robert J. Weiss, chairman of the psychiatric department, the meeting passed a resolution to the New Hampshire Medical Society requesting that the law be corrected.

When the resolution came to the Society's House of Delegates in 1961, it was referred to a special committee of three, and their recommendations were subsequently approved by the whole House. The Society is sponsoring this bill, its president stated, "because it believes that a patient should not be deprived of the right to live by statutory prohibitions."

Here was a unique moment: the first time that any state medical society had drawn up and supported an abortion-reform bill for introduction to the state legislature. Not even in Britain, with abortion reform over twenty years old, had any medical society backed statutory revision.

The Medical Society hardly suspected that it would soon be embroiled in one of the bitterest religious and political struggles in New Hampshire history. For the bill had passed unanimously through its special committee, one of whose three members was a Roman Catholic. And it had cleared the House of Delegates without a sign of opposition.

Further, the statutory amendment requested by the Society was so minute—no more than a correction of an inexplicable gap in the old law—that the possibility of real opposition seemed incomprehensible.

The first New Hampshire abortion law of 1848 resembled the statutes of most states, allowing abortion only to preserve life. But when the General Statutes were revised and consolidated in 1867, a freakish change occurred through the omission of a few key words. Since there was no recorded debate, only revision of all statutes as a package, no one knows whether the omission was purposeful or accidental.

Whatever the cause, the law ever since has prohibited abortions *before* the fetus was quick, or roughly before the fifth month of fetal growth. This change was obviously absurd by all medical standards. Not only are most abortions required in early pregnancy; medical statistics prove that they are infinitely safer in the first three months. The upshot of the law was that if medical necessity required abortion before the fifth month, a hospital could do nothing but stand by helplessly and watch the patient die, or move her to another state, as Hitchcock Hospital had recently done.

The need to extend medical abortion to early pregnancy seemed so obvious that the Medical Society expected its bill to be considered by the legislature solely on medical grounds. In addition, it had enforced the bill with safeguards that Society lawyers called "more rigid than the laws of any states we have examined." An abortion could be performed only if the attending doctor and two consulting physicians certified that the operation was necessary to save life. The certificates had to be filed with two state agencies, and the operation could take place only at an accredited hospital.

But the moment the bill was introduced into the state legislature, the Society discovered that a logical and essential medical program had been converted into a religious and political war. The attack was launched by the state's leading Roman Catholic, the Most Reverend Ernest J. Primeau, Bishop of Manchester. Speaking at a dinner on February 5, 1961, he vilified the bill and any form of abortion as "an immoral act," and demanded that "medicine should go hand in hand with morality."

In a state with a Catholic population of almost 40 per cent, the Bishop's opposition was obviously an imposing obstacle. "In the twenty-five years we have covered New Hampshire politics, we recall no instance when the Bishop got into a legislative dispute," declared a Hanover *Gazette* columnist.

The opposition, it quickly turned out, was based on more complex affiliations than religion alone. The most powerful newspaper in the state, the Manchester *Union Leader,* unleashed a steady editorial barrage against the bill. Its publisher was a close ally of former Senator Barry Goldwater, Governor Wesley Powell, and other conservative Republicans. Although Powell was Protestant, he received a major bloc of votes from the Catholic, industrialized areas of Hillsborough and Rockingham counties. And Powell soon let it be known that he wanted the abortion bill stopped.

The opposition was never concerned with logic or medical facts, but only theological dogma and tangential rhetoric. One opposition senator angrily warned the legislative body that by debating abortion, it was making itself "equal to God." The bishop's legal adviser established the standard theological line by labeling all abortion, even medical, "plain and simple murder." Other opponents constantly hammered at this theme, charging: "Any physician who performs an abortion for any reason is guilty of murder!"

Within ten days of the introduction of the bill, the Concord *Monitor* aptly described it as "a storm center."

In vain the Medical Society emphasized that the bill was only "permissive" legislation. It required no one, and certainly not the Catholic doctor or patient, to accept abortion. Many newspaper editorials tried to inject a note of patient reasoning into the furor. "The child cannot live if the mother dies," observed the *Daily Eagle*. "Therefore, are we not putting our doctors in the position of watching two lives ebb out, when they know one could be saved were they permitted to act?"

At this point the Protestant leadership agreed on a blunt answer to Catholic charges of murder and immorality. The two Protestant declarations were a significant step. Although they asked for no greater abortion reform than this limited bill, extending to New Hampshire no more than those privileges enjoyed by most states, the declarations marked the first joint support of abortion legislation by any U.S. Protestant churches. The Manchester Ministerial Association described the proposed bill as "morally right and necessary." The Executive Committee of the New Hampshire Council of Churches called it "morally right under proper safeguards."

"Indeed it is our opinion that a doctor is morally bound to perform such operations to safeguard life and protect the family," announced the Venerable Donald H. Lyons, Archdeacon of the state's Episcopal Church.

By February 22 the debate had become so heated that the opening hearing at Concord's State House was crowded to the walls with a standing audience. Dr. John Bowler, a prominent Catholic, former state representative, retired chief-of-staff at Hitchcock Hospital, and ex-president of the Medical Society, spearheaded support for the bill by deflating claims that medical abortions were no longer necessary. The need, he asserted, "is not likely to be removed." Another representative added that if the bill "saves one life, it will be worth it."

Emphasizing the importance of the mother's survival, Dr. Lyle stated: "There is nothing I know that will cause a breakdown of the family like the death of the mother." A senator testified: "My wife is the mother of six young sons. I need her—the children need her—I want the privilege of saving her life, if the occasion warrants, and not have to lose her *and* her unborn child!"

Attacking the Catholic charge of immorality, Dr. Weiss called the real immorality the "tyranny and dictatorship" of one group over another. While the bill gave every faith the freedom to use or reject medical abortion, the Catholic Church, in trying to block it, was imposing "its own beliefs on those who do not hold those beliefs."

The sharp cleavage of religious opinion on abortion was vividly demonstrated when the bill came to a vote. On March 7 the House of Representatives passed it by the resounding majority of 209 to 156, with almost every opposition ballot cast by a Catholic. Two weeks later the Senate passed it 15 to 8. All affirmative votes were either Protestant or non-sectarian; only two Protestants voted in opposition.

While the bill's passage, and particularly the margin of victory, seemed impressive on the surface, there was actually little cause to celebrate. Just before the Senate vote, Governor Powell had declared: "I cannot support this bill." If his statement portended a gubernatorial veto, neither legislative branch was likely to muster the two-thirds vote needed to override it.

In a final concerted effort to rally public opinion against a veto, twenty-one clergymen, including the Episcopal and Methodist bishops of New Hampshire, and the heads of the Baptist, Congregational, Unitarian, and Jewish congregations, issued a joint statement:

"We urge upon our church members, and indeed all citizens, to communicate their sentiments to the office of the governor immediately. . . . The religious conscience would not be jeopardized (by the bill). We believe that just the opposite applies: namely, that if the bill does not become law, the state is fettering by law the consciences of a great many physicians and patients."

The Hanover *Gazette* reported: "Bitterness over conflicting religious beliefs reached an all-time high in New Hampshire this week."

On March 29 Governor Powell announced his veto message to a hushed House of Representatives. The House attempted to override the veto, but, as all political prognosticators had expected, the vote fell short of a two-thirds majority. The abortion bill was dead.

Ironically enough, the Governor's veto quickly backfired. Although he had apparently staked his bid for re-election on pandering to the Catholic electorate in key industrial areas, he would never even reach the general elections. In the Republican primaries of both 1962 and 1964, Wesley Powell was soundly beaten.

Despite strong sentiment in the Medical Society to introduce the bill again, its chances of becoming law seem remote as long as a governor has at his command the power of veto. "This means that until this law is changed, no woman of child-bearing age has the right or the opportunity to defend her life against a pregnancy she cannot bear," states Dr. Thomas Ritzman.

Although Medical Society leadership, and the support of Protestant and Jewish ministries, marked a significant advance in abortion reform, the New Hampshire bill unfortunately presents two bitter lessons. First, the Catholic Church seems determined to block the most minute change in the present abortion system, even when a majority clearly demands it. Second, the obstacles to legislative action for reform, so vividly delineated in New Hampshire, are almost certain to occur again in any state with a sizable percentage of Catholic voters.

What these lessons accentuate in other states where abortion reform seems imminent is not only the need for resolute leadership by state and county medical societies, but also a determined program of public education, so that basic medical facts are not lost in a whirlwind of religious emotionalism. Physicians have not yet learned to reach the public through all information media, or to work with legislators in explaining the necessity of reform.

Above all, the New Hampshire struggle may mean that abortion reform must develop new techniques in states where the legislatures are an impenetrable obstacle. It may mean the start of test cases and deliberate challenges of old laws in the courts. The New Hampshire case proves that state legislatures are often the most tortuous road to progress.

XIV

The Lessons from European Abortion

Scandinavia, the Middle Way: The abortion laws of Scandinavia stand midway between the harsh rigidity of the United States and the unhampered permissiveness of Japan and most of Eastern Europe. Swedish government and social organization, once described as "the middle way," have given their stamp to all Scandinavian abortion Laws—an eminently rational system, attuned to the humanitarian instincts and moderate planning that have made these nations a model of social progress. The obvious importance of Scandinavia's "middle way" is that it offers a workable blueprint in operation at least two decades, and the first American states to adopt abortion reform will undoubtedly turn to the Scandinavian model.

Almost ignored in its isolation in the North Atlantic, tiny Iceland pioneered Scandinavian legislation with its liberal law of 1934. Public pressure, in most cases, supplied the spark. In 1929 a delegation of Danish working women petitioned Parliament to abolish the severity of the old penalties. A few years later a Copenhagen physician opened an abortion clinic for the working class. His subsequent trial and conviction spotlighted the injustice of a system sanctifying secret abortions only for the rich.

Still, Denmark had already established a government commission in 1932 to investigate the problem, which resulted in the liberal abortion law of 1939.

In Sweden, the reform movement was spearheaded by the National League for Sex Education, whose intensive campaign not only for planned parenthood but also for legalized abortion was largely instrumental in the passage of the first abortion statute in 1938. Since then, the Swedish law has been repeatedly amended and broadened.

In Norway, the Medical Association demanded a new law in 1930 with radical recommendations for reform. A few years later a government commission drafted its own bill. Although Norwegian practice on abortion was as broadly interpreted as that in the rest of Scandinavia in the intervening years, legislation was not passed until 1960. Similarly, Finland's liberal abortion policies were finally codified in law in 1950.

Despite the common misconception that Scandinavian abortion is legal on demand, legality remains strictly limited. The most common indication is medical: a serious threat to life or to physical and mental health, arising from disease, a bodily defect, or exhaustion. Since a 1946 amendment in Sweden, the last category has been extended to "anticipated exhaustion," so that even if there is no danger at the moment, the woman's total environment after childbirth may be weighed against a possible threat to her health and stability. If "her physical and mental strength will be seriously reduced by the birth and care of the child," abortion may be approved.

While the majority of Swedish and Danish abortions fall within medical categories, Norwegian law favors social indications. Abortion is permitted "when the birth of a child would be a misfortune because of serious or chronic illness of husband or children, alcoholism, criminality, lack of housing, or other specially unfavorable circumstances."

Another legal category in Scandinavia can be described as "eugenic": abortions granted for hereditary transmission of mental deficiency or disease, or other severe defects; for cases of fetal damage resulting from German measles or thalidomide poisoning; for cases of fetal damage or disease acquired in intra-uterine life.

A third category, a humanitarian one, applies to pregnancies resulting from offenses against the penal code, such as rape, incest, or impregnation in girls under fifteen or sixteen.

While the breadth of these categories appears sweeping at first glance, the actual number of abortions granted has been strongly controlled. In Sweden in 1964, for example, over 1,200 of about 4,500 applications to the Medical Board were refused. Although the "anticipated exhaustion" amendment would seem to provide an ample loophole for dubious cases, the medical history of each woman is minutely examined, so that in a typical recent year only 11 per cent of all approvals came under this category.

In fact, despite some early criticism that the new laws might be harmfully exploited, the total number of Scandinavian abortions has declined markedly in the last decade. After reaching a peak of about 6,300 in 1951, Swedish abortions have been virtually halved, rarely exceeding 3,000 in recent years. Compared with a peak of about 5,400 in 1955, Danish abortions have since averaged between 4,000 and 4,500.

Ironically, controls are so tight that a Swedish students' association early in 1965 promoted tourist trips to Poland to secure abortions in that country. The trips ended when the Swedish government announced that participants were liable to prosecution.

One explanation for the recent decrease in Scandinavian abortions is that mounting official campaigns for contraception have slowed down the need to terminate unwanted pregnancies. Another is that as physicians have become more experienced in evaluating "stress syndromes" like exhaustion, they have increasingly weeded out unqualified cases.

The most obvious reason for the decrease, however, is that Scandinavia has developed a highly systematized method of processing and approving applications, almost entirely centralized in government bureaus. With minor exceptions, all Swedish applications go to special committees of the Royal Medical Board, generally consisting of a physician, a psychiatrist, and a layman, preferably a woman. In Denmark, applications are processed through the Mothers' Aid Institution, a publicly supported organization with at least twenty local committees throughout the country. With its low fees and high standard of surgery, generally at government hospitals, the Scandinavian system is the prototype of organized planning.

The critics of even such a moderately liberal system were quick to raise the alarm that Scandinavian countries would suffer from a sharply falling birth rate and a reckless increase in immorality by granting abortions to unmarried women. Neither eventuality has proved a problem. In Denmark, for example, live births have climbed from about 78,000 in 1962 to over 83,000 in 1964. In Sweden, the birth rate has risen from 14.8 per thousand in 1955 to 16.0 in 1964.

Despite the fact that pre-marital sex relations have long been the accepted cultural pattern in Scandinavia, the number of abortions granted unmarried women in Sweden in 1964 amounted to about a third of the total, hardly an overwhelming figure, considering that no medical discrimination exists between married and unmarried cases. Over an eighteen-month period in Finland, 85 per cent of legal abortions were performed on married women. Analyzing a series of girls between fourteen and seventeen who applied for abortion in one Swedish city, the Kinsey report stated: "These figures suggest that legal abortion is not very extensively used to prevent illegitimate births in Sweden, at least among young girls."

The sharpest criticism of Scandinavian laws, however, has been leveled at their supposed failure to reduce criminal abortion. One Danish expert, explaining the difficulty of estimating a decrease or increase in illegals, admitted, "The number is very high, perhaps twelve thousand yearly." This would be over twice the number of legals, certainly far from the desired goal, but still an acceptable record. By contrast, a Norwegian study found "a decrease in the number of illegal abortions." Such conflicting reports would seem to indicate that no study can ever pierce the secrecy of the illegal system and arrive at definitive statistics.

In fact, to expect Scandinavian laws to eliminate, or even sharply reduce, criminal abortion is, under the circumstances, highly illogical. As Dr. Per Kolstad, of Norway, points out: "We must surely be allowed to reckon that at least 15 to 20 per cent of all women whose applications for abortion in hospitals are refused, have an abortion performed elsewhere—in many cases by a quack, in spite of the risk thus involved." Although the Scandinavian "middle way" has made impressive gains in granting medical, humanitarian, and social abortions, the very fact that the system is tightly controlled, and many cases rejected, makes it almost impossible to cut deeply into underworld abortion.

The Soviet Union, All the Way: A momentous yet little publicized social experiment, with an immeasurable impact on female emancipation, family life, and, above all, population trends, carries the sponsorship of political extremes—Soviet communism and Japanese democracy. While Japan became the first nation to prove that legalized abortion at the woman's request could solve a population crisis, Russia has played a unique role in different ways. Not only the first country to legalize abortion, it was also the only one to reverse its policy three times.

The Russian experiment, initiated in November 1920, stems from two concepts. Out of the revolutionary fervor for feminine equality came Lenin's insistence that no woman should be forced to bear a child against her will, and that women should be guaranteed the right of "deciding for themselves a fundamental issue of their lives." As women were encouraged to enter the professions or factory assembly-lines, the state by necessity had to provide the practical means for postponing motherhood. "In five years' time, when I am a doctor and have a job and a room, I shall have children," said one young wife, studying with her husband at Moscow Medical Institute.

Further, the grim economic conditions of the period encouraged families to limit or space their children. Professor N. A. Semashko, then People's Commissar of Health, announced that "as long as the moral survivals of the past and the hard economic conditions of the present force women to decide on this operation," the government preferred to bring "underground" abortion into the open.

The second concept, therefore, involved the government's obligation to eliminate the medical havoc of criminal abortion. The 1920 decree attacked "the mercenary and often ignorant quacks" who profited from the old system, and deplored the fact that "up to 50 per cent of such women are infected in the course of the operation, and up to 4 per cent of them die."

Legalization produced an almost instantaneous rise in hospital abortion and a corresponding decrease in criminal operations. In Moscow, legals increased fourfold by 1925, and ten times again by 1935. Announcing that the percentage of "incomplete," or mainly secret, abortions had been cut from 58 to 10 per cent, the Commissar of Health concluded: "An end has been put to the maiming of women by ignorant quacks." A Kiev physician claimed that underworld abortions in the three years following 1923 had been cut from 85 to 30 per cent. Two U.S. public-health experts visiting Russia were told that the lives of 300,000 women had been saved in a decade or so since legalization.

Despite such medical progress, Dr. Robert L. Dickinson, a noted U.S. advocate of planned parenthood, found the operations in Moscow "somewhat hurriedly done, at an eight-minute interval of time." And Dr. Abraham Stone, observing a Moscow "abortarium," reported "eight of them performed within a two-hour period, with two physicians working all the time."

This assembly-line approach, coupled with the government's seeming indifference to contraception, gradually disillusioned many

American medical observers. Although Stone saw hospital posters advising women to "go to the prophylactic center and avoid abortions," most clinics carried few contraceptive supplies or educational material, and one Stalingrad clinic had received no supplies in two years.

Apparently, the Soviets were torn between their dogmatic commitment to abortion on the basis of women's rights and health, and their fear of an open and organized population policy resulting from a contraceptive campaign. This dilemma was resolved with unexpected suddenness in 1936 when the government reversed itself and banned legalized abortion. No official explanation was ever offered. One possibility is that the mounting threat of Nazi Germany had convinced Stalin of the necessity of every potential birth to replenish the army and labor force. But it is far more likely that the ban was only part of a larger crack-down on the revolutionary enthusiasm of the old Bolsheviks. For, in the same period, Stalin also abolished such previously glorified precepts of human rights as easy divorce laws, and stamped out flourishing experiments in progressive education and avant-garde schools of music and literature.

Significantly enough, after Stalin's death and the emergence of a new freedom in public expression and consumer needs, one of the first decrees was the restoration of legalized abortion in 1955. Again, the official explanation was to remove "the harm caused to the health of the women" by the underworld system, and to grant women "the possibility of deciding by themselves the question of motherhood." The predominant cause, however, was that the Soviet government had come to grips with human reality. In the outpouring of demand, after Stalinist repression, for the smallest amenities of clothing, housing, and a standard of living slightly reminiscent of that enjoyed by the West, the most essential factor was family limitation. The average Soviet couple was desperately eager to delay another child in exchange for a private bedroom or a new suit.

"In our country the overwhelming proportion of women of productive age are occupied in work," a Soviet public-health expert explains. Since a recent study shows that the abortion rate among this employed group is over three times as large as among non-working wives, Russian women obviously depend on legalized abortion to maintain their jobs and thus contribute a second income to bolster the family living-standard.

Although the government, in contrast to the Eastern bloc, has never released abortion statistics, all evidence indicates that the Soviet abortion rate may be as high as any in the world. Dr. Tietze estimates a minimum of 2,000,000 annually, while David M. Heer, of the Harvard University School of Public Health, arrived at a figure of 5,829,000 for a recent year. In many large cities, the number of abortions equals the number of births.

An American observer at Moscow State University describes the "extraordinarily high incidence of abortions" among students—40 per cent of undergraduate women. "Amused by the look of amazement on my face upon hearing this report," the observer remarks, "a girl undergraduate laughed: 'Don't be so naïve. The real figure is probably closer to 80 per cent.'" The cost of an abortion at the university medical clinic runs about five rubles, or a dollar at the U.S. exchange rate, but in terms of purchasing power for a Russian student, this equals the price of five or six books.

Although the majority of such students are usually unmarried, one recent analysis shows the demand for abortions concentrated among married, urban women—a third of whom, in a sample of 26,000, requested the operation because of inadequate housing and lack of child-care facilities. Another 10 per cent stated they already had too many children or wanted to avoid the hardship of a new birth so soon after a previous baby. Thirty per cent of urban mothers, 40 per cent of rural, gave no cause other than opposition to childbearing at that moment.

Urbanization and the extension of higher education have boosted the abortion rate. With the average age of marriage increasing from twenty-three in 1910 to twenty-seven in 1960, women were obviously postponing marriage to complete their college and professional training. Families with three or more children today are almost always in the least educated brackets.

Despite Russia's high abortion rate, which the government periodically deplores but refuses to discuss with foreign observers, official policy still maintains the peculiar ambivalence of the 1920–36 period. Contraceptives are more accessible than they were three decades ago, but the government refrains from committing itself to a determined birth-control campaign. Modern techniques are scarce. In fact, East Germany only recently became the first Eastern-bloc nation to produce the contraceptive pill. "This can be explained by the fact that during the course of the last twenty years," a Soviet health expert observes, "research institutes, departments of obstetrics and gynecology of medical schools, and post-graduate medical training did not occupy themselves with seeking new, effective, and convenient contraceptive devices. . . ."

As a result, a study of a small Russian Republic city revealed that 52 per cent of the respondents used no contraception at all. Of those who did, only 5 per cent employed such modern techniques as diaphragm and jelly. A nationwide study shows 40 per cent of women with one or more abortions still using no contraception.

The failure in contraception stems from the government's indecision to adopt a long-range population policy. All official statements add up to a determination to hold the present birth rate, and even to raise it. Yet the government seems afraid to risk any dislocation of rising living standards. Higher fertility might mean less women in the work force. It would certainly mean huge new funds for housing, schools, and child-care facilities. "Therefore, even though the regime might abstractly prefer a higher rate of childbearing," Heer concludes, "it is probable that it is not willing to pay the price for a full-scale campaign toward this end."

Another factor in Soviet ambivalence is that the bureaucracy remains trapped in the anti-Malthusian dogma of Karl Marx. Marx always insisted that overpopulation was a curse of capitalism, rendered obsolete in the communist state. The last few years, however, have brought a sharp dissent from the original line. "Young Soviet demographers have, despite the objections of the ideologists of the older generation, scrapped the anti-Malthusian heritage," reports Lewis S. Feuer, professor of philosophy and social sciences at the University of California at Berkeley. "Both capitalist and socialist societies, they say, undertake family limitation and birth control because both experience the common influence of education, the ethic of individual happiness, and the conditions of urban life. Fortunately, the young scientists have found the fortifying authority of a later letter of Engels in which he acknowledges that even communist society may find itself 'obliged to regulate the production of human beings' and 'to achieve by planning a result which has already been produced spontaneously, without planning, in France and Lower Austria.' "

The continuing Soviet indecision over contraception reflects this theoretical struggle. Until the government resolves a firm population policy, it cannot commit itself to a vast campaign for contraception, involving clinics, education, and the development and distribution of modern techniques. Although officials infer that abortion is a temporary, emergency measure, it provides a practical compromise, answering the highly personal needs of an individual case while at the same time satisfying the objective of combatting illegal traffic. Contraception, on the other hand, has no immediate target. Moreover, an open campaign would disturb the present equilibrium, and bind the government to a population blueprint it wants to avoid.

For the Soviet Union, the present growth rate seems to answer every demand. While the birth rate at the time of the 1955 abortion decree was 25.7 per thousand, by 1964 it had dropped only to 20.8, roughly comparable to the present U.S. birth rate and higher than that of any democracy in Western Europe. Population, despite the havoc of war, expanded from 192,000,000 in 1940 to about 229,000,-000 in 1965. As post-war babies reach childbearing age, Soviet demographers expect the economy to support a three- or even four-child family by the 1970's, and the population to reach 280,000,000 by 1980.

Since this trend gives the Soviets the best of both worlds—a reasonable growth rate geared to the pace of a sluggish economy, and a solution to human needs of family limitation and higher living standards—legalized abortion rather than contraception will undoubtedly satisfy the government's aims for the foreseeable future.

Hungary and the Eastern Bloc, Prime Test-Tube of Legalized Abortion: The crucial difference between the Soviet Union and Eastern-bloc nations is that the abortion records of the latter are widely publicized and vigorously debated, making them a unique testing-ground for every aspect of the problem. Bulgaria, Hungary, and Poland followed the Soviet lead by legalizing abortion in 1956, Rumania in 1957. Czechoslovakia started with unrestricted abortions but began to tighten its controls in 1962. Yugoslavia, outside the bloc, established a similar system of modified controls in 1960. Only Albania, a mysterious enclave walled off from its communist neighbors, and East Germany, with one of the lowest birth rates in Europe, have ignored extensive legalization.

In terms of adapting abortion laws to local needs, however, each nation has plotted its own course. And none has gone farther in a frank and uninhibited pursuit of a higher living standard than Hungary.

Hungary has recently savored a modest prosperity. Compared

to other communist states, its consumers are pampered, its stores crowded with luxury goods. Budapest women pride themselves on their clothes and weekly beauty-parlor treatments. Yet the irony is that legalized abortion, a key factor in economic revival, was established by the regime of Janos Kadar, which crushed the 1956 revolt. "People in neighboring Communist countries look upon the Hungarians somewhat enviously as having 'the good life,' and Mr. Kadar himself has achieved a measure of sympathy from his people that eight years ago few would have believed," observes *The New York Times*.

The protection of health may have been basic to the original abortion decree, but the ultimate argument always comes back to human, family needs. Although "29 per cent of the women asking for induced abortion do so for health and biological reasons," Dr. Gyorgy Illes, a public-health official, points out, "the present average income possibilities only insure a reasonable living standard for a family with one child at the very best."

Women's rights were equally basic. "One cannot speak of equal rights of women, not even of the most elementary rights to freedom, if they are not allowed to determine the number of children they shall have," declared Gyula Wilmon, the deputy minister of health. "The introduction of regulations with which the state would interfere with the free decision of parents contradicts our political and moral conceptions," adds Gyorgy Peter, the government's chief statistician.

Behind the dogma and idealism, however, Hungary has staked its economic revival on the one-child family. Officials and ordinary citizens debate this phenomenon constantly in the press. A Debrecen man recalls the hardships of his eleven brothers and sisters and the "suffering our education cost." A Budapest man praises "the justified desire of young people to achieve something good which would be difficult to do with a number of children running around."

By sharp contrast to Russia's studied avoidance of the problem, Hungarian communist officials issue lengthy reports, some skeptical of the diminishing birth rate. A newspaper attacks the current dread of large families, which has permeated even to high school students, few of whom in a recent poll want even two children. Magazine cartoons occasionally satirize the one-child family, and a night-club act has been built around the theme, "A car or a child, which is more important?"

As only 131,000 babies were born in 1964, 90,000 fewer than a decade ago, the one-child family has become a reality with the average of 0.86 children per couple. In roughly the same period, legal abortions increased almost five times.

Abortion is not only the chief technique of limiting family growth (a recent study showed that 95 per cent of women requesting abortion already had two or more children); it has become the mainstay of the younger generation in Budapest and other cities, whose living standard depends on the income of a working wife. Since a child often means moving to a larger apartment, always scarce in Budapest but today, with the influx from rural areas, virtually nonexistent, the average couple postpones childbearing as long as possible.

The government has taken hesitant steps to halt this trend, extending maternity leaves from twelve to twenty weeks a few years ago. Still, at the same time as they question the value of such panaceas, officials frankly admit that allowances for children are too low. In a recent poll, asked under what conditions they would have a third child, 60 per cent of the respondents replied: "Under no conditions."

The trend has now reached the point where 140 abortions are performed for each 100 births, cutting the Hungarian birth rate from 21.4 in 1955 to 13.1 in 1963. In Bucharest, the mean rate per family is 1.3 children and only 0.7 among the educated class.

	Legal abortions		Birth rate per 1,000 population	
	1955	*1963*	*1955*	*1963*
Bulgaria	31,700	83,300	20.1	16.4
Czechoslovakia	2,100	70,700 (1964) 94,300 (1961)	20.3	16.9
Hungary	35,400	184,400 (1964)	21.4	13.1
Poland	1,400	140,500	29.1	19.1
Rumania	112,000 (1958)	220,000 (1959)	25.6	15.7
Yugoslavia	54,500 (1959)	150,000	26.9	21.4

Although all communist nations have shaved their birth rates since legalizing abortion, the imponderable question is how much of the drop can be attributed to the law alone. Hungarian and Czech statisticians have pointed out that the birth rates were already falling for years before the law. Legalization, therefore, probably only accelerated an existing trend. A special factor influencing the birth rate was no doubt the exodus of 150,000 young men after the 1956 uprising.

Poland presents the thorniest tangle in the demographic puzzle. Although its legal abortions have multiplied spectacularly from 1,400 to 140,000 since 1955, its birth rate, perhaps abnormally high in 1955, has been lowered only to the level now maintained by Russia and the United States. Further, a United Nations study predicts a population increase of 30 per cent by 1980, which would give Poland a higher growth rate than that of any Western European country despite the unlimited freedom of its abortion law.

The Czech government added another complication to the demographic puzzle in 1962 by becoming the only communist-bloc member to substitute controls for abortion on demand. It established commissions to approve each case, charged small fees except for medical indications, and required that the operation be performed in the woman's home district. These controls produced immediate complaints. "Some commissions almost compete in the number of refused requests," lamented a Prague newspaper.

But the controls apparently achieved their purpose in bolstering a falling birth rate. In contrast to 94,000 legal abortions and 220,000 births in 1961, abortions were cut to 71,000 and births rose to 236,000 in 1963.

Similarly in Yugoslavia, where commissions must approve all applications, and rejections range as high as 18 per cent, the birth rate has been shaved, but only moderately. From a high second to Poland's, it has now tapered off to the Soviet and U.S. level.

A possible limiting factor in the practice of legal abortions in Poland, Hungary, and other countries with sizable Catholic populations is the opposition of the Church. For, in contrast to Russia and Japan, which present no religious obstacles, the Eastern-bloc nations are the only testing-ground in the world where a legalized system runs headlong into the unyielding prohibitions of Catholicism.

Although no study of this conflict in human motivations has yet been made, apparently the Church's opposition has hardly deterred the abortion trend. In Hungary, Church and State coexist with reasonable equanimity; yet Catholic Action periodicals constantly attack the practice of abortion, while the Hungarian drive toward the one-child family persists.

In Poland, the conflict is more intense. With almost 90 per cent of the population nominally Catholic, a bitter cold war prevails between Church and State, and the clergy maintains a ceaseless campaign against abortion. Most government officials, of course, are non-believers, and the religious tradition is weakest among urban students and the childbearing generation. Although communist doctrine holds its firmest grip on these groups, the government must be credited with allowing open debate on abortion and the expression of individual conscience. Many Catholic doctors fought the law vehemently when it was proposed, and continue to fight it. When they are affiliated with maternity clinics, the government gives them the option of refusing to perform abortions, and the option is often exercised.

A young woman obstetrician at a Warsaw clinic explains: "I consider myself a reasonably devout Catholic, but for me, abortion is a medical problem, and I have always performed the operation. Most of the people I know feel the same way. The older generation clings more strongly to Catholic precepts. My mother, a steadfast churchgoer, was terribly upset about the abortion law ten years ago. But even she has come to see the necessity of legal abortion in many cases."

In Yugoslavia as well, where the Catholic population comprises almost 40 per cent, statistics show no diminished demand for legal abortions in Catholic areas. "When I practiced in a rural area during the war long before abortion was legalized, Catholic peasants were always begging my help to terminate unwanted pregnancies," reports a Yugoslav doctor. "If there was a little Catholic feeling against abortion then, I have seen almost none under the legal system."

The Catholic conscience in the Eastern bloc may well be eased by the fact that a predominant percentage of legal abortions are requested by married women—85 per cent, according to an official Hungarian survey. In one Rumanian city, for example, 94 per cent of legals were married women; in Yugoslavia, 78 per cent. Admittedly the secret abortion, still in practice in the Eastern bloc, remains the refuge of single girls; but, as all governments prosecute the underworld vigorously, the Church can hardly accuse the State of making promiscuity and unmarried pregnancy an easy practice.

One of the most noteworthy results of legalization is the diminution of criminal abortion. In 1958, the last year of available statistics, Russian illegal abortions were estimated at 21 per cent; Hungarian at under 20 per cent; and Polish, which reached 74 per cent before legalization, at 48 per cent by 1959.

All governments have countered the underworld, not only by insuring the phenomenal safety standards of hospital abortion (as seen in Chapter III), but also by keeping the cost at a minimum. The charge in Rumania is about $2.50; in Poland about $6, but free if husband or wife is covered by health insurance; in Hungary about $1. Abortion for medical indications is free throughout Eastern Europe.

Why, then, should women still have recourse to secret abortion? For one thing, married women, as well as single girls, dislike news of a legal operation reaching their families or friends. And though officials make every effort to cloak the procedure (Polish clinics, for example, supply the patient with a letter citing a disguised medical diagnosis for hospitalization), unfortunately, leaks through hospital clerks persist. And in a few countries like Czechoslovakia, where the operation must be performed in the woman's district, secrecy becomes particularly troublesome.

Further, the modified controls in Czechoslovakia and Yugoslavia have obviously damaged the campaign against the underworld. When the Czech government imposed restrictions in 1962, the number of secret abortions rose abruptly. Despite a reasonably broad program of legalization in Yugoslavia, secret abortions have stayed at a 37 per cent level for years, probably owing to the number of legal rejects. And in East Germany, with strict limitations on legal abortion, the number of illegals has soared in the last decade, equaling, and probably exceeding, the number of births.

On the crucial issue of contraceptive campaigns to balance their legal abortion systems, Eastern communism has recently broken with the Soviet's ambivalence and delay. In many cases the break has not yet passed the stage of official criticism and policy re-evaluation. "Now why is the propagation of birth control not in order?" demanded an influential Czech newspaper, pointing out that *coitus interruptus* is still used by 44 per cent of the people and modern contraception in short supply. In Rumania, where studies show that only the educated class—at best a third of the population—and almost no workers use the most rudimentary contraception, the government has just launched a contraceptive program. In Hungary, one study revealed that 46 per cent of legal abortion cases did not practice systematic contraception. Of white-collar workers, 27 per cent used some technique, only 7 per cent anything as modern as diaphragm or jelly. Of agricultural workers, 19 per cent were contraceptors, only 2 per cent employing the diaphragm. Although the government is now experimenting with the production of birth-control pills, an official 1964 report attacks "inadequately spread contraception and its low efficiency."

While at least 260 birth-control centers have been opened throughout Yugoslavia, and production of contraceptive materials began in 1955, a study in Slovenia in 1963 showed that about 20 per cent still used no contraception, and only about 22 per cent used the diaphragm. Still, these figures are a remarkable advance over a 1959 Slovenian study when not one respondent employed the diaphragm, and 76 per cent depended on *coitus interruptus*.

The greatest gains have been achieved in Poland, where the government recently decreed that every applicant for legal abortion must first attend educational courses at a contraceptive clinic, and have her papers stamped to prove it. Birth-control lectures are now mandatory at all hospitals with abortion cases, and this campaign of persuasion has been extended to factories, union meetings, and all groups with sizable female memberships.

With the Eastern bloc becoming a unique proving-ground for legalized abortion in the last decade, producing our first conclusive evidence that the system makes a powerful instrument for family limitation and virtually abolishes the dangers and cruelty of underworld abortion, it is particularly ironic that this experiment should take place under communism rather than in Britain or the United States. It would have been especially fitting if these words—"One cannot speak of equal rights of women . . . if they are not allowed to determine the number of children they shall have"—could have come from an American statesman rather than a Hungarian official. Even more to the point, only the Eastern bloc, and to some extent the Japanese, have grasped long before us the essential concept of the population dilemma: that legalized abortion is an emergency technique which must be carefully balanced with a basic and long-range program of birth control, and that neither alone, but only the two in unison, can ever solve the problem of human, family needs, or the population crisis already confronting so many nations.

XV

The Lesson of Japan: Abortion and the Population Crisis

Unlike Russia and the Eastern bloc, where legalization was primarily aimed at a crisis in individual, human needs, Japan apparently passed its law to cope with a national population emergency almost unparalleled in history. At the close of World War II, Japan was crushed militarily, key cities gutted, with millions of troops returning to non-existent jobs in a broken economy. Separated by defeat from a mainland empire once considered essential to support its population, Japan's 72,000,000 people were packed into a space the size of California. With only one-sixth of this area arable, Japan, in terms of land use, probably equaled South Korea as the most crowded nation in the world.

To make matters worse, Japan added 11,000,000 people in five years after the war. Combined with a low death rate and increasing longevity, resulting from skilled public-health care, the nation's high fertility rate was straining resources to the danger point.

In May 1948 the Japanese Diet, or parliament, decided to meet the crisis by passing a Eugenic Protection Law, which legalized abortions only for women whose health might be impaired from "the physical or economic viewpoint." It was the product, not of a ruling communist bureaucracy, as in Eastern Europe, but of a majority of Diet members, freely elected under a democratic system.

Although the law ostensibly protected maternal health, it was broadened by two amendments in the next few years which provided unlimited abortion at the woman's request. The results were unprecedented. From 246,000 in 1949, reported abortions rose to a peak of 1,128,000 in 1958, then tapered off to about 955,000 in the following years. Even these abortion figures may be conservative. Experts believe that some private physicians hide as many as half their operations to lower their taxable income, and that a few hundred thousand abortions a year are unreported in official records.[1]

Abortions in Japan have produced the most dramatic results in demographic history—a birth-rate cut of 34.3 per 1,000 in 1947 to 16.9 by 1961, a level generally maintained since. Never had a nation by its own choice more than halved its birth rate in so short a period.

The abortion demand was a result not only of the Japanese determination to limit their families, but also of the lack of religious and moral obstacles, in a nation whose traditions accepted even infanticide.

Further, contraception had not yet gained a sizable following. When Margaret Sanger was first invited to Japan in 1922 by progressive women's groups demanding the introduction of birth control, her visa was cancelled en route by a government already dominated by the militarist bloc and proponents of territorial and population expansion. Finally winning admittance, Mrs. Sanger lectured for weeks to overflow audiences. In her parting warning, she prophesied: "The greatest threat to the peace of the world is to be found in the teeming population of Asia."

These early gains in birth control were quickly negated by the advent of war. When Mrs. Sanger was invited to Japan again in 1950 by a revived Birth Control Association, General MacArthur temporarily blocked her admittance, probably under pressure from the Catholic Women's Club of Tokyo. After MacArthur's removal from command, she made a triumphal tour of the country, rousing the first mass enthusiasm for contraception, and aided by a government that had meanwhile developed some qualms about the unchecked surge of abortions.

The problem at this point was that contraception was so little understood by the public that the printed character commonly used in national periodicals for "birth limitation" could be interpreted as either contraception or abortion. And there were a host of other impediments. Few contraceptive supplies were available. Their price was high, their quality often deficient. In fact, abortion, costing $10 or less, was cheaper than a year's supply of even the simplest materials. Moreover, abortion was free for the worker who had industrial or government health insurance, or for those too poor to afford it.

At first, the Japanese were disillusioned and frustrated by contraception. Some techniques were ill suited to primitive, rural sanitary facilities, whereas more sophisticated methods, like diaphragm and jelly, gained acceptance only in high-income groups. One peasant woman, complaining about the use of syringe and jelly, told a public-health officer: "Don't you know that few of us possess a private room to sleep in that would permit us to put on the light without attracting the attention of the rest of the household?"[2]

By contrast, abortion was remarkably accessible. The government grants a special abortion license to specialists in obstetrics, and about 15 per cent of private physicians and almost all public and private hospitals carry this plaque of approval. Admittedly, standards of medical skill and care varied sharply. In a 200-bed hospital, operative procedures were painstaking, and patients received careful post-operative check-ups. But in a three-room clinic in a depressed industrial district, patients lined up without appointment. Prices were settled by bargaining. And surgery and antisepsis were perfunctory.

Neither these drawbacks, nor any physical or psychological repugnance to the operation itself, however, presented a problem to the Japanese mind. "A people who had the sublime opportunity of experiencing at first hand the full expression of modern war do not appear too compunctious over the removal of a few grams of fetal protoplasm from the uterus," Dr. W. T. Pommerenke, of the University of Rochester School of Medicine, concluded in his study of Japanese abortions. "They wonder over our Western sentimentality over such small matters, and over our fear that sex liberation and the ready procurability of abortions may lead to moral delinquency."[3]

By 1954, however, the government itself had become increasingly concerned about Japanese dependence on abortion. Studies conducted by the Ministry of Welfare, for example, showed that only 27 per cent used contraception, and that contraceptive techniques were obviously inadequate. An estimated 60 per cent of abortions followed contraceptive failure.

Even more disturbing was the fact that many women became pregnant again within six months. Although no conclusive study of the dangers of repeated abortions has ever been made in either Japan or Eastern Europe, the Ministry of Health feared that frequent operations "necessarily produce undesirable effects upon the health of mothers."

A new population policy was recommended by Dr. Yoshio Koya, the director of the National Institute of Public Health and, later, president of the Family Planning Federation of Japan. Koya concluded that "no argument against abortion is effective in overcoming their (the people's) determination to limit their children to the number they can adequately support and educate in accordance with their cultural concepts." Restrictions on the present abortion law would simply drive abortions underground. Thus, the only method of reducing the high abortion rate was by means of the most intensive campaign of contraceptive education and supplies ever conducted.

Supported by the government, Koya decided to concentrate on a series of pin-pointed tests in specific areas and groups. He would establish clinics and lecture programs, distribute posters and leaflets, and guarantee the services of trained doctors and midwives. It would be the first real proving-ground for a contraceptive campaign (the Eastern European experiments came later), aimed at reducing the abortion rate of a nation that had turned to legalization in a moment of crisis.

Koya purposefully chose the most difficult groups—rural villages, which traditionally valued large families; people on public relief; coal miners noted for their record of fertility. In every test, his results were striking.

The crude birth rate in the coal-mining area was reduced by half in five years; in three villages of farmers and fishermen, by half over seven years. Working with 80,000 employees of the Japanese National Railways, Koya cut the crude birth rate 37 per cent at a minimum.

All these reductions were achieved by converting the participants to contraception, and virtually eliminating the need for abortion. Among coal miners, for example, 90 per cent of the families practiced contraception after five years. In the coal-mining and village tests, the abortion rate dropped two-thirds below the original level. In the national program, contraceptive use proved 67 per cent greater in areas receiving intensive education by health officers than in those receiving none.[4]

The most recent national polls, sponsored by the Mainichi newspapers, soon proved that although abortion remained a dominant factor in family limitation, the contraceptive campaign had produced lasting results. Seventy per cent of all couples now approved contraception either with or without qualifications. By the time of their third or fourth child, 80 per cent approved.

While in 1950, 21 per cent used contraception and 69 per cent did not, by 1961, 44 per cent were regular contraceptors, 30 per cent not. Thus, in ten years, contraceptive practice had more than doubled.

The trend now showed a strong tendency to "bunch" births at an early age as more groups applied contraception to the small-family concept. The professional class, with its ambitions to rise to the top, the "white-collar" class, bent on maintaining its suburban-apartment living standard, invariably adopted birth control after a second child and before the wife reached thirty years of age.

Although far fewer Japanese than Americans used contraception in early marriage, over 50 per cent turned to contraception after their second child, and the number of abortions in these groups had dropped sharply. The problem still remained to educate the great mass of Japanese in modern techniques. Unfortunately, by 1965 the government had still not approved the oral pill or the "Lippes loop."

A recent survey showed that 40 per cent continued to depend on the condom, almost 39 per cent on the rhythm method, and 7 per cent on withdrawal. With jelly, or diaphragm and jelly, employed by only 11 per cent, the dependence on poor techniques, and particularly on the husband's responsibility, left a vast possibility of continued contraceptive failure and meant that far too many couples would have to fall back on legal abortion.[5]

The impact of legalized abortion in halving the birth rate, together with the gains from contraceptive campaigns, presents a remarkable demonstration of applied demographic principles. In fact, Japan's achievement has been so significant, it seems incredible that such lessons have not been applied to other nations with population problems. India, a case in point, recognized the threat of over-population and began issuing ringing pronouncements shortly after independence; yet it wasn't until 1965 that the government considered legalized abortion. Also, India's avowed commitment to birth control has been so timid and perfunctory that the government can be accused of almost toying with the crisis until the country was buried by it.

Meanwhile, India's population increased by about 122,000,000 from 1951 to 1965, and has now reached the staggering total of about 480,000,000. Although its land area is only about two-fifths the size of the continental United States, India's population ranks second only to communist China. At its present rate, its population should double in the next thirty-five years.

India was handicapped from the start by the opposition of Mahatma Gandhi, who believed that birth control would weaken the moral fibre of his people, and expected them to follow his own unique idealism, limiting their families by self-restraint. Later, Nehru's contraception campaigns not only lacked force and adequate financial support; they were run by a spinster Health Minister, who was decidedly unenthusiastic about the subject. The only impressive headway in these early years—the founding of big-city clinics, and a constant flow of motorized clinics to the distant vastness of rural India—was organized by private family-planning associations under the resourceful guidance of Lady Dhanvanthi Rama Rau.

When the Indian government finally appealed for help to the United Nations, the best it could get from the World Health Organization, handicapped by Roman Catholic member-nations, was a team of experts to teach the "rhythm" method. The method is dubious enough in itself, because of the variation in menstrual cycles, and the difficulty of calculating fertile and infertile days. But the experts failed to consider the complexities of human nature when they distributed to distant villages flamboyant "rhythm" necklaces made up of 28 beads, one for each day of the menstrual cycle.

Although the women had been taught to move one bead each day to calculate their "safe" period, they soon complained that they could not distinguish the red beads, marking unsafe days, in the middle of the night. The experts changed the color to a square shape, having to add a safety catch to prevent the beads from moving in both directions around the necklace. The chief problem, however, was that many women forgot to move the beads. Others refused to wear them for fear of criticism by neighbors. A few even thought that moving the bead itself prevented conception, and failed to inform their husbands of unsafe nights. "Needless to say, the rhythm method failed to bring down the birth rate," concludes Professor S. Chandrasekhar, director of the Indian Institute for Population at Madras.

Each new experiment in contraception was launched with fanfares of publicity, only to flounder on similar obstacles. The diaphragm, for example, required rural women to travel to distant clinics for fittings; but when they returned home, application proved impractical in houses without bathrooms, light, and running water. The foam tablet, heralded for its cheapness, depended on diligent application. The oral pill, once considered a magic solution, not only demands daily remembrance, but is still too expensive for most Indians. Further, the government, which has refused to accept Western tests through innate conservatism, never ran any major test of its own or approved the pill officially.

From the start, the government also failed to recognize the necessity of sterilization as part of its total attack on a soaring birth rate. This surgical procedure (known as vasectomy for the male, tubal ligation for the female) particularly fits the needs of couples firmly set against further children. Although three Indian states adopted sterilization programs almost a decade ago, the government has just granted nationwide support. Nearly a million operations have been performed so far, but many unfortunately after the family had grown too large. "Had India embarked on this policy fifteen years ago with fervor, the country by now could have cut its birth rate by half," Chandrasekhar insists.[6]

Only recently, the Indian government committed itself to a contraceptive technique, the "Lippes loop," which is both promising and practical. The loop is a plastic, S-shaped device, generally kept permanently in the uterus. It prevents fertilization, or implantation of the fertilized ovum in the uterus. After intensive tests on 3,500 Indian women, 5 per cent had the loop removed because of discomfort. Another 5 per cent expelled the device naturally. In the remaining 90 per cent, the loops prevented pregnancy in 99 per cent of all cases.

Although the loop requires insertion by an expert, which means that trained teams still have to reach remote villages, its superiority is that in most cases it supplies, at the cost of only a few cents, lasting contraception until the couple wants a child. Spurred on by private U.S. aid, and now manufacturing the loop locally, the government plans to distribute 2,000,000 in the next year or so, and 5,000,000 annually by 1967.

Still, some experts doubt that the loop can seriously dent the Indian birth rate. A device that will take years to distribute to women of procreative age can hardly be expected to roll back an avalanche of population now increasing at the rate of 11,000,000 annually. While contraception is essential in any long-range policy, the Indian government continually fails to deal with the population crisis as a total entity. The frightening mathematics of population growth overwhelms piecemeal solutions and timidity. No government, particularly of an underdeveloped nation, can solve a population crisis without combining legalized abortion with a permanent and intensive contraception campaign.

Lady Rama Rau, who has devoted a lifetime to contraception education, now insists that "legal abortion is necessary primarily as a back-up measure when population pressures are critical." And Professor Roger Revelle, noted director of Harvard University's Center for Population Studies, states: "Any contraceptive program probably needs to be backed up by a system of legal, safe and inexpensive abortion, such as exists in Japan, the Soviet Union, and the Scandinavian countries."

Unhindered by religious opposition, the government nevertheless delayed fifteen years before studying legalization. This in spite of the fact that 75 per cent of the women who sought help at the first planned-parenthood clinics were already pregnant, and insisted that attending doctors should terminate their pregnancies. Even now, the government is just polling national opinion on abortion. Such arguments as a shortage of doctors and hospitals provide officials with more excuses to delay a necessary decision.

The basic tragedy of a halting and fragmented population policy, particularly in underdeveloped nations, is its destructive impact on economic and social modernization. No matter how fast new industries are developed or agricultural methods updated, no matter how much foreign aid the United States may pour into a local economy, a runaway population negates these advances almost faster than they can be initiated. Capital investment is siphoned off into rising consumer demands for food, clothing, and housing. The economy may expand vigorously, but particularly in nations like India, already far behind the industrialized Western world, such growth can never keep pace with a soaring birth rate.

The per capita income of India could be increased nearly 40 per cent if its birth rate were cut in half, two population experts have pointed out. Mohammed Ayub Khan, President of Pakistan and a devoted supporter of family limitation, asserts: "All the effort that is being mounted in new countries like mine will be wasted if we can't keep our population within reasonable bounds." In Latin America, where the problem is equally acute, Venezuela's birth rate of 44 per 1,000 population has recklessly outraced the country's economic growth despite huge natural wealth in oil. The average Venezuelan income in 1962 was $25 less than five years before.[7]

The relationship of fertility to economic progress becomes increasingly crucial as the population of underdeveloped nations expands from 70 per cent of world population in 1960 to an estimated 80 or 85 per cent by the end of the century. And population growth is intensified by a constantly declining death rate. For centuries, pestilence and disease were largely responsible for keeping a reasonable balance between births and deaths. Malaria, for example, killed thousands of Asians each year until the introduction of DDT. "Today if you want to meet a mosquito in Ceylon or India, you have to go to a zoo," Chandrasekhar observes. As a result of medical advances and public-health care, Western nations have helped to slash the death rate in underdeveloped areas to about seventeen per 1,000 at the same time as births have soared to two and three times this rate.

No real economic progress is possible, therefore, until underdeveloped areas adopt drastic solutions. Foreign aid and local economic efforts become almost inconsequential without total and rigorous fertility control, based on a crash program of legalized abortion. "And since the goal of anti-nationalist policies in the underdeveloped world must be to achieve fertility decline *before* rather than after full social and economic modernization," sociologist Dennis H. Wrong concludes, "it ill behooves Westerners to frown on the adoption of methods like sterilization and abortion."[8]

The population crisis in Latin America, certainly comparable to India in its soaring birth rate, is further complicated by the prevalence of illegal abortion, so rampant that it presents a health problem of alarming severity.

At the municipal maternity hospital in Caracas, Venezuela, thirty-five women are admitted daily for abortion-caused emergencies in contrast to ninety admitted for childbearing. Dr. Robert Santiso, chief of gynecology at Latin American Hospital, Guatemala, calls his rate "one of the highest percentages of provoked abortions in the world."

In Chile, where illegal abortions have multiplied four times in the last fifteen years, a University of Chile School of Public Health study revealed that 35 to 40 per cent of all pregnancies ended in abortion. And for each case seen in hospitals, two had occurred without official cognizance. Illegals now cause two of every five deaths among pregnant women, and account for almost a third of hospital obstetrical budgets. This high death and injury rate results from the fact that almost 40 per cent of the women resorted to the most dangerous techniques: self-abortion or abortion by amateur midwives.

The Uruguayan rate, possibly unequaled anywhere, now runs almost two and a half times the number of annual live births. Even this figure may be "conservative," according to Dr. Hector Rozada, of the University of Montivedeo Medical School, who considers underworld abortion "a worse scourge than polio or tuberculosis." Dr. Ofelia Mendoza, of the International Planned Parenthood Federation, regards illegal abortion in Latin America as a whole "a critical health problem."

The poor in particular, virtually cut off from contraception information by the opposition of the Catholic Church, have been forced into underworld abortion in their struggle for family stability and economic survival. Population growth throughout Latin America has reached such heights that most nations will double their populations in about twenty-seven years, according to Dr. Mendoza. Brazil and Venezuela are expected to double in twenty years. Guatemala with 49, Mexico with 45 births per 1,000, rank as two nations having the highest birth rates in the world. In fact, the birth rates of every Central American country are at least twice as high as that of the United States.

Such explosive population growth condemns a large proportion of Latin Americans to an endless cycle of poverty, passed on from generation to generation, as the poorest couples invariably produce the largest families. Over half the residents of Caracas, for example, live in abject squalor. Nicaragua cannot provide even primary schooling for two thirds of its children. Guatemala has the highest infant mortality rate in the world.

By its rigid strictures, the Catholic Church has not only intensified the demand for illegal abortion as the only outlet for desperate women, but has also blocked the development of family-planning campaigns. Sex education in public schools and scientific discussion of contraception in the press are virtually prohibited throughout Latin America. Even medical schools, with one or two exceptions, omit contraceptive training.

In the last decade, however, the planned-parenthood movement has slowly reached the urban masses, and recent studies in Haiti, Jamaica, Mexico, and Peru, to name a few, reveal an overwhelming popular demand for government-sponsored birth control. One study in Chile showed that 70 per cent of the women wanted birth-control services, although over half attended Catholic church at least once a week.[9]

After thirty years of struggle, private planned-parenthood organizations in Puerto Rico have built the largest chain of clinics in Latin America. Contraception has gained such popular support that when the Church threatened to excommunicate any member voting for a governor known to be an advocate of birth control, he was elected anyway by a resounding majority.

Now the Church has given signs of softening its position. The delegates at a recent Central American Medical Congress, almost all Roman Catholics, passed a resolution urging their governments to include contraception in public-health services. Even more significant, the first birth-control conference in Latin America, organized by eminent public officials and medical leaders, was convened in Colombia in August 1965. Not only did the presiding officer, ex-president Alberto Lleras Camargo, of Colombia, come out forcefully for population control; the delegates included a sizable number of priests. "And many of the delegate-priests not only sat through speeches sharply attacking previous positions of the Church on birth control," reported The New York Times, "but they also submitted some of the best and boldest papers on the subject."

Although private planned-parenthood groups have made remarkable gains, the establishment of sixty clinics in fourteen of twenty Latin American countries can hardly be expected to stem the flood of population. At least in India and most underdeveloped nations, the program has government support. In Latin America, with its religious and cultural obstacles, family planning at best will require two or three decades before it makes a pronounced impression on the birth rate. Meanwhile, increasingly, illegal abortion takes a toll of health and mortality. Sociologists and medical officials wring their hands over the statistics. U.S. foreign-aid funds dwindle away in a tide of new births. Everyone but desperate mothers ignores the ultimate reality, that only legalized abortion can cut to the core of the problem. As long as Latin America and other underdeveloped nations continue to ignore the lesson of Japan, they will be submerged even deeper in the population morass.

We have reached the point where warnings are no substitute for a decisive population policy. "Probably never in history," James Reston, Associate Editor of The New York Times, declares succinctly, "has so obvious and significant a fact been so widely evaded. . . ." Delude ourselves as we may with optimistic experiments in contraception in Pakistan, South Korea, Tunisia, and elsewhere, these are only essential starting-points. They chip away at the periphery while the gloomy arithmetic of population growth races almost faster than the mind can grasp.

While it took 1,840 years since the time of Christ for the world population to reach one billion, we tripled this figure in little more than a century. And at the present explosive birth rate, the present 3 billion is expected to double to 6 billion from 1960 to 2000.

The grand delusion among Western nations, particularly in the United States, is that we are divinely protected from the population crisis, whereas in fact the U.S. growth rate, which has equaled or exceeded that of many underdeveloped areas, now adds 3,000,000 people each year. As a result of the baby boom after World War II, and a sharp increase in the number of women of procreative age, the U.S. population should double in the next forty or fifty years.

Beyond the problem of economics and food supply, the brutal reality is that the world will eventually run out of space to hold a population that keeps doubling at the present rate. General Eisenhower, an *opponent* of family-planning aid during his presidency, has this to say today: ". . . Since the earth is finite in area and physical resources, it is clear that unless something is done to bring an essential equilibrium between human requirements and available supply, there is going to be in some regions not only a series of riotous explosions but a lowering of standards of all people, including our own."

XVI

A Blueprint for Changing U.S. Abortion Laws

"The statesman knows that laws should be like clothes, made to fit the citizens that make up the state," observed Clarence Darrow, the noted trial lawyer.

"Criminal law which is not enforced practically is much worse than if it was not on the books at all," added Judge Learned Hand.

Although our abortion laws fit only a minority of religious dogmas, and have proved unenforceable throughout the nation, even among a large segment of Catholics, they remain unchanged, a monument to political fear. Next to the women themselves, many medical groups are most intimately affected, and constantly demand reform. In his inaugural address as president of the New York County Medical Society in 1965, Dr. Carl Goldmark, Jr., called for revision of New York State's "archaic" abortion laws and foresaw "an enlightened society" 100 years hence wherein it would be possible for any woman to be legally aborted for an unwanted pregnancy.

The New York Academy of Medicine calls our laws "unsupported by medical logic." Seventy per cent of doctors questioned by the San Francisco *Chronicle* at the 1964 meeting of the American Medical Association wanted abortion laws liberalized. In the *Medical Tribune's* study of 1,300 physicians, a national sampling by geographic distribution and professional specialization, over 40 per cent favored legalized abortion for medical reasons alone, almost 60 per cent for social and economic reasons as well.

"It's time we had something to offer the mother of the unwanted child besides platitudes or the address of an abortionist in Hong Kong," stated a California surgeon. "No child should be forced into this world to unwanted parents," concluded a Nebraska pediatrician.

In a study of all New York State obstetricians and gynecologists —specialists closest to the problem—85 per cent of 1,417 responding endorsed the proposals for the legislative reform urged by the American Law Institute.[1]

Probably the most significant demand for abortion reform has come from the American Medical Association, previously noted for its conservatism on all methods of population control. In a report cleared by the board of trustees in November 1965, the AMA's Committee on Human Reproduction urged enactment of the legislative reforms of the American Law Institute. Although the AMA's House of Delegates deferred final action, Dr. Percy Hopkins, chairman of the board, concluded: "It's an historic statement."

Labeling the present law "barbarous" and "certainly an example of man's inhumanity to man—or, more directly, to woman," *The New York Times,* in a series of editorials, placed on its final "must" list for the state legislature: "Liberalization of the cruel law depriving doctors and hospitals of needed discretion on abortions."

While the majority continues to be tyrannized by laws supported by minority dogmas, our legislatures until recently took only two hesitant steps toward reform. One, in New Hampshire, was defeated in 1961. The other, a reform bill passed by both houses of the New York State legislature, was vetoed by Governor Thomas E. Dewey. Not one state has actually adopted a single piece of reform legislation. Although in Britain a large bloc of Members of Parliament vigorously demand a new law, not one member of the U.S. Congress has ever introduced the question of abortion reform in the Senate or House since the passage of the Comstock law in 1873.

The first real impetus for legislative action stems from a masterful document of the American Law Institute, one of the nation's eminent legal societies. After ten years of intensive labor and debate by a corps of judges, professors, criminologists, lawyers, and other judicial experts, the ALI approved in 1962 a Model Penal Code, intended to serve as a blueprint for revision and reform of almost every aspect of penal law. In its section of the code applying to abortion, the ALI proposed that abortion be legalized for three causes:

1. When continuation of pregnancy would gravely impair the physical or mental health of the mother,

2. When the child might be born with a grave physical or mental defect,

3. When pregnancy resulted from rape, incest, or other felonious intercourse, including illicit intercourse with a girl below the age of sixteen.

Since ALI members represent every shade of opinion of the American Bar, their suggested reforms are the result of judicious molding and compromise. They constitute a program based to some extent on the tested Scandinavian system, yet far more conservative than the Scandinavian middle way. They offer a national and modest formula that should be acceptable to any state legislature.

Still, with all these factors in their favor, the ALI abortion proposals have been considered by the legislatures of only five states, and not adopted even by one!

In Illinois, when the whole Penal Code came up for debate, such pressure was brought against the most controversial sections that abortion reform was quickly abandoned to clear less sensitive parts of the code.

Although the Kansas State Senate passed an abortion-reform bill in 1963, it was killed two weeks later in the House Committee on Judiciary. A similar reform bill in Minnesota shared the same fate.

A New York bill in 1965, which unfortunately failed to meet the standards of the ALI code, never reached the floor of either house. A new bill, following the ALI model, has been introduced at the 1966 session by Senator Manfred Ohrenstein and Assemblyman Percy Sutton. Although its chances of passage in the next few years are considered slim, it offers a rallying-point for reform forces in the state.

The importance of such a focus has already been demonstrated in California, the fifth state to consider an abortion bill and the prime area where abortion has become a heated public issue. After an early reform attempt in 1961, Assemblyman Anthony Beilenson, who calls the present law "inadequate, discriminatory, and hypocritical," introduced a new bill in 1963. Beilenson believed he had a clear majority in committee to send the bill to the Assembly with a "do pass" recommendation. Then each committee member was deluged with mail ranging from the highest levels of the Catholic hierarchy to the vituperative scrawls of parishioners. One assemblyman, a known supporter of the bill, was warned: "May God in Heaven strike you dead and damn your immortal soul to hell for eternity . . ." Another assemblyman reported receiving "hundreds and hundreds of letters, the nastiest mail ever . . ." As a result of what the San Francisco *Chronicle* called the "tremendous pressure" of the Catholic Church, the Beilenson bill was killed in committee in 1963 and succeeding years.

Nevertheless, the overwhelming importance of these bills and hearings was that abortion was finally thrust into the forefront of public debate. Two Los Angeles grand juries have already called for reform. Not only the House of Delegates of the California Medical Association, but also the Los Angeles Obstetrical and Gynecological Society and other medical organizations, including 1,000 specialists, have supported new legislation, broadening indications from "life" to "health" according to the ALI formula. Nearly 1,300 Protestant and Jewish clergymen in 334 cities and towns came out for reform. Even the California Junior Chamber of Commerce, probably the first business group involved in the campaign, backed the Beilenson bill.

The first specialized organization to concentrate on the problem is the Society for Humane Abortion, with headquarters in San Francisco. Founded by Patricia M. Maginnis, the Society devotes itself primarily to educating the public as to the inadequacies of present laws, staging a continuous series of radio and television debates and public meetings, particularly on college campuses. Its most ambitious project was a conference on abortion and human rights, held in San Francisco in January 1966 and attended by delegates from every part of the state.

The Society, however, remains critical of the Beilenson bill, calling it not a forward step but a side step. Although the bill generally follows the ALI formula, it adds a complex system of committee approval. A woman requesting abortion must first obtain the written consent of two physicians. Then her case must go before a committee of five members, four of them medical specialists. Crowded medical schedules may involve the woman in tortured delays. Besides, since the bill does not stipulate the religion of committee members, a few Catholics could block most affirmative decisions.

In cases of rape or incest, the procedure is even more cumbersome. Such cases must be certified by the county district attorney, or, if he refuses, the patient may petition the superior court—two steps that could entangle a woman in a further agony of red tape. As a result, the bill hardly touches even the periphery of the problem, and Beilenson himself admitted that it would affect only "2 to 5 per cent of the 50,000 to 100,000 illegal abortions performed in California" annually.

What the Society particularly attacks is the concept that a doctor's relations with his patient should be regulated by the penal code rather than by the health and safety code, as is customary in all other medical procedures.

The Society's platform, as liberal as any yet enunciated, demands that abortion become "a decision which the person or family involved should be free to make as their own religious beliefs, values, emotions, and circumstances may dictate," and that the operation "should be available at a cost that is not prohibitive, and in a manner that is in no way humiliating nor discriminatory." It supports as indications for abortion "some compelling reason . . . physical, psychological, mental, spiritual, or economic," a range that comes close to making abortion available on request.

More broadly based than this California group is a second, specialized organization, the Association for the Study of Abortion, with headquarters in New York City but membership throughout the country. Founded in 1964, the Association already lists among its officials Dr. Robert Hall, its president and associate professor of obstetrics at Columbia-Presbyterian Medical Center; Cass Canfield, chairman of the executive committee of Harper & Row; the Reverend Joseph F. Fletcher, professor of Christian Ethics at Episcopal Theological School, Cambridge, Mass.; Dr. Carl Goldmark, Jr.; Dr. Alan F. Guttmacher, president of the Planned Parenthood Federation; Theodore Kheel and Harriet Pilpel, both noted lawyers; and Dr. Helen B. Taussig, winner of the President's Medal of Freedom.

The Association uses the influence of its many medical experts to educate the public toward reform with speakers appearing regularly at civic meetings and on radio and television. It concentrates particularly on professions related to the abortion problem. Its committees on religion and social work already include hundreds of clergymen, sociologists, and social-welfare aides. Its medical committee carries its reform program to hospitals. Its research committee has extended the first study of medical opinion among New York State obstetricians to a national poll of psychiatrists.

After the dismal record of legislative action in California, the Reverend Lester Kinsolving declared: "Some Catholics are insisting that their particular beliefs be forced upon all Californians. This is no more valid than if the legislature were asked to outlaw pork because of Jewish beliefs or imposing the Christian Scientist's view on medicine or the Jehovah's Witnesses' objections to blood transfusions on everyone." But whether in California, New Hampshire, or elsewhere, Catholic opposition to new laws has been particularly effective on state representatives from marginal districts where religious blocs hold special power. The Church has fought even minute steps to reform, and enlisted its chief spokesmen, like Bishop Primeau in New Hampshire, in debates reaching the point of vehemence. With such pressure on legislators, it remains doubtful that a meaningful bill can be passed in any state before 1970.

As a result, an influential group of lawyers, with Morris Ernst, Cyril Means, and Harriet Pilpel as spokesmen, asserts that the most practical technique of reform is through the determined insistence of the medical profession on its rights within existing laws. Ernst claims that the profession has scared itself into a negative position, remaining "in substantial default through silence." Pessimistic doctors say, "The glass of wine is half empty while the realist calls it half full." In actuality, Ernst concludes, "abortions are legal but may become illegal," and the present laws are only what the doctors and the courts make them.

"One might even go so far as to argue that the figures on illegal abortion reveal that the failure of the legitimate medical profession to take over in this area constitutes as great a threat to life as many of the major diseases we as a nation are trying to eradicate," Mrs. Pilpel adds.[2]

What these lawyers demand is a forthright program by hospitals and doctors to perform abortions as required by good medicine without constantly looking over their shoulder at the law. The pessimist may call this "stretching" the law. The realist, however, knows that only the medical profession can apply the law on a daily basis. "A great profession may someday feel that one honest man can defeat a legion of cowards," Ernst points out. And that day may be reasonably close.

Already many hospitals are performing abortions for German measles in early pregnancy, to cite the most obvious case. Few authorities would claim that the birth of a deformed child generally endangers the mother's life. In fact, such abortions are approved mainly to protect the potential child, rather than the mother, from a life of tragedy. As more and more important hospitals accept German-measles abortions, the procedure will undoubtedly become standard throughout the country within a few years.

An even more noteworthy example of progress is the bold policy in the last decade of two prominent Buffalo hospitals, affiliated with the State University of New York. Without fanfare, these hospitals have quadrupled the number of their abortions from an average of about fifteen a year in the 1943–49 period to about fifty-five a year between 1960 and 1964. Not only is this a marked contrast to the diminishing rates of most hospitals; the types of cases accepted "reflect a very liberal interpretation of the law," two staff obstetricians, Drs. Kenneth R. Niswander and Morton Klein, reported to a recent AMA meeting.

The most striking aspect of their report is that most abortions are performed for "psychogenic" reasons, that vague category of emotional, social, and economic pressures which almost every hospital studiously rejects. At these Buffalo hospitals, however, psychogenic abortions have soared from 13 per cent of the total in 1943 to almost 88 per cent in 1963.

"When the moral pressure of society threatens the mental health of the mother or the wellbeing of the family," Niswander and Klein state, "we are likely to interpret the law as liberally as possible. A forty-year-old divorced woman with two young teen-agers cannot have an out of wedlock child and maintain her social status. Some might insist that she deserves no help, but what of her children? Must they be punished for her deed? A fourteen-year-old who is pregnant by rape would also seem to deserve help. Even in a puritanical sense this patient has done no wrong, and to allow the pregnancy to ruin her life seems unthinkable. Such tragic social situations account for many of our 'psychogenic' abortions."

Another impressive mark of courage in these Buffalo hospitals is their increasing concern with the plight of the single patient. By contrast with most institutions, where such abortions are rare, the Buffalo hospitals in recent years performed over 41 per cent of their operations on single, separated, or divorced women.

These hospitals have shown particular courage in accepting the single girl under twenty. Compared to the 1940's, when no single teenage case was accepted, the Buffalo hospitals now perform almost 15 per cent of all abortions in this group.

What makes this bold and liberal policy a significant blueprint for other hospitals is that it developed without plan or debate at the administrative level, motivated solely by the desire of the obstetrical staff to practice good medicine. The chief of obstetrics, to begin with, refused to allow his staff to be cowed by an abortion committee, and the administration never interfered. Abortion requests need only the approval of two appropriate consultants. "Certainly the physician who knows the patient is in a better position to judge the status of her disease and its relation to pregnancy than are not necessarily more competent consultants who may see the patient only briefly," Niswander and Klein point out.

Even more important, this policy has proved that the possibility of community opposition is slight. Although the population of Buffalo is over 50 per cent Catholic, and the abortion report to the AMA convention was widely publicized in leading Buffalo newspapers and reprinted across the country, little criticism has come from religious spokesmen. Interestingly enough, the abortion rate for Catholics in the study ranged from almost 24 to 38 per cent of all operations.

"No matter how effective the contraceptive, unwanted pregnancies will occur, and when all else fails, abortion may be the only answer," Niswander and Klein conclude. "Should the medical profession force desperate women to risk their lives by evading the law?"

These Buffalo hospitals have simply accepted a responsibility that most hospitals and doctors have too long evaded. By making "a very liberal interpretation of the law," they have saved hundreds of women from injury and death in underworld abortion. When two respected Buffalo hospitals can perform abortions for psychiatric or any other reasons deemed medically necessary, no other hospital in New York State has the right to continue hiding behind a rigid and antiquated interpretation of the law.[3]

Few doctors realize that the scope of medical judgment has already been decisively broadened by court decisions. Frequently in the last decades, high courts have handed down opinions in abortion cases which define and enlarge the meaning of statute law, and thus grow into a body of "case law" integral to the protection of the medical profession.

The courts have repeatedly stressed that the profession itself has a unique right to set the standards for physicians in the community. As far back as 1929, a Washington court called an abortion justified "if the appellant in performing the operation did something which was recognized and approved by those reasonably skilled in his profession practicing in the same community. . . ." *(State v. Powers)* In 1944, the Supreme Judicial Court of Massachusetts ruled a doctor's judgment in abortion correct when following "the general opinion of

competent practitioners in the community in which he practices."
(*Commonwealth v. Wheeler*)

These decisions have an obvious relevance to the blueprint developed in Buffalo; for, if ever questioned about its policy, a smaller hospital can point to the Buffalo standards as its model.

Another important decision was handed down in 1953 by the Oregon Supreme Court. Following the legislature's passage of a Medical Practice Act, which specifically defined the physician's prerogatives in abortion, Dr. George H. Buck was convicted under the criminal code. This code allows abortions only to preserve life, whereas the new Medical Act gives doctors far wider discretion to preserve health. Buck insisted that his operation, performed on health grounds, must be judged under the Medical Act. The court not only upheld him, but pointedly ruled that it was "the intention of the legislature to place medical physicians and surgeons in a class by themselves, as far as abortions, as defined by the Medical Practice Act. . . ." (*State v. Buck*)

In view of this decision, the wonder is that every state and county medical association has not demanded that abortion standards be spelled out explicitly in their own health and medical codes. Most penal laws on abortion were passed a hundred years ago, long before the medical profession had made it a safe and simple operation. To continue to lump doctors together under the penal code with non-medical abortionists becomes a frontal insult to the entire profession.

Two other court decisions gave doctors far greater leeway in defining the threat to a patient's life than the profession generally realizes. When a family doctor in Iowa was accused of performing an abortion on a girl whose life did not appear in immediate peril, the appeals court ruled: "It was not essential that the peril to life should be imminent. It was enough that it be potentially present even though its full development might be delayed, to a greater or less extent." (*State v. Dunklebarger*)

This decision was further amplified by London's noted Bourne case in 1938. And it is particularly significant that in the 1959 trial of Dr. Francis E. Ballard, an obstetrician, the California District Court of Appeals reaffirmed the principle that peril to life need not be imminent, and then went on to cite both the Dunklebarger and the Bourne case. (*People v. Ballard*)

In another Ballard trial in 1963, the court extended the range of medical protection by ruling that it was the responsibility of the state to prove an abortion unnecessary. Previously, the doctor presumably had to substantiate necessity. *(People v. Ballard)*

Finally, the Wheeler opinion, already cited, ruled: "For the purpose of this case at least, we may assume that in general a physician may lawfully procure the abortion of a patient if in good faith he believes it to be necessary to save her life or to prevent serious impairment of her health, mental or physical. . . ." Here is the first significant statement by an American high court linking *health* to life as a basis of abortion—an interpretation that the medical profession should seek throughout the country.

All these cases are landmarks too often neglected. Although decisions in one state are not necessarily accepted as precedents in others, the crucial decisions of high courts traditionally leave a broad imprint on all case law, as we have seen in California's Ballard ruling. These six cases should provide a strong defensive bulwark when the crucial test-case in abortion reaches the courts.

The Buffalo formula offers one, eminently effective method of attack on the present abortion system. Hospitals in other states, afraid to follow it, or deterred by legal obstacles, might consider the alternate method of attack through test cases, modeled after the Bourne trial and after a whole series of cases which insured the development of the birth-control movement from 1918 on.

In the most noted of these cases, *U.S. v. One Package*, in which Ernst and Mrs. Pilpel served as counsel, the key points were: (1) whether a physician had the right to import a foreign contraceptive for the health of his patient despite the flat prohibition against the importation of "any article whatever" for the prevention of conception; and (2) whether the physician was "excepted by implication from the literal terms of the statute," as the Federal Circuit Court put it.

The court not only disregarded the literal terms of the statute and gave physicians this right; it specifically emphasized that contraceptives "might intelligently be employed by conscientious and competent physicians for the purpose of saving life or promoting the wellbeing of their patients."

Thus, this test case, which was foreshadowed by earlier decisions, involved interpretation of the law not at all indicated by its language, and gave the medical profession a vastly broadened scope for contraceptive use under the all-important word "wellbeing." "No law is free from ambiguity," Mrs. Pilpel insists. "Our abortion laws today, like birth control laws in the past, must be interpreted by the courts. We can reasonably assume that a test-case in abortion might give physicians enlarged freedom of judgment in the abortion field just as the *One Package* case did in the birth control field in 1936."

Such a case, possibly supported by the Association for the Study of Abortion, should enlist a group of eminent physicians to testify in court that the abortion sought or denied was essential to the good practice of medicine to protect the woman's life.

Their testimony would add substantial support to the thesis long enunciated by the World Health Organization, the New York Academy of Medicine, and other distinguished medical groups: that the preservation of life requires a state of complete physical and mental wellbeing, not merely the absence of disease or infirmity.

A theoretical test-case might deal with what Scandinavian laws unofficially call the "worn-out-mother" syndrome. Let us presume that a woman of thirty-five, mother of six children within a ten-year period, becomes accidentally pregnant by her husband, who is an alcoholic and contributes almost no care or money to his family. Neither parent wants another child. The mother, working as a cleaning woman, cannot afford to lose her salary, and fears that another child will push her physically and emotionally to the breaking point.

In this theoretical case, the woman's physician and a team of specialists would declare in court that they approved abortion to protect her life. The threat of a complete physical and mental collapse, though not imminent, appeared so certain in their medical judgment that an abortion was essential under the terms of the Dunklebarger, Ballard, and other opinions.

If such a theoretical case was carried to a high court, perhaps even the U.S. Supreme Court, and the judges confirmed a broad interpretation of the meaning of a threat to life, undoubtedly a landmark in abortion decisions would be reached. Thenceforth, the medical profession would have the right to evaluate each patient in the widest range of factors threatening her physical and emotional life. "Maybe only one case will be needed to have our jurisprudence bring clarification to the problem of abortion so that the honorable leaders of the medical profession need not refer all their patients to the so-called abortionists," Ernst concludes.

XVII

The Century of the Wanted Child

When nations are ready to assume their ultimate responsibility, this age, once characterized as the Century of the Common Man, must become the Century of the Wanted Child. For too long our only concern has been with the rights of the embryo and the endless creation of rivers of humanity. Now, in our revolt against servitude to uncontrolled fertility, and a reckless flood of children born as accidents and out of ignorance, we at last have recognized that survival of the embryo is not enough. Our laws must not demand that conceptions be brought to term without being equally concerned about the child who is born. As crucial as his right to be born is his welfare as a human being.

"Our welfare agencies, our foster homes, the whole vast machinery of public and private institutions dedicated to child care have been involved almost wholly with picking up the pieces," asserts Sophia M. Robison, professor-emeritus of Columbia University's School of Social Work. "Instead, we should attack the root of the problem—the needs and rights of the child to be born with a fair chance for social as well as physical development. Our responsibility is to guarantee that no child comes into this world unwanted, unloved and uncared for."

Although contraception remains the most desirable method of achieving this ideal, unfortunately it has never gained universal acceptance, nor been scientifically perfected to meet every requirement of dependability, cost, and esthetic preference. It is to be hoped that some day every woman requesting it will have a simple, inexpensive contraceptive that prohibits pregnancy until she and her husband decide on a child. The long-sought technique may be one pill that lasts for months or years until counteracted by another pill, or it may be an injection with similar characteristics. However, until medical research discovers the final solution, abortion is the essential emergency measure, the inalienable right of all women in a free society.

We will only defeat ourselves by producing an endless cycle of unwanted children. Those born in slums, for example, denied even the smallest share of education and economic opportunity, have little chance of realizing their full potential as citizens. One-third of all children on welfare today come from neglected homes, ignored and unwanted by either parent, states Mrs. Katherine Oettinger, chief of the U.S. Children's Bureau.

"When unwanted children become parents, they are more likely than others to be poor parents themselves and breed another generation of unwanted children," observes Dr. Garrett Hardin, professor of biology at the University of California at Santa Barbara. "This is a vicious circle if there ever was one. It is ruinous to the social system."

But it is a grave error to believe that unwanted children are only poor kids in poor families," adds Dr. Emanuel K. Schwartz, of New York's Postgraduate Center for Mental Health. "The 'unwanted' are found in large numbers among the most affluent members of our society." And these affluent, unwanted children eventually contribute heavily to the population of our mental institutions.

Society can make the mother bring her pregnancy to term, but it can never keep her bitterness from poisoning her relationship with this child, or the rest of her family. Nor can it fool the child. "Nothing is more tragic, more fateful in its ultimate consequences than the realization of the child that he is unwanted," states Dr. Karl Menninger, of the Menninger Clinic, Topeka, Kansas.

Society's awareness of its ultimate responsibility will come only with the recognition that family limitation is an affirmative, creative policy. All birth-control measures, including abortion, can bring the richest fulfillment to a woman's life. "A woman who aborts this year because she is in poor health, neurotic, economically harassed, unmarried, on the verge of divorce, or immature," Hardin points out, "may well decide to have another child five years from now—a wanted child. The child that she aborts is always an unwanted child.

If her need for abortion is frustrated, she may never know the joy of a wanted child."

Above all, society must grasp the grim relationship between unwanted children and the violent rebellion of minority groups. In analyzing the problems behind the 1965 race riots in Los Angeles, *The New York Times* concluded: "The leading cause was considered to be financial trouble, that the poverty-beset Negroes have families beyond their ability to provide support."

No matter how extensive the funds poured into depressed areas, whether Negro Harlem or white Appalachia, all the community centers, nurseries, and job-training projects can do little more than pick up the pieces. What must be effected is a guarantee to every child, whether rich or poor, of an equal right to family care, education, and economic advancement. The Office of Economic Opportunity, the government's anti-poverty program, and all public and private agencies must eventually recognize that this right depends on the right of family planning. And that in accidental and unwanted conceptions, the poor as well as the rich must have equal access to safe and low-cost hospital abortion.

State Senator Alvin Weingand, of Santa Barbara, California, recently predicted: ". . . I think one day that the people of this state will accept some kind of program of therapeutic abortion as just part of a birth control program, and that responsible parenthood is becoming far more important than any other consideration."

As long as a reasonable chance of contraceptive failure persists, however, abortion must be included as part of birth control to insure every child's becoming a wanted child. Describing the problem of teaching contraception in a remote Georgia county, one clinic official presented a not untypical patient who "has used contraceptives for the last fifteen years of various kinds, pills, diaphragms, with the best of intentions. Today she has fourteen children." The patient added: "Well, I really did use all of them, but I don't know why I have so many kids."

Social workers continually report such cases in both rural and urban areas where patients lack the education, language skill, or motivation to apply contraception accurately over extended periods. No matter how strongly these women desire to limit their families, contraceptive misuse and failures persist. Abortion becomes the last resort.

The problem may even be accentuated by faulty medical advice. A twenty-two-year-old Illinois mother, pregnant again after two children in the first two years of marriage, continually requested birth-control help from her family doctor, who insisted that her husband's contraception was the best solution. Now desperately searching for an abortionist, she writes: "I feel that if I do have another one (a child) so soon I will certainly have a nervous breakdown."

Above all, the continuing need for abortion stems from the fact that no contraceptive technique has proved scientifically infallible. The "Lippes loop," for example, inserted by a doctor or nurse and recommended by most birth-control authorities, still has a significant percentage of failure. In a comprehensive national study of 5,326 women over a period of a year, the loop showed a failure rate of 2.4 per cent, indicating that of every 1,000 women using the loop, twenty-four became pregnant.

The oral pill, used conscientiously, comes closest to the measure of infallibility; whereas other techniques, like foams and jellies, have a far higher failure rate than the loop, running up to 20 per cent.[1]

"No matter how good a method of contraception is, we can never expect it to be perfect," Hardin observes. "Even one with a 1 per cent failure rate produces a quarter of a million unwanted children a year." To force these women to bear a child against their will, as a result of contraceptive failure, becomes the cruelest and most illogical sentence that society can inflict.

The indications for abortion also arise in those tragic cases of force or criminal intercourse, when the woman is denied the chance for contraceptive protection. These cases, including rape, incest, and intercourse with a child under fifteen, are far more common than opponents of abortion would like to believe. In one borough of New York City, five women were raped in a period of a week or so in 1965. A few days later, a nineteen-year-old college student admitted having raped thirty girls in the previous year. More than a dozen rape cases in early 1965 were attributed to Oklahoma City teen-agers, one the son of a former Bar Association president, another the son of a medical-school professor.

According to the Federal Bureau of Investigation, there were 20,550 forcible rapes or assaults in 1964, possibly only part of the total, since many go unreported through "fear or embarrassment on the part of the victims." With medical studies showing a 2 to 4 per cent probability of conception from one act, a minimum of 600 women annually, and perhaps far more, are forced into bearing a child as a result of rape.[2]

Further, even birth-control methods as close to perfection as the pill or the diaphragm can be invalidated by human, emotional factors. "In our effort to discuss sexual matters calmly and dispassionately," Hardin points out, "we forget sometimes that the act that produces conception is not always the result of the same careful foresight, deliberation and planning that characterize the purchase of a home, say." During a fertility span of almost three decades, the most conscientious woman may well forget her pill occasionally, or misuse a diaphragm. "We will always need a method of birth control that can serve as an afterthought, to prevent a natural but undesired consequence of unforeseen events," Hardin concludes. "Abortion is the much-needed backstop in the system of birth control."

Still another factor emphasizing the need for legalized abortion is the failure of federal and local governments to make birth control available to every woman in the nation. Until recently, birth control was organized and financed primarily by one private group, the Planned Parenthood Federation. By 1965, it operated 120 affiliates with about 250 clinics, a remarkable record of private initiative.

Still, these efforts have barely reached the teeming slums. In New York City, for example, PPF sends one mobile clinic, a small blue station wagon equipped with laboratory and examining table, to six neighborhoods where a majority of families subsist on incomes officially recognized as the poverty level. "But in a city of eight million, faced with a staggering population explosion," Marion Sanders, associate editor of *Harper's,* points out, "one tiny blue station wagon touring three boroughs is no more than a beaver dam trying to hold back Niagara."

Although more than a quarter of a million women in New York exist on Aid to Dependent Children allowances, the city government has paid little more than lip service to birth-control education for welfare clients. "It is a bitter irony that here in New York, where some of the most revolutionary research in birth control methods has been carried out, where the most enlightened efforts of the Planned Parenthood movement are based, hundreds of thousands of mothers still live in as dark ignorance as the peasants of a remote Pakistani village," Mrs. Sanders concludes.

The prime failure in supporting birth control rests on the federal government. Although the Office of Economic Opportunity has been authorized to support community family planning, and $525,000, a fraction of the need, was allotted nine projects by October 1965, these efforts proceed at a dishearteningly sluggish pace.

The application for federal support from the Indiana Association for Family Planning, approved not only by prominent Catholics on its board but by the mayor of Indianapolis and all U.S. representatives and senators from the state, was still pigeonholed in Washington six months after it had been filed. "How many unwanted children will be born while inefficient and reluctant bureaucrats are shuffling and reshuffling 4,071 applications?" demands Dr. Irving Rosenbaum, of Indianapolis.

Further, the O.E.O. continues to place severe restrictions on approved programs. It prohibits physicians from advocating a particular method of contraception, and using federal funds to publicize the program. It limits distribution of materials to one year, not to exceed $12 a patient, and confines government-financial supplies to married women living with their husbands. Dr. Rosenbaum concludes: "We have almost despaired of developing a meaningful birth control program with O.E.O. funds...."

Federal efforts have also been hampered by the opposition of the National Catholic Welfare Conference, which claims that government birth-control aid constitutes discrimination against the poor, since they will feel coerced to adopt contraception.

"Is not the true situation just about the opposite of this?" demands Dr. John T. Edsall, professor of biology at Harvard University. "Today it is the poor who in most parts of the country are denied access to information.... Government support will correct this inequity and put us all eventually on an even footing in this respect."

The striking gains resulting from government support are evident in Corpus Christi, Texas, whose Planned Parenthood Center received the first federal grant. Although the clinic has been operating five years, federal money established four one-day-a-week birth-control centers in the most depressed neighborhoods, where the average resident of twenty-six has five children, a third-grade education, and an income of about $35 a week. "A family of two, three or four children holds together," a local physician observed. "But when there are six, seven and eight, it seems to fall apart at the seams."

Among its patients, mainly of Spanish extraction, the birth-control clinic produced two significant results. Births were reduced 28 per cent in a period of four years. Illegal abortions, previously estimated at 1,000 annually for the county, and mainly performed by unskilled midwives, were cut 41 per cent in the same period. The clinic's physicians are convinced that women who formerly depended on abortion are now being reached by contraceptive education for the first time. The Corpus Christi clinic offers added proof to Dr. Koya's experiments in Japan that an intensive contraception campaign quickly lowers the abortion rate.

In regard to the government's anti-poverty program, O.E.O. family-planning grants prohibit "any surgical procedures intended to result in sterilization." And voluntary sterilization is an essential supplement to contraception and abortion in making every child a wanted child.

Already an estimated 1,500,000 living Americans have obtained sterilization, with another 100,000 added each year. In a recent nationwide survey, one out of every ten wives between eighteen and thirty-nine reported that she or her husband had secured the operation.

Sterilization requires the most painstaking decision. Although the operation may be reversible at a later date, and fertility restored in about 50 per cent of all men and women, no couple should gamble on such odds. A husband and wife should be completely convinced they want no more children before deciding on the operation.

At the same time, finality is sterilization's greatest advantage. Whether performed on male or female, the voluntary operation offers unqualified protection against fertility.

Despite the popular belief that men are deprived of sexual potency, and women of sexual desire and femininity, no physiological basis exists for these fears. Neither operation requires the removal of any organs, nor interferes with female menstruation or production of male sperm cells. In addition, freed from the worry of conceiving unwanted children, and the routine of contraception, many couples may find renewed sexual enjoyment.

Tubal ligation, the female operation, often performed after childbirth, since it is easier for the surgeon and less expensive for the patient, involves cutting both Fallopian tubes and tying off the separated ends. This prevents an egg's passing from ovary to womb. Costing about $200, it is no more complex than an appendectomy.

Vasectomy for the male, even simpler and costing about $100, involves two small incisions in the scrotum, and the cutting and tying of both tubes through which sperm passes from testis to urethra. It can be performed in a doctor's office under local anesthesia, with the patient returning to work the following day.

Voluntary sterilization is legal in all fifty states. Only Connecticut and Utah specifically require proof of medical necessity. Virginia and North Carolina, on the other hand, specifically approve it for family limitation. The key point, however, is that voluntary sterilization must be clearly differentiated from the involuntary operation, which the Association for Voluntary Sterilization, the national information center in New York, vigorously opposes.

For some women, sterilization is incidental to relieving a gynecological condition such as cancer or fibroids. For others, it may be suggested for medical protection. A mother with a heart condition, for example, may decide on sterilization to avoid the physical complications another pregnancy might bring. A few couples who know they may pass on a genetic defect like hemophilia may prefer sterilization to the risk of transmitting the disease to their children.

Most couples, however, choose sterilization as the surest method of birth control. Whether they have two, five, or seven children already, whether they cannot afford to rear and educate more, or consider themselves past the childbearing age, such couples have come to the conclusion that their family must remain at present size.[3]

Although the Roman Catholic Church opposes sterilization as vehemently as it does abortion, religious dogma is not the only obstacle to creating a world of wanted children. Many critics of legalized abortion base their opposition on moral grounds. Obsessed with the erosion of moral barriers, they claim that women will depend on abortion almost exclusively if it becomes too easy to obtain.

Such fears are groundless by any standard of human behavior. No woman will go out of her way to seek surgery. An operation and hospitalization, in addition to being costly and unpleasant, are instinctively avoided. Wherever dependable, inexpensive contraception is available, a woman will choose it over abortion for every emotional and esthetic motive.

In Hungary and other countries with widespread abortion, the primary cause is a failure in contraceptive education and a lack of access to supplies. Japan, on the other hand, has proved that a people, once dependent on abortion, adopt contraception when education, supplies, and, above all, free choice are available.

The moralists are equally obsessed with the impact of legalized abortion on promiscuity, particularly in the case of the single girl.

Their argument is that fear of pregnancy provides the chief deterrent of intercourse, an argument rarely borne out by reality. ". . . This factor can hardly be a significant influence on the rate of illicit sexuality in a society where contraceptives offer reasonable assurance against need for the unpleasant and expensive prospect of abortion," observes the American Law Institute's analysis of its Model Penal Code.

Even if the single girl were ignorant of birth-control methods, the risk of conception from one act presents too small an obstacle. Further, real morality can never be based on fear, as Reverend Raible and other ministers have stressed. Our puritanical insistence that morality can be legislated should have ended with the failure of the Volstead Act.

"Let the theologians, both celibate and senile, give way to a new generation of men who are alive to today's world and today's needs," points out the Reverend Felix Danford Lion, of the Palo Alto, California, Unitarian Church. "We live in a world where adults are relatively free to decide what their own sexual behavior shall be. We may not approve, but this is the fact of the matter."

"It is no wonder that the risk of pregnancy is so poor a deterrent to love-making," Hardin concludes, "that we may rightly doubt if the complete legalization of abortion would significantly increase promiscuity."

The chief attack on legalized abortion, however, remains focused on protecting the fetus as a human being, endowed with a rational soul, and invariably equates abortion at any point with murder. Still, the emphasis of this attack has shifted in recent years. Since Catholic spokesmen now brush over the question of the exact moment at which a soul enters the fetus, they increasingly stress the legal rights of an unborn child, and argue the beginnings of human life on biological grounds.

The legal-rights theory is based on recent cases in which a child recovered damages in court as a result of an automobile collision or other accident suffered before birth. The theory presumes that since an unborn child can be protected by the court, he is already considered a person by the court. Catholic spokesmen, attacking the Beilenson bill in California, specifically cited the McPheeters case. (*Scott v. McPheeters*)

"However, the McPheeters case was a suit by a surviving child for damages suffered in a prenatal injury," points out the unofficial

Beilenson-bill report of the California legislature. "This has nothing to do with the problem involved here.

"Recovery is allowed because the injured party must live under a handicap, and may need the support of the state if other compensa- is not forthcoming," the report continues. "An unborn child that is never born alive does not suffer this handicap, and the reasoning of these cases has no application to therapeutic abortion laws."

"There has never been any recognition in our law of the right to life before birth," emphasizes Ephraim London, a prominent New York lawyer who has tried many key civil-liberties cases before the U.S. Supreme Court. "It would be absurd to draw any parallel be- tween the claim of a living child to recover damages and the claim that an embryo has the right to be born no matter what the hardships and injury to the family and the child itself."

The biological approach to the subject of abortion is based on equally twisted logic. Armed with Keber's discovery a century ago that the male spermatozoa enter the female ovum, and with recent information concerning the process of conception, some theologians now argue that soul cannot be separated from physical form, and a new human personality comes into existence the moment a living cell is created.

Despite new biological terminology, the old argument is still wrapped in semantics. The core of the problem remains the meaning of the word "life." If the theologian insists that the meeting of sperm and ovum produces life, the pragmatist can point out with equal validity that life already exists in both the unfertilized egg and the spermatozoa. "What escapes most people is that life is never created," Hardin states. "It is simply passed on, or snuffed out."

Life is a continuing process, and both sperm and egg are part of the endless transmission-belt of existence. Under the microscope, a spermatozoon is so alive to the expert biologist that he can see in it the impact of disease and illness. Yet the average male kills about 100,000,000 spermatozoa each day; and a woman cuts off the life of an egg almost every month.

The state of being thus remains a strictly religious interpretation of a biological process. Each religion preserves the full rights to its own interpretation. But since our pluralistic American society guar- antees equal rights to all beliefs, only the common agreement of so- ciety can give a specific belief the sanction of law.

On the questions of what constitutes human life before birth, whether taking of fetal life is an offense, and how it should be punished, if at all, religious and ethical opinion cover a vast range of conflicting positions, as we have seen in Chapter XI. An even broader diversity exists among individuals. One family may consider a piece of fetal tissue human life when it has grown for two months; another, when it has grown for three. Still another may see the beginning of life in the emergence of the child from the womb.

Every shade of belief must be protected under our democratic system, including the belief of the Catholic or anyone else that life starts at the moment of conception. The whole basis of abortion reform is to insure that all rights are respected.

No religion or group, on the other hand, should impose its position on the rest of the nation. No religion, by demanding adherence to the status quo, by refusing to allow the slightest legal reform, should use the power of law to force its belief on others.

The California legislature's committee on the Beilenson bill states: "Clearly the Legislature cannot pass a resolution decreeing that life begins at conception. But to base legislation solely on this premise would in reality be the same thing, and so would retaining existing legislation for that sole reason."

In its unyielding opposition to abortion reform, the Catholic Church is thus maintaining its dogma of conception through present laws. Its campaign bears a striking parallel to a theoretical attempt by the Christian Science Church, for example, to force its medical principles on the rest of the country. No one would deny the right of the Christian Scientist to preach such beliefs from the pulpit, the press, or any other public medium. But there is an enormous difference between information and persuasion, and the tactics used by the Catholic hierarchy in New Hampshire and other states, where every type of political in-fighting was directed at legislators and governors to block reform legislation. If these tactics had been used by the Christian Science Church, or any other small denomination, the national reaction would have been instant and violent.

Richard Cardinal Cushing, the Roman Catholic Archbishop of Boston, has already proclaimed in eloquent language: "Catholics do not need the support of civil law to be faithful to their own religious convictions and they do not seek to impose by law their moral views on other members of society." Unfortunately, the Cardinal's pronouncement remains unheeded by most of the Catholic hierarchy.

As long as the Catholic Church, or any faith, continues to block legislation allowing individual conscience and free choice in abortion, the core of our democratic system is crippled. The right to abortion is the foundation of Society's long struggle to guarantee that every child comes into this world wanted, loved, and cared for. The right to abortion, along with all birth-control measures, must establish the Century of the Wanted Child.

XVIII

Legalized Abortion: The Final Freedom

"The most far-reaching social development of modern times," Margaret Sanger declared in 1920, "is the revolt of woman against sex servitude." Feminine suffrage, the climb toward equality in business and the professions, and, above all, the control of fertility through contraception, are all steps in this long quest. The ultimate freedom remains the right of every woman to legalized abortion.

"No woman can call herself free who does not own and control her body," Mrs. Sanger stated. "No woman can call herself free until she can choose consciously whether she will or will not be a mother."

The laws that force a woman to bear a child against her will are the sickly heritage of feminine degradation and male supremacy. "The residue of an ancient world in which women were, quite literally, put in a legal class with children, idiots and slaves," Hardin calls it. "The desire of the male to dominate is all too readily apparent beneath the thin veil of ethical rhetoric."

The laws forcing a woman to conception, whether aimed at birth control or abortion, are man-made laws. Their roots go back to the primeval past, when man struggled for survival against the violence of nature, famine, disease, and early death. Woman, to a great extent, was prized only as a breeder and child-rearer. She was trapped by a biological fact, harnessed to the demands of rulers and statesmen for new armies and new populations to fill their territories. Right through the era of America's expanding frontiers in the nineteenth century, the pioneer expected his wife to breed until exhaustion, and often replaced her after an early death with more wives to continue the procreative process.

And when the American woman, particularly the middle-class after the Civil War, turned to crude methods of contraception and abortion in her search for economic stability, education, and a better life for herself and her family, the lawmakers stopped her with the Comstock Act and similar statutes in almost every state. These legislatures consisted only of males, elected by males. No male legislator has ever had the honesty to suggest a feminine referendum to approve or abolish such prohibitions.

The neglect of man-made laws to grant the choice of motherhood not only condemns women to the level of brood animals, but disfigures the sanctity of birth itself. By making birth the result of blind impulse and passion, our laws ensure that children may become little more than the automatic reflex of a biological system. Not only woman, but all humanity, is degraded.

We have advanced through the centuries toward a peak of dignity by increasing the role of reason in our lives. Civilization itself has been built on the taming of nature. "To me, the main purpose of man's existence is to fight these very evils of pain, sickness and unhappiness, to engage in endless and constant struggle with the forces of nature until he makes them the servant of his will and the ministers of his delight," the late Lord Buckmaster told the House of Lords in 1926.

The culmination of this struggle, the triumph of reason over blind instinct, can come only when procreation is entrusted to each man and woman, not to the state, not to the church or synagogue, not to any instrument of authority.

"Until a child is actually born into this world," declares Rabbi Margolies, "it does not belong to society, nor has it been accepted into any faith. Its existence is purely and entirely the business and concern of its parents, whether they are married or not."

"Only completely legalized abortion can untangle the unhappy mess that seventy-five years of blind and inhuman legislation has created," *Southern Medicine and Surgery* announced as early as 1942.

In a ringing credo shortly before his election as president of the Association for the Study of Abortion, Dr. Robert E. Hall wrote:

> My answer as an obstetrician is that doctors should not be asked to determine which women qualify for abortions. We are no more qualified to do so than accountants or streetcleaners. Nor do I think that lawyers, psychologists, or theologians are better suited. Who then? Who but the prospective parents them-

selves? They know as much about animate and inanimate fetuses as the highest priest and a great deal more about their own ability and desire to raise a child than the fanciest physician. They are not going to create a pregnancy for the sole purpose of destroying it; yet if its destruction seems imperative to them, they will be spared a great deal of otherwise inevitable guilt if their society sanctions what they do.

"Any woman at any time should be able to procure a legal abortion without even giving a reason," Hardin concluded in his noted Berkeley speech.[1]

The complete legalization of abortion is the one just and inevitable answer to the quest for feminine freedom. All other solutions are compromises. The American Law Institute code offers a practical plan that might eventually be accepted by a few state legislatures. But it evades the real problem, touching only a fraction of essential cases, and leaving the average woman chained to a tenuous and possibly unmanageable law, and the medical profession still struggling to decide what cases can be accepted under the vague definition of "health."

Even the recent British formula, supported by part of the Abortion Law Reform Association, falls short of a total solution. This formula demands a return to the old common law in operation in Britain before 1803 and in most of the United States before the Civil War. While abortions under the common law would be permitted before quickening, the act of procreation would still be controlled by the state. And if a pregnancy had to be terminated after quickening, both patient and physician would continue to be entangled in the present morass of laws.

Following an intensive study of both legal and civil-rights aspects of abortion, the New York Civil Liberties Union recently became the first prominent organization to support complete legalization. A proposed revision of the penal code, drafted by a committee with Ephraim London as chairman, and approved by the CLU board on October 5, 1965, condenses the law to a few simple words: "A person is guilty of abortion if he is not a duly licensed physician and intentionally terminates the pregnancy of another otherwise than by a live birth."

By punishing only the abortionist who is not a licensed physician, this proposed law grants total freedom of choice to the woman and the medical profession. Its one objective—the only humane and logical objective in eliminating the brutality and chaos of our present system—is to protect a woman's health and life against the ignorance of an unlicensed practitioner. The CLU proposal not only offers a rallying point for women in their revolt against enforced procreation; it embodies the supreme morality of our time, the guarantee that every child shall become a wanted child.

What a few perceptive lawyers have begun to emphasize is that the feminine quest for legalized abortion involves constitutional principles of vast impact. "Does it not constitutionally deny a woman's life, liberty and the pursuit of happiness," demands Harriet Pilpel, "if despite her wishes and the opinions of concurring doctors, she is forced to bear a child she doesn't want and, objectively, shouldn't have?"

The first court test involving these constitutional principles is New York's Manhattan State Hospital case, cited in Chapter V. (*Williams v. State*) An unmarried woman mental patient, raped by another inmate, was denied a hospital abortion, and ultimately gave birth to a baby girl. Since both mother and father may be confined to mental hospitals for the rest of their lives, the care and education of the child depends on the mother's parents, who are not only aged but indigent.

The immediate basis of the suit is the negligence of the State of New York in not preventing the rape and its liability for failing to terminate the pregnancy, thereby causing the birth of a child who will be deprived of normal home life and parental care. But beyond this lie far deeper issues, affecting the responsibility of the state for forcing an unwanted birth. Can the state refuse any abortion when the child's life will be gravely damaged? demands Norman Roy Grutman, attorney for the child. In forcing an unwanted birth, does not the state incur responsibility for the child's education and support?

A decision in the Manhattan State Hospital case, unprecedented in any U.S. court, was handed down on June 25, 1965. The New York Court of Claims ruled that the child had the right to recover damages from the state. Now the state is appealing. If a higher court upholds the Court of Claims, Grutman believes the decision will be broad enough to define the responsibility of the state to perform abortions. "If upheld, it will establish New York as the first state to recognize a cause of action for wrongful birth," concludes *The New York Times*.[2]

A second test, involving similar constitutional principles and still pending in the courts in 1965, should clarify the rights of a mother whose request for abortion when she contracted German measles was refused, and whose baby was born deformed as a result. *(Stewart v. Long Island College Hospital)* What is this hospital's responsibility if the infant needs expensive treatment, or even custodial care for the rest of its life? Or if the mother needs expensive treatment caused by the trauma of bearing a deformed child?

The answers are to be found in the case of a Brooklyn mother whose daughter came down with German measles in April 1964. When the mother developed the same symptoms, her family doctor diagnosed them also as measles. In addition, he suspected she might be pregnant, and tests proved positive.

Since the risk of bearing a deformed child runs about 20 to 50 per cent for a mother with measles in early pregnancy, both parents in consultation with their doctor agreed on the necessity of abortion. The doctor gave them a letter verifying measles and pregnancy, and sent them to the nearest city hospital. The hospital asked the mother to wait until all traces of measles had disappeared. When she returned a few days later, the hospital asked her to wait until a specific obstetrician was available for the operation, a delay repeated each time she returned during the next ten days.

Concerned by these postponements, the woman's doctor sent her in mid-May, again with a verifying letter, to a nearby voluntary hospital. Here she was admitted for abortion with the approval of three staff physicians and both the diagnosis and the approval entered on the hospital records. However, a week passed and she was still pregnant. Finally, the woman was informed that her uterus was too large for an effective dilatation and curettage. She was not only discharged, but encouraged to bring the pregnancy to term with the assurance that her baby would be born normal, a strange and hazardous assumption even under routine circumstances.

Tragically, the prognosis proved wrong. A baby girl was born in January 1965, afflicted with all the measles-related malformations ranging from congenital cataracts and congenital heart disease to severe deafness.

Now the mother, also represented by Grutman, is suing the voluntary hospital for denial of her constitutional rights. The issues go even beyond those in the Manhattan State Hospital case. Not only was the mother denied freedom to seek proper medical treatment on the advice of her physician and the hospital's doctors; she was also forced to bear a child against her will, a child whose life may be physically and emotionally blighted, and who may require a lifetime of costly medical care.

Extending the constitutional argument to cases of rape, Cyril Means, a New York lawyer, insists that no abortion law in any state can be interpreted as preventing the victim of rape from seeking legal termination of her pregnancy. Could any state enact a statute prohibiting a woman confronted with a would-be rapist from defending herself or even killing in self-defense? "No American court would hold such a statute constitutional," he declares. "The woman's right to kill an attacker in self-defense is a natural right and one that the Constitution would protect."

Why, then, is a state law that prevents a woman from terminating the aggression initiated by rape not equally unconstitutional? "The victim of rape, who resorts to abortion, is simply exercising her right of self-defense against an embryo which becomes part of the same criminal aggression," Means concludes. "Her self-defense against the embryo is a common-law right as valid as her self-defense against its father, and no legislature can constitutionally deprive her of it."[3]

Although the Manhattan Hospital case is the first court test touching on these constitutional principles, the 1965 U.S. Supreme Court decision overthrowing the Connecticut birth-control law by a 7-to-2 vote upholds basic liberties that seem integral to all methods of family limitation. (*Griswold v. Connecticut*)

In delivering the opinion of the Court, Justice William O. Douglas cited the Fourth and Fifth Amendments "as protection against all governmental invasions 'of the sanctity of a man's home and the privacies of life,'" and the Fourth Amendment as creating a "right of privacy, no less important than any other right carefully reserved to the people." Justice Douglas concluded: "The present case, then, concerns a relationship lying within the zone of privacy created by several fundamental constitutional guarantees."

In his concurring opinion, Justice Arthur J. Goldberg, joined by Chief Justice Warren and Justice Brennan, declared that "the right of marital privacy is protected, as being within the protected penumbra of specific guarantees of the Bill of Rights. . . ." He cited the liberty protected by the Fifth and Fourteenth Amendments in particular, and added, as had Justice Douglas in his opinion, that the liberty protected was not confined "to rights specifically mentioned in the first eight amendments." For the Ninth Amendment provides: "The

enumeration in the Constitution, of certain rights, shall not be con-
strued to deny or disparage others retained by the people."

"In sum," concluded Justice Goldberg, "I believe that the right
of privacy in the marital relation is fundamental and basic—a personal right 'retained by the people' within the meaning of the Ninth
Amendment."

Since the Court laid such emphasis on rights retained by the
people, it might well be asked whether abortion does not fall within
this category. The ten amendments protecting these retained rights
were passed in 1791. Since the right of abortion before quickening
was included in the common law until 1827 in Illinois, and in most
states until the Civil War and after, there would seem good reason
to conclude that abortion, as well as marital privacy, deserves the
protection of the Constitution.

Now that the Court has guaranteed marital privacy in contraception, lawyers may also ponder whether this same right does not apply
to all techniques of family limitation. The question remains whether
marital privacy is better protected by preventing an unwanted pregnancy than later, when conception has taken place.

The line between these situations may often be blurred. The
Lippes loop, for example, fast becoming one of the most widely used
contraceptive devices, may actually be an abortifacient. Scientists
are still not certain how the device works. One theory holds that it
prevents the female egg, already fertilized, from becoming attached
to the uterus, or that it even displaces an egg recently attached. If
this theory is confirmed, the Court's decision in the Connecticut case
may result in the ambiguity of covering a presumed contraceptive
that in fact turns out to be an abortifacient.

Scientific research, in fact, may eventually become as much a
part of the feminine quest for the right of abortion as constitutional
guarantees sought through the courts. The development of an abortifacient pill, taken orally shortly after pregnancy has been determined, could solve the abortion problem. Prescribed by the woman's
physician—and in this way preserving a completely private relationship between patient and doctor—the pill would be taken at home,
within "the right of marital privacy." Further, it would eliminate
surgery involved in the present dilatation and curettage. And the
very act of surgery, with its possible emotional trauma, has presented an obstacle of varying degrees to almost every patient. Above
all, by eliminating hospital abortion committees, the pill would separate abortion from the realm of bureaucracy and officialdom.

Some of these advantages, of course, are more imaginary than real. An abortifacient pill taken shortly after conception produces the same end as surgery at two months; but in the woman's mind, there is a vast difference. The fact that she herself performs the act makes it far more acceptable. Also, she has not only made the decision; she has carried it through without a coterie of medical judges looming over her shoulder. Spared the operating room and other frightening symbols, she can free herself from the possible stigma and guilt that hospital surgery may inflict on any woman who considers abortion a right as simple and personal as the regular use of contraception.

Unfortunately, research to produce an abortifacient, conducted primarily by Dr. J. B. Thiersch, clinical professor of pharmacology at the University of Washington, Seattle, is still far from its objective. Thiersch has worked for fifteen years to develop a chemical compound that will destroy the fetus without causing any injury or side-effects to the woman. Because the early fetus has a high rate of protein synthesis, he has concentrated on anti-metabolites or amino-acid, purine and pyrimidine analogues which interfere with the natural "building-blocks" of protein in the developing cells.

Thiersch's medical papers report varying degrees of success. In one series of experiments, he produced chemical abortion in ten of twelve cases during the first three months of pregnancy, but failed to produce immediate abortion in three older fetuses. In another series, he produced abortion in eleven of thirteen cases within twenty days. In a series of tubercular patients, he was successful in only half the cases, calling his compound still "too uncertain."

Although several compounds in his tests on rat litters were found to be over 90 per cent effective at various stages of pregnancy, these animal experiments do not rule out possible malformation in the human embryo in case of drug failure. U.S. Food and Drug regulations now limit further studies in this direction. As a result, drug companies have been discouraged from supporting research with sizable financial grants.

Still, the abortifacient pill remains as vital to the abortion problem as the contraceptive pill was to birth control during its first, experimental obstacles. "Research must find a compound with so vast a margin between the dangerous dose and abortive effect that it proves absolutely harmless for human use," concludes Dr. Sheldon Segal, director of the Population Council's Biomedical Division. "I'm certain it can be found and eventually applied without risk."[4]

In the meantime, the feminine request for legalized abortion depends partly on legislative reform, partly on the courage of the medical profession to extend the Buffalo blueprint to every possible hospital, but, above all, on court cases aimed at a broader definition of our constitutional liberties and guarantees.

If such organizations as the New York Civil Liberties Union and the Association for the Study of Abortion are to carry this campaign through the courts, women themselves must bear the special responsibility of rallying opinion behind reform, standing up and making their demands for justice known throughout the country. Nothing is stronger than the moral power of an idea once it has come of age. And the moral power of legalized abortion will surely prevail when women have directed their anger against the superstitions of centuries, and cried out for the final freedom of procreative choice.

Although more than a million American women each year are forced by inhuman laws to crawl through the horror of secret abortions, almost none has protested publicly against the laws that defiled her. Almost no men, whose rights are equally at stake, have risen up to attack a system which makes a mockery of free people in a free society.

"When rulers have inverted their functions and enacted wickedness into a law which treads down the inalienable rights of man to such a degree as this," abolitionist minister Theodore Parker of Boston declared after passage of the Fugitive Slave Bill in 1850, "then I know no ruler but God, no law but natural Justice."

What rulers are we to acknowledge today? We have remained silent too long. We pay obeisance on the surface to laws we disregard in secret. We maintain a system by hypocritical silence when the time has come to seek natural justice. If men and women are going to break U.S. abortion laws at least a million times a year, let them declare their freedom boldly. Let them announce it at their clubs and town meetings and proclaim it in the press. Let them affirm with conviction: No law is a real law that prohibits the inalienable rights of human beings.

"In my humble opinion, religion in the highest sense calls upon each of us to disavow the old taboos that suggest that abortion and planned parenthood are sinful," concludes Rabbi Margolies, "and assert honestly and proudly that, as creative partners of God, we reserve the right to create families purposefully and joyfully, not accidentally and reluctantly. Let us help build a world in which no human being enters life unwanted and unloved."

Notes and Special References

In order to avoid a hopelessly large collection of notes, and to make this study as readable as possible, I have tried to limit the numbered citations in each chapter to the most essential references. Further, I have followed the practice of grouping all references in a paragraph, and occasionally in a few preceding paragraphs, under one numbered citation.

In addition to the notes, most chapters include a list of special references. These are sources of a more general nature on which sections of the chapter are based.

In a few cases, such as Chapter XIV, "The Lessons from European Abortion," all materials and sources are listed under Special References to avoid the confusion of four or five sources for one paragraph which might have had to be repeated a few paragraphs later.

CHAPTER ONE
The System

[1] Mary S. Calderone (ed.): *Abortion in the United States* (New York: Paul B. Hoeber, Inc.; 1958), p. 180; Marie E. Kopp: *Birth Control in Practice* (New York: Robert M. McBride & Co.; 1934), p. 222.

[2] Paul H. Gebhard *et al: Pregnancy, Birth and Abortion* (New York: Harper & Row–Hoeber, Inc.; 1958), pp. 137, 147.

[3] Christopher Tietze and Clyde E. Martin: "Foetal Deaths, Spontaneous and Induced...," *Population Studies*, Vol. XI, No. 2 (November 1957), pp. 170–76; Ruth Roemer: "Due Process and Organized Health Services," *Public Health Reports* (August 1964); Edwin M. Gold *et al:* "Therapeutic Abortions in New York City: A Twenty-Year Review," New York Department of Health, Bureau of Records and Statistics (October 14, 1963).

[4] The figure 8,000 has been estimated by Dr. Tietze on the basis of hospital abortions in New York City, the only major municipality keeping abortion statistics fully, and applied proportionate to population to the rest of the country. See Gold, Ibid. The figure is verified by Dr. Hall's study showing 2 hospital abortions per 1,000 live births. See

Robert E. Hall: "Therapeutic Abortion, Sterilization and Contraception," *American Journal of Obstetrics and Gynecology,* Vol. 91 (February 15, 1965), pp. 518–32.

[5] See Kopp: *Birth Control,* Ibid, in whose study 26 per cent were Catholics; Hall: "Therapeutic Abortion," Ibid, in whose study 22 per cent of white patients were Catholics; records of Dr. G. L. Timanus, formerly a prominent Baltimore abortionist whose records, analyzed by the author, show 22 per cent of 3,320 patients to be Catholics. Kenneth R. Niswander and Morton Klein: "Changing Attitudes Towards Therapeutic Abortion" (unpublished) (June 30, 1965) shows 24 to 38 per cent of abortions at two Buffalo hospitals were Catholics.

Special References:

Unofficial Report of Committee Staff, Committee on Criminal Procedure of California State Assembly, Bill AB 2614 (1964), p. 34.

Alan F. Guttmacher: "Legal and Moral Status of Therapeutic Abortion," *Progress in Gynecology,* Vol. 4 (New York: Grune & Stratton, Inc.; 1963), p. 293.

Raible sermon delivered October 20, 1963.

Case No. 9, Letters sent to British Abortion Law Reform Association, London.

The Abortion Problem, Proceedings of Conference under auspices of National Committee on Maternal Health (Baltimore: Williams & Wilkins Co.; 1944), for Kleegman quotation.

Henry J. Langston (ed.): "Abortion and the Law," *Southern Medicine and Surgery* (July 1942), p. 408.

Margie Anson, as told to Cal Bernstein: "A Night of Terror," *Coronet* (June 1956).

Alan F. Guttmacher: *Babies by Choice or by Chance* (New York: Avon Books; 1961), p. 138, on Baltimore rape case.

Nikolas A. Janovski *et al:* "Soap Intoxication Following Criminal Abortion," *New York State Journal of Medicine,* Vol. 63, No. 1 b, (May 15, 1963), p. 1463; Ronald Smith *et al:* "Soap-Induced Abortion," *Obstetrics and Gynecology,* Vol. 20, No. 2 (August 1962).

Margolies' speech delivered at New York Academy of Medicine, meeting of Association for the Study of Abortion, February 24, 1965.

CHAPTER TWO

A Farce in Phoenix

This chapter is based primarily on personal interviews with Mr. and Mrs. Robert Finkbine and study of their personal memoranda, letters, and newspaper-clipping files on the case; on an article bv Joseph Stocker in *Redbook,* January 1963, and additional research and memoranda from Mr. Stocker.

Authorities in Phoenix close to the case, including editors, lawyers, religious leaders, hospital executives, and physicians, also supplied memoranda which have been kept anonymous by request.

Judge Yale McFate's opinion is taken from Memorandum No. 140504 of Superior Court of State of Arizona, County of Maricopa, July 31, 1962.

Rabbi Israel Margolies' statement is from sermon of October 20, 1962, in New York.

For information on thalidomide, see particularly Dr. Howard Rusk: "Thalidomide Tragedy II," *The New York Times* (August 12, 1962), p. 56; and Dr. Helen B. Taussig: "The Thalidomide Syndrome," *Scientific American* (August 1962), and articles in the *Arizona Republic* from July 23 through August 4, 1962.

CHAPTER THREE
How Safe Is Hospital Abortion?

[1] Antonin Černoch: "Experiences in Czechoslovakia with the Effects and Consequences of Legalized Artificial Termination of Pregnancy" (unpublished paper delivered at U.N. World Population Conference, Belgrade; August 30–September 10, 1965). Further Černoch references in chapter apply to this paper.

K.–H. Mehlan: "Family Planning in the Eastern European Socialist Countries," *Family Planning Programs—Proceedings of an International Conference, August 1965* (Illinois: University of Chicago Press; ·1966).

Christopher Tietze: "The Demographic Significance of Legal Abortion in Eastern Europe," *Demography,* Vol. 1, No. 1 (1964), pp. 119–25; Christopher Tietze and Hans Lehfeldt: "Legal Abortion in Eastern Europe," *Journal of the American Medical Association,* Vol. 175 (April 1, 1961), pp. 1149–54.

[2] Roy O. Greep (ed.): *Human Fertility and Population Problems,* (Cambridge, Mass.: 1963; Schenkman Publishing Co.), p. 233; K.–H. Mehlan: "The Effects of Legislation of Abortion on Health of Mothers in Eastern Europe," 7th International Congress of Planned Parenthood (Singapore; February 1963) estimates the Swedish, Finnish, and Danish death rate from abortion as 14 to 18 per 100,000; but Tietze considers the Scandinavian average closer to 40 per 100,000.

[3] Since viability is an indefinite period, ranging from 24 to 28 weeks of pregnancy, medical schools usually prefer the measurement adopted by the World Health Organization, which considers it abortion when

a fetus weighs 500 grams or less (slightly over a pound). If a fetus weighs between 500 and 999 grams, it is called delivery of an immature fetus. If a fetus weighs between 1,000 and 2,499 grams, it is called a delivery of a premature fetus.

[4] Alan F. Guttmacher: "Techniques of Therapeutic Abortion," *Clinical Obstetrics and Gynecology,* Vol. 7, No. 1 (March 1964) (Harper & Row–Hoeber, Inc., New York), pp. 100–07; John Rock and Armand Maillot: "Abortion," *Gynecology and Obstetrics,* Vol. 1, Ch. 10 (Hagerstown, Md.: W. F. Prior Co.; 1963); Gorm Wagner *et al:* "Induction of Abortion by Intra-Ovular Instillation of Hypertonic Saline," *Danish Medical Bulletin,* Vol. 9, No. 5 (August 1962), p. 137.

[5] Jan Lindahl: *Somatic Complications Following Legal Abortion* (Stockholm: Scandinavian University Books; 1959). Further Lindahl references apply to this paper.

[6] Per Kolstad: "Therapeutic Abortion," *Acta Obstetrica et Gynecologica Scandinavica,* Vol. 36, Supplement 6 (1957). Further Kolstad references apply to this paper.

[7] Per Arén: "Legal Abortion in Sweden," *Acta Obstetrica et Gynecologica Scandinavica,* Vol. 36, Supplement 1 (1958).

[8] Mary S. Calderone (ed.): *Abortion in the United States* (New York: Harper & Row–Hoeber, Inc.; 1958), p. 62.

[9] Two preceding paragraphs from Harold Rosen (ed.): *Therapeutic Abortion* (New York: The Julian Press, Inc.; 1954), pp. 12, 31, 196, 279, 292.

[1] Jerome M. Kummer: "Post-Abortion Psychiatric Illness—a Myth?" *American Journal of Psychiatry,* Vol. 119, No. 10 (April 1963), p. 983. Further Kummer references apply to this paper.

[2] Martin Ekblad: "Induced Abortion on Psychiatric Grounds," *Acta Psychiatrica et Neurologica Scandinavica,* Supplement 99 (1955).

[3] Gebhard, *Pregnancy,* Ibid, p. 209.

[4] Calderone, *Abortion,* Ibid, p. 135.

[5] Calderone, *Abortion,* Ibid, p. 981.

Special References

Techniques of abortions are described in Larsson-Cohn: "Legal Abortion by Percutaneous Intra-Amniotic Salt Injection," *Svensk. Lakartidn.,* Vol. 61 (June 3, 1964), pp. 1881–84 (summary in English); Chernyak, A. A.: "Artificial Termination of Pregnancy with a Vacuum Aspirator," *Zdravookhranenie Belorusii* (Minsk), Vol. 9 (May 1963), pp. 28–30 (in Russian; author's address–Scientific Research Institute for Mother and Child Care, Minsk, Belorussian S.S.R., U.S.S.R.).

All references in Kinsey study in Paul H. Gebhard *et al: Pregnancy, Birth and Abortion* (New York: Harper & Row–Hoeber, Inc.; 1958), pp. 205, 211.

Anthropological references are from William Graham Sumner: *Folkways* (Boston: Ginn & Co.; 1907), pp. 320–27; George Devereux: *A Study of Abortion in Primitive Societies* (New York: Julian Press., Inc.; 1955).

Hardin quotation and all further Hardin references from lecture of April 29, 1964, at University of California, Berkeley.

CHAPTER FOUR

Hospital Abortion: A System of Fear and Privilege

[1] All quotations from the results of a survey made by Dr. William Ober, of Knickerbocker Hospital, New York City, and the author, henceforth to be called the Ober-Lader survey. Questionnaires were sent to 700 diplomates in obstetrics and gynecology across the country. Every eighth name was selected from the official directory, representing a reasonable geographic cross-section. The tabulation includes 338 usable replies. Forty-one returns were unusable because of physician's death, lack of proper address, etc.

[2] First quotation from Harold Rosen (ed.): *Therapeutic Abortion* (New York: Julian Press, Inc.; 1954), p. 291; second quotation from Ober-Lader survey. Further Rosen references are from pp. 239–40, 287, 289.

[3] Sloane statistics from Robert E. Hall: "Therapeutic Abortion, Sterilization and Contraception," *American Journal of Obstetrics and Gynecology*, Vol. 91 (February 15, 1965), pp. 518–32; New York City statistics from Edwin M. Gold *et al:* "Therapeutic Abortions in New York City: A Twenty-Year Review," New York Department of Health, Bureau of Records & Statistics (October 14, 1963).

[4] New York statistics from Hall: "Therapeutic Abortion," *Ibid*; Los Angeles from Keith P. Russell: "Changing Indications for Therapeutic Abortion," *Journal of the American Medical Association*, Vol. 151 (January 10, 1953), p. 108.

[5] Virginia statistics from Gunnard A. Nelson and James J. Hunter, Jr.: "Therapeutic Abortion," *Obstetrics and Gynecology*, Vol. 9 (1957), p. 284; California from Lewis K. Savel and Irving K. Perlmutter: "Therapeutic Abortion and Sterilization Committees," *American Journal of Obstetrics and Gynecology*, Vol. 80 (2), No. 2 (1960), p. 1192; New York from Hall: "Therapeutic Abortion," *Ibid*.

[6] University of Pennsylvania quotation from Stanley H. Boulas, Robert H. Preucel, and John H. Moore: "Therapeutic Abortion," *Obstetrics and Gynecology*, Vol. 19, No. 2 (February 1962), p. 222.

[7] Gold: "Therapeutic Abortions," Ibid; 1964 statistics from *Journal of Public Health*, Vol. 55, No. 7 (July 1965), p. 964.

[8] Previous two paragraphs from Hall: "Therapeutic Abortion," Ibid.

[9] New York statistic from Alan F. Guttmacher: "Legal and Moral Status of Therapeutic Abortion," *Progress in Gynecology*, Vol. 4 (New York; Grune & Stratton, Inc.; 1963); Los Angeles from Edmund W. Overstreet (ed.): "Therapeutic Abortion and Sterilization," *Clinical Obstetrics and Gynecology*, Vol. 7, No. 1 (March 1964).

CHAPTER FIVE

The Doctor's Dilemma

[1] Edmund Overstreet and Herbert F. Traut: *Postgraduate Medicine*, Vol. 9 (1951), p. 16; J. G. Moore and J. H. Randall: "Trends in Therapeutic Abortion," *American Journal of Obstetrics and Gynecology*, Vol. 63, No. 1 (1952), p. 28.

[2] Herbert L. Packer and Ralph J. Gampell: "Therapeutic Abortion: A Problem in Law and Medicine," *Stanford Law Review*, Vol. 2 (1959), p. 417.

[3] Harold Rosen (ed.): *Therapeutic Abortion* (New York: Julian Press, Inc.; 1954), pp. 232–35.

[4] Edwin M. Gold *et al:* "Therapeutic Abortions in New York City: A Twenty-Year Review," New York Department of Health, Bureau of Records and Statistics (October 14, 1963); and *Journal of Public Health*, Vol. 55, No. 7 (July 1965), p. 964.

[5] Rosen, *Therapeutic Abortion*, Ibid, p. 193; further quotations from Mandy, Jenkins, and Lidz from Rosen, pp. 243, 282, and 292.

[6] "Symposium on 'The Social Problem of Abortion,'" *Bulletin of the Sloane Hospital for Women*, Vol. 11 (fall 1965), pp. 68–71.

[7] For fetal damage caused by German measles, see Gian Tonduri: "On the Damage Which May Derive to the Human Embryo from Virus Action," *Journal of the International Federation of Gynecology and Obstetrics* (April–July 1964), p. 230.

For risk of fetal damage, see John Rendle-Short, professor of child health, University of Queensland, in 1964 annual report of British Law Reform Association, p. 9; Margaret M. Manson *et al:* "Rubella and Other Virus Infections during Pregnancy," *Ministry of Health Reports on Public Health and Medical Subjects*, No. 101 (London; 1960); Mary D. Sheridan: "Final Report of a Prospective Study," *British Medical Journal*, Vol. 2 (August 29, 1964), pp. 536–39; National Foundation–March of Dimes report on Dr. Gilbert M. Schiff *et al*, Society for Pediatric Research and American Pediatric Association, Philadelphia (May 4–6, 1965); Schiff: "Studies on Congenital Rubella," *American Journal of the Diseases of Children*, Vol. 110 (October 1965), pp. 441–43; and J. B. Avery (pp. 444–46) and J. L. Sever (pp. 453–54) in same issue. For statistics on measles incidence, see Schiff and National Foundation reports cited above, and personal communication with Dr. Saul Krugman, New York University Hospital; Dorothy M. Horstmann: "Rubella and the Rubella Syndrome," *California Medicine*, Vol. 102: pp. 397–403 (1965); *The New York Times* (Oct. 27, 1965).

[8] For New York statistics in previous paragraphs, see Edwin M. Gold *et al:* "Therapeutic Abortions in New York City," Ibid.

Special References:

Suicide statistics from Mary S. Calderone (ed.): *Abortion in the United States* (New York: Harper & Row–Hoeber, Inc.; 1958), pp. 140–41.

Sidney Bolter quotation from "The Psychiatrist's Role in Therapeutic Abortion," *American Journal of Psychiatry*, Vol. 119, No. 4 (October 1962).

Impact of emotional illness on pregnancy from J. G. Moore and J. H. Randall: "Trends," Ibid, p. 28; Jerome M. Kummer: "Psychiatric Contraindications to Pregnancy," *California Medicine*, Vol. 79, No. 1 (July 1953), pp. 31–35.

Socio-economic factors in abortion from Edmund Overstreet and Herbert F. Traut: *Postgraduate Medicine*, Vol. 9 (1951), p. 16; Alan F. Guttmacher: "Therapeutic Abortion: The Doctor's Dilemma," *Journal of Mt. Sinai Hospital*, Vol. 21 (May–June 1954), p. 111; and Mary Calderone (ed.): *Abortion*, Ibid, p. 138.

CHAPTER SEVEN

Methods of Reaching the Skilled Abortionist

[1] Christopher Tietze: "Induced Abortion and Sterilization as Methods of Fertility Control" (in press); *National Institute of Mental Health Record*, Vol. XVI, No. 25 (December 15, 1964), p. 1.

[2] David M. Heer: "Abortion, Contraception, and Population Policy in the Soviet Union," *Demography*, Vol. 2 (June 1965); Hungarian statistic from Hungarian Press Survey, No. 1347 (1963), of Free Europe Committee, New York; Czechoslovakian statistic from Czechoslovakian Press Survey (1963), of same office.

Special References:

Kinsey statistics from Paul H. Gebhard *et al: Pregnancy, Birth and Abortion* (New York: Harper & Row–Hoeber, Inc.; 1958), pp. 60, 97, 98, 119.

Illegitimacy statistics from Clark E. Vincent: *Unmarried Mothers* (Free Press of Glencoe, Inc.; 1961), p. 53; and personal communication,

Robert Mackreth, New York City Bureau of Foster Care. See also Elizabeth Herzog: "Unmarried Mothers," *Child Welfare* (October 1962), p. 342. Even these figures are minimal. See Hannah M. Adams and Ursula M. Gallagher: "Some Facts and Observations about Illegitimacy," *Children*, Vol. 10, No. 2 (March–April 1964), pp. 43–48.

Helen Dean: *Unmarried Parenthood* (Welfare Council of Metropolitan Los Angeles; 1964), p. 30.

Leontine Young: *Out of Wedlock* (New York: McGraw-Hill Book Co., Inc.; 1954), p. 32.

For babies available for adoption, see Pearl Buck: *Children for Adoption* (New York: Random House; 1964), p. 175; see also unpublished survey made by Child Welfare League, New York.

For percentage of colored adoptions, see Vincent: *Unmarried Mothers*, Ibid, p. 13; New York statistics from Mackreth, Bureau of Foster Care; Adams and Gallagher: "Some Facts," Ibid; *The New York Times* (January 17, 1965).

For cost of welfare support, see *The New York Times* (August 3, 1964), p. 30.

For damage to illegitimate child, and parent of, see Buck, *Children*, Ibid, p. 12; "Children of Illegitimate Birth Whose Mothers Have Kept Their Custody," U.S. Department of Labor Publication No. 190, p. 2; Virginia Wimperis: *The Unmarried Mother and Her Child* (London: George Allen & Unwin, Ltd.; 1960), pp. 98–107.

CHAPTER EIGHT

The Underworld of Abortion

[1] N.Y. county study and cases from Jerome E. Bates and Edward S. Zawadzki: *Criminal Abortion* (Springfield, Ill.: Charles C. Thomas; 1964), pp. 95, 154–66, 183, 184, 202.

[2] Christopher Tietze: "Abortion as a Cause of Death," *American Journal of Public Health*, Vol. 38, No. 2 (October 1938), p. 1434; Edwin M. Gold *et al:* "Therapeutic Abortions in New York City: A Twenty-Year Review," New York Department of Health, Bureau of Records and Statistics (October 14, 1963); and *Journal of Public Health*, Vol. 55, No. 7 (July 1965), p. 964.

[3] "Case 29–1961," *New England Journal of Medicine*, Vol. 264, No. 2 (April 27, 1961), p. 877; Frank R. Dutra *et al:* "Criminal Abortions Induced by Intrauterine Paste," *Journal of the American Medical Association*, Vol. 143, No. 10 (July 8, 1950), p. 865.

[4] Alan F. Guttmacher: *Babies, by Choice or by Chance* (New York: Avon Books; 1961), p. 137; "Law and Criminal Abortion," *Indiana Law Journal*, Vol. 32 (1956–57), p. 1932.

5 New York State Supreme Court, Kings County: *A Presentment on the Suppression of Criminal Abortion by the Grand Jury for the Extraordinary Special and Trial Term* (New York: The Hamilton Press; 1941).

6 Paul H. Gebhard *et al: Pregnancy, Birth, and Abortion* (New York: Harper & Row–Hoeber, Inc.; 1958), pp. 197, 198, 212; Marie E. Kopp: *Birth Control in Practice* (New York: Robert M. McBride & Co.; 1934).

Special References:

For prohibitions on potassium, etc., see U.S. Food and Drug Administration *Register* (Washington, D.C.; August 23, 1960).

For drugstore sale of catheters and lack of pregnancy tests, see Guttmacher: *Babies,* Ibid, p. 169.

CHAPTER NINE

The Origins of Abortion Chaos

1 Both the Chinese and Egyptian techniques are cited in Norman Himes: *Medical History of Contraception* (Baltimore: Williams & Wilkins Co.; 1936); the Hammurabi code and the biblical reference from Exodus 21: 22–23, King James version, are analyzed in Immanuel Jakobovits, *Jewish Medical Ethics* (New York Philosophical Library; 1959); William E. H. Lecky: *History of European Morals from Augustus to Charlemagne* (London: Longmans, Green & Co.; 1869), 2 vols.

2 Early Greek and Roman techniques from George Devereux:*A Study of Abortion in Primitive Societies* (New York: Julian Press, Inc.; 1955); Soranus citations from O. Temkin: *Soranus' Gynecology* (Baltimore: Johns Hopkins University Press; 1956), and Alan F. Guttmacher: "Techniques of Therapeutic Abortion," *Clinical Obstetrics and Gynecology* (New York: Harper & Row, Hoeber Medical Division; March 1964), Vol. 7, No. 1.

3 T. N. A. Jeffcoate: "Indications for Therapeutic Abortion," *British Medical Journal* (February 27, 1960), p. 413; Roger J. Huser: *Criminal Abortion in Canon Law* (Washington, D.C.: Catholic University of America Press, Canon Law Studies No. 162; 1942); James F. Stephen: *History of the Criminal Law of England* (London: Macmillan & Co. Ltd.; 1883), Vol. 1, p. 25.

4 Eugene Quay: "Justifiable Abortion—Medical and Legal Foundations," *The Georgetown Law Journal,* Vol. 49, No. 3 (spring 1961), pp. 414, 415, 419, 425; John T. Noonan, Jr.: *Contraception* (Cambridge, Mass.: Harvard University Press; 1965), pp. 21, 23 *fn,* 86.

5 Noonan: *Contraception,* Ibid, pp. 88, 91, 232; for list of penances, see Noonan: p. 164; Edvard Westermarck: *Origin and Development of*

Moral Ideas (London: Macmillan & Co., Ltd.; 2nd ed., 1924), Vol. I, p. 416, *fn* 4.

6 Stephen: *History,* Ibid, Vol. I, p. 54; Noonan: *Contraception,* Ibid, p. 216; Quay: "Justifiable Abortion," Ibid, p. 431.

7 "The Law of Criminal Abortion," *Indiana Law Journal,* Vol. 32 (1956–57), pp. 193–94; *43 George 3, c. 58* in *A Collection of the Public General Statutes passed in the 43rd Year of the Reign of His Majesty King George III* (London: George Eyre & Andrew Strahan; 1803).

8 Noonan: *Contraception,* Ibid, pp. 362–63; Huser: *Criminal Abortion,* Ibid, pp. 62–63, 75–78, 103–05.

9 Noonan: *Contraception,* Ibid, p. 405; Professor Noonan has stated in a personal letter of July 22, 1965: "For purposes of determining whether someone has committed the sin of abortion, the general rule is that the sin is committed by destroying a fetus at the moment of conception or afterwards (Arthur Vermeersch, *Theologiae moralis principia—responsa—consilia,* 3rd ed. 1945, Vol. II, no. 580–581; Bernard Haring, *La Loi du Christ,* French translation 1959, Vol. III, p. 366). For the purposes of the canonical penalties, some writers think the old rule of the 40- and 80-day period might apply (Charles Augustine, *Commentary on the Code of Canon Law* [1920] Vol. IV, pp. 489–490). Haring, at the place cited, says that today 'almost all theologians' believe that conception is the moment when the soul is infused and that the old rule is no longer a tenable opinion."

On this same point, Reverend Huser, in a personal letter of July 31, 1965, states: "Pius IX's apostolic constitution, 'Apostolicae sedis,' abolished the 40-80 theory in regard ONLY to incurring the *censure* of excommunication for the crime of abortion. It simply disregarded entirely the matter of incurring an *irregularity* (prohibition to exercise or receive 'orders') and certain other penalties. Hence, canonists almost universally admitted that the animation-distinction remained applicable in the church law relative to incurring irregularity, etc., for the crime of abortion down to the present Code of Canon Law enacted in 1918. This law relative to irregularity for abortion was that of Popes Sixtus V and Gregory XIV."

1 Arthur W. Meyer: *The Rise of Embryology* (Palo Alto, Calif.: Stanford University Press; 1939), pp. 132–37; Noonan: *Contraception,* Ibid, p. 365.

2 Noonan: *Contraception,* Ibid, pp. 76, 132, 150, 194, 227, 275, 372, 421, 422, for references in three preceding paragraphs.

Special References:

For medico-legal analysis of quickening, see J. A. Gonzales, M. Vance, M. Helpern, and C. J. Umberger: *Legal Medicine, Pathology and Toxology* (New York; 1954), 2nd ed., p. 566.

For Draper report, see *The New York Times* (November 26, 1959), p. 43.

For link between Keber and dogma of conception, see Cyril Means' letter to *The New York Times* (April 9, 1965), p. 2 of scientific addenda (unpublished).

For Jeremy Bentham on contraception, see "Situation and Relief of the Poor," in Arthur Young, ed.: *Annals of Agriculture and Other Useful Arts*, 29 (1797), p. 423.

For impact of disease and infanticide on population, see William L. Langer: "Europe's Initial Population Explosion," *American Historical Review*, Vol. 69 (October, 1963).

For further discussion of delayed animation, see Richard A. McCormick: *America* (June 19, 1965), p. 879.

CHAPTER TEN

Probing the U.S. Legal Maze

[1] Laws in preceding paragraphs from Eugene Quay: "Justifiable Abortion—Medical and Legal Foundations," *The Georgetown Law Journal*, Vol. 49, No. 3 (spring 1961), pp. 395–526; the original volume of Revisers' Notes of New York statutes of 1828 were found by Cyril Means at the Association of the Bar of the City of New York; British statutes are 9 Geo. 4, c. 31; 7 Will. 4 & 1 Vict., c. 85, 1837; 24 & 25 Vict., c. 100, 1861.

[2] Glanville Williams: *The Sanctity of Life and the Criminal Law* (New York: Alfred A. Knopf; 1957), p. 154; later quotation from Williams, p. 156.

[3] Robert W. Haney: *Comstockery in America* (Boston: Beacon Press; 1960), pp. 18, 20–21; *Congressional Globe*, 1872–73, Part 2, 42nd Congress, 3rd session, p. 2005; Heywood Broun and Margaret Leech: *Anthony Comstock: Roundsman of the Lord* (New York: Albert & Charles Boni; 1927).

CHAPTER ELEVEN

The Religious Position on Abortion

[1] As to theologians brushing over the exact moment the soul enters the fetus, Reverend Roger Huser states in a personal letter of July 31, 1965: "Yes, I think that is generally true. After the late nineteenth century, the contrary opinion was almost entirely neglected."

[2] Godin and Hanley: *Hospital Ethics* (1957), p. 62, quoted in Monroe Trout: "Therapeutic Abortions Need Therapy," *Temple Law Quarterly*, Vol. 32, No. 2 (winter 1964); Paul Blanshard: "The Roman Catholic Church in Medicine, Sex and Education," pamphlet reprint (New York: *The Nation;* 1947).

Speaking in the British House of Commons on February 10, 1961, Kenneth Robinson (St. Pancras North) stated: "That doctrine (of the

Catholic Church) lays down perfectly clearly that, if it is a question of choice between the life of a child and the life of a mother, then, unfortunately, the mother must die. I think that is not a view which would commend itself to the rest of the people of this country."

[3] Frederick L. Good and Otis F. Kelly: *Marriage, Morals, and Medical Ethics* (New York: P. J. Kennedy & Sons; 1951), pp. 22–26.

[4] Joseph F. Fletcher: *Morals and Medicine* (Princeton, N.J.: Princeton University Press; 1954), pp. 153, 156; Glanville Williams: *The Sanctity of Life and the Criminal Law* (New York: Alfred A. Knopf; 1957), p. 202.

[5] Canon Henry de Dorlodot, in E. C. Messenger (ed.): *Theology and Evolution* (London; 1949), p. 279, quoted in Alice Jenkins: *Law for the Rich* (London: Victor Gollancz Ltd.; 1961), p. 17.

Special References.

For Catholic Church on fetal burial, etc., see Lester Kinsolving: "What About Therapeutic Abortion?" *The Christian Century* (May 13, 1964).

For prohibitions on abortions in Catholic hospitals, see Harold Rosen (ed.): *Therapeutic Abortion* (New York: Julian Press, Inc.; 1954), p. 164; Charles J. McFadden: *Medical Ethics,* 2nd ed. (Philadelphia: F. A. Davis Co.; 1951).

The best summaries of the Jewish position on abortion are Isaac Klein: *Responsa* (New York: The Rabbinical Assembly); Solomon B. Freehof: *Recent Reform Responsa* (Cincinnati: Hebrew Union College Press; 1963); Rosen (ed.): *Therapeutic Abortion,* Ibid, p. 171.

For Baptist position paper, see William H. Genné: "Abortions," *Concerns for Christian Citizens,* Vol. 5, No. 4 (January 1965), pp. 1–2; personal letter from Elizabeth J. Miller of June 18, 1964.

For embryological wastage, see George W. Corner: *Ourselves Unborn: An Embryologist's Essay on Man* (New Haven; 1944), p. 93; Gerald Leach: *New Statesman* (June 11, 1965).

CHAPTER TWELVE

Britain's Bourne Case: The Struggle for Reform

[1] Preceding paragraphs from Alice Jenkins: *Law for the Rich* (London: Victor Gollancz Ltd.; 1961), pp. 24, 32, 46; Max Hodann: *History of Modern Morals* (London: William Heinemann Ltd.; 1937).

[2] G. P. R. Tallin: "*R. v. Bourne,*" *Canadian Medical Association Journal,* Vol. 87 (August 4, 1962), p. 207.

[3] Polls in preceding paragraphs from *ALRA Newsletter,* No. 2 (London; April 1963), p. 4; No. 11 (summer 1965), pp. 2–3.

[4] Preceding paragraphs from Jenkins: *Law*, Ibid, p. 14; Parliamentary Debates (Hansard) Vol. 634, No. 51 (February 10, 1961), pp. 859–60, 874.

Special References:

Aleck Bourne: *A Doctor's Creed* (London: Victor Gollancz Ltd.; 1962).

The Lancet (July 9, July 23, July 30, September 24, 1938).

British Medical Journal (July 9, July 23, July 30, August 13, 1938).

The New York Times (June 29, July 2, July 19, July 20, 1938).

London Times (July 2, July 19, July 20, 1938).

Daily Express (London; August 9, 1962), Bourne's reflections on the trial.

Paul Ferris: "The Doctors' Dilemma," *The Observer* (London; October 17, October 24, 1965).

D. E. Zarfas: "Psychiatric Indications for the Termination of Pregnancy," *Canadian Medical Association Journal*, Vol. 79 (August 15, 1958), p. 230.

CHAPTER THIRTEEN

Storm over New Hampshire

This chapter is based on the files of the New Hampshire Medical Society at Concord, N.H.; on hearings before the state legislature on the abortion bill; on interviews with officers and lawyers of the Medical Society and with doctors who participated in the campaign for the bill; on interviews with members of the state legislature, with the New Hampshire Council of Churches, and with reporters who covered the bill; and on the files of the Manchester *Union Leader*, Hanover *Gazette*, and other newspapers.

CHAPTER FOURTEEN

The Lessons from European Abortion

Special References:

Scandinavia

Christopher Tietze: "Some Facts about Legal Abortion," in *Human Fertility and Population Problems,* ed. by Roy O. Greep (Cambridge, Mass.: Shenkman Publishing Co.; 1963), pp. 222–35.

———: "Legal Abortion in Scandinavia," *Obstetrics and Gynecology* (October–December 1959), pp. 227–230.

———: "Induced Abortion and Sterilization as Methods of Fertility Control" (New York: National Committee on Maternal Health; June 1964), unpublished.

Per Kolstad: "Therapeutic Abortion," *Acta Obstetrica et Gynecologica Scandinavica,* Vol. 36, Supplement 6 (1957), pp. 1–72.

Kerstin Höök: "Refused Abortion," *Acta Psychiatrica Scandinavica,* Vol. 39, Supplement 168 (1963), pp. 1–156.

Paul H. Gebhard *et al*: *Pregnancy, Birth and Abortion* (New York: Harper & Row–Hoeber, Inc.; 1958), pp. 222, 225, 226, 229–230.

Mary S. Calderone (ed.): *Abortion in the United States* (New York: Harper & Row–Hoeber, Inc.; 1958), pp. 15–16, 19, 21, 27, 209.

Martin Ekblad: "Induced Abortion on Psychiatric Grounds," *Acta Psychiatrica et Neurologica Scandinavica,* Supplement 99 (1955).

————: "The Socio-Psychiatric Indications for Legal Termination of Pregnancy in Sweden," *Fourth International Conference on Planned Parenthood,* (1953), pp. 88–89.

Soviet Union

Rudolf Schlesinger: *The Family in the USSR* (London: Routledge & Kegan Paul Ltd.; 1949), pp. 18, 44, 172 *ff.*, for early Soviet policy.

Mark G. Field: "Re-Legalization of Abortion in Soviet Russia," *New England Journal of Medicine,* Vol. 255 (August 30, 1956), pp. 421–27, for early and later policy.

Calderone: *Abortion,* Ibid, pp. 207–08.

The Abortion Problem, conference of National Committee on Maternal Health (Baltimore: Williams & Wilkins Co.; 1944).

Lawrence Lader: *Margaret Sanger and the Fight for Birth Control* (New York: Doubleday & Co., 1955), p. 282. Preceding three references report reactions of U.S. doctors visiting USSR.

David M. Heer: "Abortion, Contraception and Population Policy in the Soviet Union," *Demography,* Vol. 2 (1965), pp. 531–39, the most complete analysis of Russian population studies.

David Robert: "Moscow State University," *Survey,* No. 51 (April 1964), pp. 28–29, for student abortion.

Lewis S. Feuer: "Problems and Unproblems in Soviet Social Theory," *Slavic Review,* Vol. 23, No. 1 (March 1964), p. 123, for Engels' letter on population planning. See second preface to *Das Kapital* for Marx's views on population.

Christopher Tietze: "The Demographic Significance of Legal Abortion in Eastern Europe," *Demography,* Vol. 1, No. 1 (1964), pp. 123–24.

K.–H. Mehlan: "Family Planning in the East European Socialist Countries," *Family Planning Programs—Proceedings of an International Conference, August, 1965* (University of Chicago Press; 1966), for most recent study of Soviet abortion rates and relationship between abortion and contraception.

Eastern Europe

K.–H. Mehlan: "Family Planning," Ibid.

————: "The Effects of Legalization of Abortions," *Third Conference of the Region for Europe, Near East and Africa of the International Planned Parenthood Federation* (1962), pp. 209–19.

————: "The Effects of Legalization of Abortion on the Health of Mothers in Eastern Europe," *Seventh International Conference on Planned Parenthood* (1963), pp. 214–22.

————: "Legal Abortions in Rumania," *Journal of Sex Research*, Vol. 1 (March 1965), pp. 31–38.

Lidija Andolsek: "Current Status of Abortion and Family Planning in Yugoslavia," *Fourth Conference of International Planned Parenthood Federation* (1964), Paper 38.

Christopher Tietze: "The Demographic Significance," Ibid.

————: and Hans Lehfeldt: "Legal Abortion in Eastern Europe," *The Journal of the American Medical Association*, Vol. 175 (April 1, 1961), pp. 1149–54.

Herak-Szabo, J.: "Legal and Illegal Abortion in the People's Republic of Croatia," *Third Conference of the Region for Europe, Near East and Africa of the International Planned Parenthood Federation* (1962), p. 222.

Mojic A.: "Abortion as a Method of Family Planning: Experiences of the Yugoslav Health Service," *Third Conference*, etc. (1962), pp. 77–79.

Antonin Černoch: "Experiences in Czechoslovakia with the Effects and Consequences of Legalized Termination of Pregnancy" (Belgrade: U.N. World Population Conference; 1965), unpublished.

András Klinger: "Demographic Effects of Abortion Legislation in Some European Countries" (Belgrade: U.N. World Population Conference; 1965), unpublished.

Karoly Miltényi: "Social and Psychological Factors Affecting Fertility in a Legalized Abortion System (Hungary)" (Belgrade: U.N. World Population Conference; 1965), unpublished.

"No Children Welcome (Hungary)," *Youth and Freedom*, Vol. 6, No. 4 (New York: Institute of International Youth Affairs; 1964), p. 9.

Eastern European References from Files of Free Europe Committee, New York:

"The Abortion Problem in Hungary: A Survey" (April 7, 1964).

Hungarian Press Survey No. 1334 (1963), survey from Central Statistical Bureau.

Hungarian Press Survey No. 1347 (1963).

Hungarian Press Survey No. 1462 (1964).

Hungarian Press Survey No. 1488 (1964), article by Dr. Gyorgy Illes.

Hungarian Press Survey No. 1530 (1964).

Hungarian Press Survey No. 1562 (1964), report of Presidential Committee for Demography.

Polish Press Survey No. 1675 (1964); and unnumbered report, *Glos Pracy* (January 2, 1965).

Czechoslovakian Press Survey No. 1242 (1963).

Czechoslovakian Press Survey No. 1306 (1963).

Czechoslovakian population reports from *Rude Pravo* (February 21, 1964; June 27, 1964; January 23, 1965).

Bulgarian Press Survey No. 540 (1964).

Issues of *East Europe* with pertinent articles: (February 1963), p. 35; (March 1963), p. 39; (July 1963), p. 36; (March 1964), p. 21; (October 1964), p. 23.

The New York Times (August 3, 1965), p. 4; (August 21, p. 2; August 22, 24, 1965).

CHAPTER FIFTEEN

The Lesson of Japan: Abortion and the Population Crisis

[1] Yoshio Koya: *Pioneering in Family Planning* (Tokyo: Population Council, New York and Japan Medical Publishers, Inc.; 1963), pp. 26 and 63; Minoru Muramatsu: "Effect of Induced Abortion on Reduction of Births in Japan," *Milbank Memorial Fund Quarterly*, Vol. 38, No. 2 (April 1960), p. 153.

[2] Irene B. Taeuber: *The Population of Japan* (Princeton, N.J.: Princeton University Press; 1958).

[3] W. T. Pommerenke: "Abortion in Japan" *Obstetrical and Gynecological Survey*, Vol. 10, No. 2 (April 1955), pp. 157, 161–62.

[4] Koya: *Pioneering*, Ibid, pp. 5, 6, 8, 9, 23, 41, 69, 121, 168 in particular, but the whole study is essential to an understanding of Japanese abortion.

[5] "Sixth Opinion Survey on Family Planning and Birth Control" (June 1962), and "Seventh Opinion Survey" (June 1963), made by the Population Problems Research Council of the Mainichi Newspapers (available from International Planned Parenthood Federation, Western Region, Tokyo); Shigemi Kono: "What Will Decide the Birth Rate in Japan?" *Asahi Journal* (September 8, 1963), available from IPPF, Tokyo; Minoru Tachi: "Implication of Population Trends" (Tokyo: English Pamphlet Series No. 58, Institute of Population Problems; February 1, 1964); Yoshio Koya: "Some Essential Factors

for Fertility Control in Japan," paper delivered at United Nations Population Conference (August 30–September 10, 1965), unpublished.

[6] S. Chandrasekhar: "A Billion Indians by 2000 A.D.?" *The New York Times Magazine* (April 4, 1965), pp. 110, 117.

[7] Ansley Coale and Edgar M. Hoover: *Population Growth and Economic Development in Low Income Countries* (1958).

[8] Dennis H. Wrong: "Population Myths," *Commentary* (November 1964), p. 63.

[9] Latin American statistics and quotations are based primarily on the following studies of the International Planned Parenthood Federation, New York:

Ofelia Mendoza: "Chile Adds Family Planning Services as Part of National Public Health Program"; "Population Growth and Family Planning in Latin America" (February 10, 1964); "What Are the Factors in Latin American Culture That Might Stimulate or Discourage Fertility Control?" (7th International Conference, IPPF, Singapore, February 12, 1963);

Hector Rozada: "National Problems and Plan in Family Planning in Uruguay" (2nd Family Planning Seminar for Latin American Leaders, IPPF, October 7–19, 1963);

Guillermo Adriasola: "Protection of the Family in Chile" (2nd Family Planning Seminar).

Papers delivered at 4th Conference of IPPF, April 19–27, 1964:

Ralph A. St. C. Hoyte: "Abortion at the General Hospital, Port of Spain" (Paper 58);

Roberto Santiso: "Contraceptives as a Means of Combatting Illegal Abortions" (Paper 7);

Rolando Armijo and Tegualda Monreal: "Epidemiology of Provoked Abortions in Santiago, Chile" (Paper 32);

Arturo Aldama: "Report about Family Planning in Mexico" (Paper 51);

Nydia G. Ferrarotti and Carmen G. Varela: "Research on Illegal Abortion, Buenos Aires" (Paper 12);

Martiniano Fernandes: "Family Planning in Prevention of Criminal Abortion, Brazil" (Paper 47).

Special References:

P. K. Whelpton: "Outlook for Control of Human Fertility in Japan," *American Sociological Review*, Vol. 15, No. 1 (February 1950), p. 34.

Lawrence Lader: *Margaret Sanger and the Fight for Birth Control* (New York: Doubleday & Co.; 1955), pp. 186, 329 ff.

Emerson Chapin: "Japan's Birth Rate—The Trend Turns," *The New York Times Magazine* (October 25, 1964), p. 44.

Thomas K. Burch: "Induced Abortion in Japan under the Eugenic Protection Law of 1948," *Eugenics Quarterly,* Vol. 2, No. 3 (September 1955), pp. 140–51; "Patterns of Induced Abortion and Their Socio-Moral Implications in Postwar Japan," *Social Compass,* Vol. 3 (1955), pp. 178–88.

Kimura, M.: "Induced Abortions in Japan in 1953-1954," *Milbank Memorial Fund Quarterly,* Vol. 37 (April 1959), pp. 154–73; "A Review of Induced Abortion Surveys in Japan," *International Population Conference* (New York; 1961), pp. 77–85.

CHAPTER SIXTEEN

A Blueprint for Changing U.S. Abortion Laws

[1] Robert E. Hall and ten professors of obstetrics and gynecology at New York State medical schools, a study of attitudes toward American Law Institute abortion code (to be published by *American Journal of Obstetrics and Gynecology*).

[2] Morris Ernst, all quotations from "There Is a Desperate Need of Medical Wisdom to Deal with the Problem of 'Abortion,'" *New Medical Materia* (July 1962), pp. 21–23.

Harriet Pilpel, speech delivered at Columbia-Presbyterian Medical Center, New York (March 20, 1964), unpublished.

[3] Kenneth R. Niswander and Morton Klein, "Changing Attitudes Towards Therapeutic Abortion," presented at the annual convention of the American Medical Association, New York, June 20–24, 1965 (unpublished).

Special References:

New York Academy of Medicine: Committee on Public Health, "Therapeutic Abortion," *Bulletin of the New York Academy of Medicine,* Vol. 41 (April 1965), pp. 406–09.

American Medical Association poll from *San Francisco Chronicle* (June 25, 1964), p. 12.

Medical Tribune poll (October 31–November 1, 1964), pp. 21–22.

The New York Times, editorials on abortion (February 13, April 7, June 2, 1965).

CHAPTER SEVENTEEN

The Century of the Wanted Child

[1] Christopher Tietze: "Fifth Progress Report of the Cooperative Statistical Study for the Evaluation of Intra-Uterine Contraceptive Devices," National Committee on Maternal Health (February 28, 1965), summarizes failure rate for the loop. The failure rate of the oral contraceptive runs only about 1 per 1,000.

[2] *Uniform Crime Reports for the United States, 1964,* issued by the F.B.I. (Washington, D.C.: U.S. Government Printing Office), p. 9; "Probability of Pregnancy Resulting from Single Unprotected Coitus," *Fertility and Sterility,* Vol. 11 (September–October 1960), pp. 485–88.

[3] Robert W. Laidlaw and Medora S. Bass: "Voluntary Sterilization as It Relates to Mental Health," *American Journal of Psychiatry,* Vol. 120, No. 12 (June 1964), pp. 1176–80. All other studies on sterilization from the Association for Voluntary Sterilization, New York.

Special References:

"Regional Report: Birth Control," National Educational Television Network (September 29, 1965), for Weingand and Sanders quotations.

Santa Barbara News-Press (Calif.; July 27, 1965), for Dr. Hardin on failure rate.

The New York Times (September 7, 1965), letter column for Dr. Rosenbaum; (September 5, 1965), letter column for Dr. Edsall.

Reverend Lion quotation from sermon of April 19, 1964.

Therapeutic Abortion (unofficial report of the Committee on Criminal Procedure of the California State Legislature on Assembly Bill 2614), pp. 26, 42–43 for analysis of protection of unborn child by the courts.

CHAPTER EIGHTEEN
Legalized Abortion: The Final Freedom

[1] *Southern Medicine and Surgery* (July 9, 1942), p. 408; Robert E. Hall: "Thalidomide and Our Abortion Laws," *Columbia University Forum,* Vol. 6, No. 1 (winter 1963); Garrett Hardin: lecture at University of California, Berkeley (April 29, 1964).

[2] *The New York Times* (June 26, 1965), p. 1.

[3] Cyril Means: letters to American Civil Liberties Union (April 21, 1965), and *The New York Times* (June 26, 1965), unpublished. For justification of "a woman killing one who attempts to ravish her," see Blackstone: *Commentaries on the Law of England,* 1st ed., Vol. 4, p. 181.

[4] J. B. Thiersch: "Therapeutic Abortion with a Folic Acid Antagonist (4 Amino P.G.A.) Administered by the Oral Route," *American Journal of Obstetrics and Gynecology,* Vol. 63, No. 6 (June 1952), pp. 1298–1304.

———: "The Control of Reproduction in Rats with Antimetabolites," *Acta Endocrinologica,* Supplement 28 (1956), pp. 37–45.

———: "Effect of Lipopolysaccharides of Gram Negative Bacilli in the Rat Litter in Utero," *Proceedings of the Society for Experimental Biology and Medicine,* Vol. 109 (1962), p. 429.

————: "Effect of Substituted Mercaptopurines in the Rat Litter in Utero," *Journal of Reproduction and Fertility,* Vol. 4 (1962), p. 291.

————: "Effect of Podophyllin and Podophyllotoxin on Rat Litter in Utero," *Proceedings of the Society for Experimental Biology and Medicine,* Vol. 113 (1963), p. 124.

————: "Effect of Substituted 2, 4–Diamino–Pyrimidines on the Rat Fetus in Utero," *Proceedings of 3rd International Congress of Chemotherapy* (Stuttgart: Georg Thieme Verlag; 1964), pp. 367–72.

Special References:

Margaret Sanger: *Woman and the New Race* (New York: Truth Publishing Co.; 1920), pp. 1, 94.

Dorothy Thurtle: *Abortion: Right or Wrong?* (London: T. Werner Laurie Ltd.; 1940), for Buckmaster quotation.

Harriet Pilpel: speech at American Civil Liberties Union convention (Boulder, Colo.; June 1964), unpublished.

Bibliography and Sources

The authoritative books on abortion are surprisingly few. Although some are partly out-dated, the following studies have been of great help to me:

Mary S. Calderone (ed.): *Abortion in the United States.* New York: Harper & Row–Hoeber, Inc.; 1958.

Paul H. Gebhard *et al*: *Pregnancy, Birth and Abortion.* New York: Harper & Row–Hoeber, Inc.; 1958.

Harold Rosen (ed.): *Therapeutic Abortion.* New York: Julian Press, Inc.; 1954.

Harold Rosen (ed.): *Therapeutic Abortion.* New York: Julian Press, Inc.; 1954. Reissued in paperback as *Abortion in America.* Boston, Beacon Press; 1967.

Frederick J. Taussig: *Abortion, Spontaneous and Induced.* St. Louis: C. V. Mosby Co.; 1936.

Glanville Williams: *The Sanctity of Life and the Criminal Law.* New York: Alfred A. Knopf; 1957.

Of particular value to me were recent medical papers, usually listed under Notes and Special References. I have repeated only the most significant titles in this Bibliography.

Further, an exhaustive reference on abortion is included in *Bibliography of Fertility Control*, edited by Christopher Tietze and published in 1965 by the National Committee on Maternal Health, New York. As the Gebhard and Rosen studies cited above contain excellent bibliographies, I have sought to avoid repetition by confining my bibliography to those works on which I have drawn most heavily.

Finally, one of my prime sources has been personal communications from the Ober-Lader survey, and interviews with hundreds of physicians, sociologists, lawyers, police officers, abortionists and their patients. Owing to the confidential nature of their testimony, it has been necessary in all but a few cases to keep these sources anonymous.

American Law Institute: *Model Penal Code*, Proposed Official Draft, Sec. 230.3:2. Philadelphia: American Law Institute; 1962.

Arén, Per: "Legal Abortion in Sweden." *Acta Obstetrica et Gynecologica Scandinavica*, Vol. 36, Supplement 1 (1958).

Bloch, Iwan: *Sexual Life of Our Time*. New York: Rebman & Co.; 1920.

Boulas, Stanley H.; Preucel, Robert H.; Moore, John H.: "Therapeutic Abortion." *Obstetrics and Gynecology*, Vol. 19, No. 2 (February 1962).

Browne, Stella: "The Right of Abortion." *Journal of Sex Education*, Vol. 5 (1952).

Burton, Richard T.: *Religious Doctrine and Medical Practise*. Springfield, Ill.: Charles C. Thomas; 1958.

Calderone, Mary S.: "Illegal Abortion as a Public Health Problem." *American Journal of Public Health*, Vol. 50, No. 7 (July 1960).

Chesser, Eustace: *Society and Abortion*. London: Abortion Law Reform Association; 1949.

————: "The Doctor's Dilemma." *New Statesman* (June 7, 1958).

Clemmesen, Carl: "State of Legal Abortion in Denmark." *American Journal of Psychiatry*, Vol. 112 (2), No. 8 (February 1956).

Davies, D. Seaborne: "The Law of Abortion and Necessity." *The Modern Law Review*, Vol. 2 (1938).

Deutsch, Helene: *The Psychology of Women*. Vol. 2. New York: Grune & Stratton; 1945.

Devereux, George: *A Study of Abortion in Primitive Societies*. New York: Julian Press; 1955.

Eastman, Nicholas J.: Editorial comment on Per Kolstad study, *Obstetrical and Gynecological Survey*, Vol. 13, No. 4 (August 1958).

Ekblad, Martin: "Induced Abortion on Psychiatric Grounds." *Acta Psychiatrica et Neurologica Scandinavica*, Supplement 99 (1955).

Eliasberg, Wladimir C.: "Psychiatry in Pre-Natal Care and the Problem of Abortion." *Medical Woman's Journal*, Vol. 58, No. 1 (January–February 1951).

Ellis, Havelock: *Studies in the Psychology of Sex*. Vol. 2. New York: Random House; 1936.

Ernst, Morris L., and Lindey, Alexander: *The Censor Marches On*. New York: Doubleday, Doran & Co.; 1940.

Fisher, Russell: "Criminal Abortion." *Journal of Criminal Law, Criminology and Police Science*, Vol. 42, No. 2 (July–August 1951).

Fletcher, Joseph: *Morals and Medicine*. Princeton, N.J.: Princeton University Press; 1954.

Freeman, Lucy (as told to by Dr. X): *The Abortionist*. New York: Doubleday & Co.; 1962.

Friedman, J. H.: "The Vagarity of Psychiatric Indications for Therapeutic Abortions." *American Journal of Psychotherapy*, Vol. 26 (April 1962).

Fultz, G. S.: "Therapeutic Abortions." *Southern Medical Journal*, Vol. 47 (January 1954).

Gampell, Ralph J.: "Legal Status of Therapeutic Abortion and Sterilization in the U.S." *Clinical Obstetrics and Gynecology*, Vol. 7 (March
1964).

Genné, Elizabeth S. and William H. (eds.): *Foundations for Christian
Family Policy—The Proceedings of the North American Conference
on Church and Family*. New York: National Council of Churches of
Christ in the U.S.A.; 1961.

Greenhill, J. P.: "World Trends of Therapeutic Abortion and Sterilization."
Clinical Obstetrics and Gynecology, Vol. 7 (March 1964).

Greep, Roy O. (ed.): *Human Fertility and Population Problems*. Cambridge, Mass.: Schenkman Publishing Co.; 1963.

Gunnard, A. Nelson, and Hunter, James, Jr.: "Therapeutic Abortion: A
Ten-Year Experience." *Obstetrics and Gynecology*, Vol. 9 (1957).

Guttmacher, Alan F.: *Planning Your Family*. New York: Macmillan Co.;
1961.

————: "Techniques of Therapeutic Abortion." *Clinical Obstetrics and
Gynecology*, Vol. 7, No. 1 (March 1964).

————: "Induced Abortion." *New York State Journal of Medicine*, Vol. 63,
No. 16 (August 15, 1963).

————: "Therapeutic Abortion: The Doctor's Dilemma." *Journal of Mt.
Sinai Hospital*, Vol. 21 (May–June 1954).

————: "Legal and Moral Status of Therapeutic Abortion." *Progress in
Gynecology*, Vol. 4 (1963).

————: "Therapeutic Abortion in a Large General Hospital." *Surgical
Clinics of North America*, Vol. 37 (April 1957).

————: "Therapeutic Abortion: Physician's Viewpoint." *Obstetrics and
Gynecology*, Vol. 16 (October–December 1959).

Haire, Norman: "Abortion in Australia." *Journal of Sex Education*, Vol. 2,
No. 4 (February–March 1950).

Halevi, H. S., and Brzezinski, A.: "Incidence of Abortion among Jewish
Women in Israel." *American Journal of Public Health*, Vol. 48 (May
1958).

Hall, Robert E.: "Therapeutic Abortion, Sterilization, and Contraception."
American Journal of Obstetrics and Gynecology, Vol. 91 (February
15, 1965).

————: "Thalidomide and Our Abortion Laws." *Columbia University
Forum*, Vol. 6 (winter 1963).

Hamilton, Virginia C.: "Medical Status and Psychologic Attitude of Patients Following Abortion." *American Journal of Obstetrics and Gynecology*, Vol. 41 (1941).

————: "Some Sociologic and Psychologic Observations on Abortion."
American Journal of Obstetrics and Gynecology, Vol. 39, No. 6
(1940).

Heer, David: "Abortion, Contraception, and Population Policy in the Soviet Union." *Demography*, Vol. 2 (1965).

Hewetson, John: "Birth Control, Sexual Morality and Abortion." *Twentieth
Century Magazine* (winter 1962–63).

Himes, Norman: *Medical History of Contraception.* Baltimore: Williams & Wilkins Co.; 1936.

Höök, Kerstin: "Refused Abortion." *Acta Psychiatrica Scandinavica,* Vol. 39, Supplement 168 (1963).

Houghton, Vera: "Medical Termination of Pregnancy Bill." *The Eugenics Review,* Vol. 53 (July 1961).

Huser, Roger J.: *The Crime of Abortion in Common Law.* Canon Law Studies No. 162. Washington, D.C.: Catholic University of America Press; 1942.

Israel, S. L.: "Therapeutic Abortion." *Postgraduate Medicine,* Vol. 33 (June 1963).

Janovski, Nikolas A.; Weiner, Louis; and Ober, William B.: "Soap Intoxication Following Criminal Abortion." *New York State Journal of Medicine,* Vol. 63, No. 1b (May 15, 1963).

Jenkins, Alice: *Law for the Rich.* London: Victor Gollancz Ltd.; 1961.

Kinsolving, Lester: "What About Therapeutic Abortion?" *The Christian Century* (May 13, 1964).

Kolstad, Per: "Therapeutic Abortion." *Acta Obstetrica et Gynecologica Scandinavica,* Vol. 36, Supplement 6 (1957).

Kopp, Marie E.: *Birth Control in Practice.* New York: Robert M. McBride & Co.; 1934.

Koya, Yoshio: *Pioneering in Family Planning.* Tokyo: Population Council, New York and Japan Medical Publishers, Inc.; 1963.

Kummer, Jerome M.: "Don't Shy Away from Therapeutic Abortion." *Medical Economics* (April 11, 1960).

———: "Post-Abortion Psychiatric Illness—A Myth?" *American Journal of Psychiatry,* Vol. 119, No. 10 (April 1963).

———, and Leavy, Zad: "Criminal Abortion—A Consideration of Ways to Reduce Incidence." *California Medicine,* Vol. 95 (September 1961).

———: "Psychiatric Contraindications to Pregnancy." *California Medicine,* Vol. 79 (July 1953).

Langer, William L.: "Europe's Initial Population Explosion." *The American Historical Review* (October 1963).

Leavy, Zad, and Kummer, Jerome M.: "Criminal Abortion." *Southern California Law Review,* Vol. 35, No. 2 (winter 1962).

Lederman, J. J.: "The Doctor, Abortion, and the Law." *Canadian Medical Association Journal,* Vol. 87 (August 4, 1962).

Levine, A. S.: "The Problem of Psychiatric Disturbances in Relation to Therapeutic Abortion." *Journal of the Albert Einstein Medical Center,* Vol. 6 (March 1958).

Lindahl, Jan: "Somatic Complications Following Legal Abortion." Stockholm: Scandinavian University Books; 1959.

Mathew, J.: "The Present State of the Law of Abortion." *Medicine, Science and the Law,* Vol. 4 (July 1964).

Meyer, Arthur: *The Rise of Embryology*. Palo Alto, Calif.: Stanford University Press; 1939.

Moore, J. G., and Randall, J. H.; "Trends in Therapeutic Abortion." *American Journal of Obstetrics and Gynecology*, Vol. 63, No. 1 (1952).

Mumford, Robert S.: "An Interdisciplinary Study of Four Wives Who Had Induced Abortions." *American Journal of Obstetrics and Gynecology*, Vol. 87, No. 7 (December 1, 1963).

National Committee on Maternal Health, Proceedings of Conference under: *The Abortion Problem*. Baltimore: Williams & Wilkins Co.; 1944.

New York Academy of Medicine: Committee on Public Health: "Therapeutic Abortion." *Bulletin of the New York Academy of Medicine*, Vol. 41 (April 1965).

Niswander, Kenneth R., and Klein, Morton: "Changing Attitudes Towards Therapeutic Abortion." Unpublished.

Noonan, John T., Jr.: *Contraception*. Cambridge, Mass.: Harvard University Press; 1965.

Novak, F.: "Effect of Legal Abortion on the Health of Mothers in Yugoslavia." *Seventh International Conference on Planned Parenthood* (1963).

Overstreet, Edmund W. (ed.): *Clinical Obstetrics and Gynecology*, Vol. 7, No. 1. New York: Harper & Row–Hoeber, Inc. (March 1964).

———, and Traut, Herbert F.: *Postgraduate Medicine*, Vol. 9 (1951).

Packer, Herbert L., and Gampell, Ralph J.: "Therapeutic Abortion: A Problem in Law and Medicine." *Stanford Law Review*, Vol. 11 (1959).

Quay, Eugene: "Justifiable Abortion." (2 parts) *The Georgetown Law Journal*, Vol. 49, Nos. 2 and 3 (winter and spring 1960).

Robinson, William J.: *The Law against Abortion*. New York: Eugenics Publishing Co., Inc.; 1933.

Rock, John, and Maillot, Armand: "Abortion." *Gynecology and Obstetrics*, Vol. 1. Hagerstown, Md.: W. F. Prior Co.; 1963.

Rongy, A. J.: *Abortion: Legal and Illegal*. New York: Vanguard Press; 1933.

Routledge, J. H., Sparling, D. W., and MacFarlane, K. T.: "The Present Status of Therapeutic Abortion." *Obstetrics and Gynecology*, Vol. 17, (February 1961).

Royal Commission on Population, Papers of. Vol. 4. London: Report of the Biological and Medical Committee; 1950.

Russell, Keith P.: "Changing Indications for Therapeutic Abortion." *Journal of the American Medical Association*, Vol. 151 (January 10, 1953).

———: "Therapeutic Abortion in a General Hospital." *American Journal of Obstetrics and Gynecology*, Vol. 62 (August 1951).

————, and Moore, J. G.: "Maternal Medical Indications for Therapeutic Abortion." *Clinical Obstetrics and Gynecology*, Vol. 7 (March 1964).

Savel, Lewis K., and Perlmutter, Irving K.: "Therapeutic Abortion and Sterilization Committees." *American Journal of Obstetrics and Gynecology*, Vol. 80, No. 2 (1960).

Schur, Edwin M.: *Crimes without Victims.* Englewood Cliffs, N.J.: Prentice-Hall Inc.; 1965.

Shaffer, Helen B.: "Abortion in Law and Medicine." *Editorial Research Reports* (Washington, D.C.), Vol. 11, No. 13 (October 6, 1965).

Siegel, I., and Kanter, A. E.: "Therapeutic Abortion: A Five-Year Survey at Mt. Sinai Hospital." *Chicago Medical School Quarterly*, Vol. 21 (March 1960).

Sim, M.: "Abortion and the Psychiatrist." *British Medical Journal*, Vol. 2 (July 20, 1963).

Simms, Madeleine: "Abortion—A Note on Some Recent Developments in Britain." *The British Journal of Criminology* (July 1964).

Sloane Hospital for Women, Transactions of Annual Meeting of Alumni, "Symposium on 'The Social Problem of Abortion.'" *Bulletin of the Sloane Hospital for Women*, Vol. 11 (fall 1965).

Smith, Ronald and Leonard F., and Tenney, Benjamin: "Soap-Induced Abortion." *Obstetrics and Gynecology*, Vol. 20, No. 2 (August 1962).

St. John-Stevas, Norman: *The Right to Life.* London: Hodder & Stoughton; 1963.

Storer, Horatio R.: *Criminal Abortion in America.* Philadelphia: J. B. Lippincott & Co.; 1866.

Studdiford, William E.: "Common Medical Indications for Therapeutic Abortion." *Bulletin of the New York Academy of Medicine*, Vol. 26 (November 1950).

Sulloway, Alvah: *Birth Control and Catholic Doctrine.* Boston: Beacon Press; 1959.

Thurtle, Dorothy: *Abortion: Right or Wrong?* London: T. Werner Laurie, Ltd.; 1940.

Tietze, Christopher, *et al: Quarterly Review of Surgery, Obstetrics and Gynecology*, Vol. 16 (October–December 1959).

————: "Abortion as a Cause of Death." *American Journal of Public Health*, Vol. 38, No. 2 (October 1948).

————: "Introduction to the Statistics of Abortion." *Pregnancy Wastage.* Springfield, Ill.: Charles C. Thomas; 1953.

————, and Martin, C. E.: "Foetal Deaths, Spontaneous and Induced in the Urban, White Population of the U.S." *Population Studies*, Vol. 11, No. 2 (November 1957).

————: "The Demographic Significance of Legal Abortion in Eastern Europe." *Demography*, Vol. 1, No. 1 (1964).

————, and Lehfeldt, Hans: "Legal Abortion in Eastern Europe." *Journal of the American Medical Association*, Vol. 175 (April 1, 1961).

———: "Legal Abortion in Scandinavia." *Obstetrics and Gynecology* (October–December 1959).

Trout, Monroe: "Therapeutic Abortions Need Therapy." *Temple Law Quarterly*, Vol. 37, No. 2 (winter 1964).

Williams, Glanville: "The Legalization of Medical Abortion." *Eugenics Review*, Vol. 56 (April 1964).

Woodside, Moya: "Attitudes of Women Abortionists." *The Howard Journal* (London; 1963).

Bibliography of Legal Cases

UNITED STATES

Commonwealth v. Bangs, 9 Mass. (Tyng) 387, 388 (1812)
Commonwealth v. Parker, 50 Mass. (9 Met.) 263, 43 Am. Dec. 396
Commonwealth v. Wheeler, 315 Mass. 394, NE 2d 4, 1944
Evans v. People, 49 N.Y. 86, 90, 1872
Foster v. State, 182 Wis. 298, 196 N.W. 233, 1923
Griswold v. Connecticut, 381 U.S. 479 (1965)
Mills v. Commonwealth, 13 Pa. 621, 1850
Mitchell v. Commissioner, 78 Ken. 204, 210, 1879
People v. Ballard, 167 Cal. App 2d 803, 355 P 2d 204, 1959
People v. Ballard, 218 Cal. App 2d 295, 32 Cal. Rptr 233, 1963
Scott v. McPheeters, 33 Cal. App 2d 629, 92 P 2d 678, 1939
State v. Buck, 200 Ore. 87, 262 P 2d 495, 1953
State v. Cooper, 22 N.J.L. 52 (Sup. Ct. 1849)
State v. Dunklebarger, 206 Iowa 971, 221 NW 592, 1928
State v. Murphy, 27 N.J.L. 112 (Sup. Ct. 1858)
State v. Powers, 155 Wash. 63, 283 P 439, 1929
State v. Siciliano, 21 N.J. 249, 121 A 2d 490, 1956
Stewart v. Long Island College Hospital (pending in Supreme Court, Kings County, N.Y., as of November 1965)
U.S. v. One Package [86F (2d) 737 (C.C.A. 2d 1936) affirming 13 F. Supp. 334 (S.D.N.Y. 1936)]
Williams v. State, 46 misc 2d 824, unofficial 260 N.Y. supp. 2d 953, 1965

GREAT BRITAIN

R. v. Bourne (1938) 3 All E.R. 615 (K.B.); (1939) 1 K.B. 687 (1938); 108 L.J.K.B. 471 (1939)

Acknowledgments

The subject of abortion touches on so many specialized fields from medicine to law, and from religion to sociology, that few experts have encompassed the total concept. It was my good fortune to have my manuscript read by two highly respected authorities: Dr. Robert E. Hall, president of the Association for the Study of Abortion and associate professor of obstetrics and gynecology at Columbia-Presbyterian Medical Center; and Dr. Garrett Hardin, professor of biology at the University of California, Santa Barbara. Both gave invaluable counsel and criticism.

Dr. Christopher Tietze, of the National Committee on Maternal Health, offered his time unstintingly in almost every statistical analysis and in researching such areas as Eastern Europe and Japan.

On legal aspects, I have had the generous counsel of three eminent New York attorneys: Mrs. Harriet Pilpel, Ephraim London, and Cyril Means, to whom I am deeply indebted.

Dr. William Ober, of New York's Knickerbocker Hospital, contributed his knowledge and facilities for a national survey that provided a unique insight into the attitudes of obstetricians and gynecologists.

I received wise and frequent advice from many friends and associates in the Association for the Study of Abortion, including Dr. Edwin M. Gold, professor of maternal and child health at Flower and Fifth Avenue Hospitals; Dr. Carl Goldmark, Jr., president of the New York County Medical Society; Dr. Alan F. Guttmacher, president of the Planned Parenthood Federation; Dr. Robert Laidlaw, of New York's Roosevelt Hospital; Rabbi Israel Margolies, of New York; Dr. Wardell B. Pomeroy, of New York; and Professor-Emeritus Sophia Robison, of Columbia University's School of Social Work. Miss Patricia Maginnis, president of the Society for Humane Abortion in San Francisco, was particularly helpful on abortion research in California, as was Assemblyman Anthony C. Beilenson, of Beverly Hills, Calif.

For material on Britain, I am indebted to Glanville Williams, of Jesus College, Cambridge University, and to the officers of the British Abortion Law Reform Association; for material on the Soviet Union, to Professor Lewis S. Feuer, of the University of California, Berkeley, and to Stephen F. Cohen, of Columbia University; for material on India, to Lady Dhanvanthi Rama Rau, of Bombay, president of the International Planned Parenthood Federation.

Dr. Ofelia Mendoza, of IPPF's New York office, and Mrs. Celestina Zalduonda, of the Family Planning Association of Puerto Rico, were a faithful source of research on Latin American abortion.

I also wish to thank particularly: Irving Clark, attorney of Seattle, Washington; Morris Ernst, New York attorney; Reverend William H. Genné, of the National Council of Churches, New York; Frederick Jaffe, vice-president of Planned Parenthood Federation; Dr. Jerome Kummer, of the University of California Medical Center, Los Angeles; Dr. Robert Mumford, of Roosevelt Hospital, New York; Dr. Kenneth R. Niswander, of Children's Hospital, Buffalo, N.Y.; Dr. Edmund Overstreet, of the University of California Medical School, San Francisco; Dr. Sheldon Segal, of the Population Council, New York; Joseph Stocker, of Phoenix, Arizona; and Dr. G. Loutrell Timanus, of Rehoboth Beach, Delaware.

Above all, I am deeply grateful to Jack Harrison Pollack, Mrs. Roberta Pryor, and Mort Yarmon for their never-failing encouragement and advice during three years of an exhausting project.

Further appreciation is due to the following publishers for the use of quotations and excerpts from the books listed: Harvard University Press, *Contraception,* by John T. Noonan, Jr.; Harper & Row–Hoeber, Inc., *Pregnancy, Birth and Abortion,* by Paul H. Gebhard *et al,* and *Abortion in the United States,* edited by Mary Calderone; Alfred A. Knopf, *The Sanctity of Life and the Criminal Law,* by Glanville Williams; Charles C. Thomas, *Criminal Abortion,* by Jerome E. Bates and Edward S. Zawadzki; and the Julian Press, Inc., *Therapeutic Abortion,* edited by Harold Rosen, and *A Study of Abortion in Primitive Societies,* by George Devereux.

Index

Abortifacients, 68-70, 90, 91, 173-174
Abortion: by age, 2, 99; Baptist attitude toward, 101; deaths, 3, 66; and early Christians, 77-79; and false pregnancy, 73-74; and Hippocratic oath, 76; history of, 75-76; in hospitals (*see* Abortion, legal); *vs.* illegitimacy, 60; incomplete, 22, 28, 66; in Japan, 57-58, 134-136; Judaic position on, 87-89, 101-102; medical definition of, 18; and morality, 113, 114, 119; philosophers on, 76; in Poland, 58; premarital, 20; in primitive cultures, 23; Protestant position on, 58, 99-102; psychological injury from, 3; rate, 57, 59, 135-136; Roman Catholic position on, 75, 94-97, 101-102, 164 165; self-induced, 3, 67-69, 73, 140; and Shintoism, 23; in Soviet Union, 58, 121-122; techniques, 18-19, 46, 47, 76, 83, 85, 121-122, 134; "therapeutic," 3; and unmarried women, 4; in U.S., 2, 85; and women's rights, 99, 167-173
Abortion, illegal: in Chile, 140; in Eastern Europe, 129; in Latin America, 140; in Mexico, 57; rate of, 7-8, 160-161; and restrictive abortion laws, 135; in Soviet Union, 121; in Sweden, 120; in Uruguay, 141
Abortion, legal: and abortion committees, 3, 24; and age, 150; annual rate in Soviet Union, 123, in U.S., 12, 24, 27; in Buffalo hospitals, 150; and Catholics, 95, 96; cost of (*see* Cost, of abortions); curtailment of, 24-25, 26-28, 34, 119; deaths from, 17-18; and economic discrimination, 29-30; and economic problems in India, 139; and fertility, 19, 20; and fetal quickening, 75, 77, 78, 86, 89, 112, 169; and Finkbine, Sherri, 14-15; in Great Britain, 87, 107; ——grounds for, 6-7, 24; ALRA proposal, 108; and Beilenson bill, 147-148; and birth-control failure, 158; and British law of 1861, 105; diabetes, 36; German measles, 36, 37, 38-39, 98, 149, 171; medical, 6, 24, 39-40, 100, 114; and Model Penal Code, 145-146; opinion polls on, 108; pernicious vomiting, 36; and poor social classes, 30; psychological, 7, 8, 24, 25-26, 32, 34-35, 98, 150; rape, 4, 5-6, 34-36, 146, 147, 170, 172; Rh factor, 40; in Scandinavian nations, 118; socio-economic, 40, 41; "stretching," 149; and suicide danger, 32-33, 34; and threat to mother's life, 111; "worn-out mother" syndrome, 154; in India, 94, 136, 139; in Japan, 2, 133, 134; medical procedures, 18; and monthly quota system, 27; and morality, 162-163; opinion polls on, 108, 135-

Abortion, legal—*Cont.*
grounds for—*Cont.*
136, 139, 144; physical complications after, 19; and population problems, 89, 132-136, 139; psychiatric after-effects of, 20-23; rate for Catholics, 39, 132-133, 151; repeated, 134; and social class, 8, 29; in Soviet Union, 120-125; in Sweden, 119; and sterilization, 30-31
Abortion committees: abolishment of, 150-151; and Catholic Church, 25; and curtailment of abortions, 34; reasons for, 26, 27; and role of physician, 32; standards of, 28-29; and state laws, 26; and sterilization, 30-31; and ward patients, 29-30
Abortionists: actual professions of, 64; advertisements for, 91; Cuban, 54; in Mexico, 57; open, 53; part-time, 52; and police, 52, 57, 72-73; Restell, Madame, 85, 91; in San Juan, 56; skilled, 44-45, 46-47, 53-55, 58-59; stereotypes of, 43; in Tokyo, 57
——underworld: description of, 65-66; and nonpregnant women, 74; and police abortion squads, 70; and poorer classes, 64; in Scandinavian countries, 120; and Smith, Jacqueline, 64; and tax returns, 44; techniques of, 67; *see also* Timanus, Dr. G. Loutrell
Abortion Law Reform Association, 104, 107, 108, 169
Abortion laws: abolishment of, 100; and abortion underworld, 4; in ancient Greece and Rome, 76, 77; and Anglo-Saxons, 78-79; British, 16; Canadian, 106-107; Catholic Church attitude toward, 93; in code of Hammurabi, 75; and Comstock, Anthony, 90-91; in Eastern Europe, 125-131; and fetal quickening, 75, 77, 78, 86, 89, 112, 169; in Great Britain, 82-84, 87-88, 103-110; in Hungary, 125-127; in Israel, 58; in Japan, 23, 57; and Jews, 75; lack of protest against, 8-9; liberal interpretation of, 148-151; in Maryland, 49; and medical profession, 92; in Mexico, 57; in New Hampshire, 112; in Poland, 23; and politics, 3-4, 112, 126; in primitive tribes, 23; and puritanical codes, 90; purpose of, 88-89; in Scandinavia, 117-120; in several states, 3n.; and Society for Humane Abortion, 147; in Soviet Union, 120-125; as stimulus to abortifacient manufacture, 70; in Sweden, 58; in Switzerland, 58; and unmarried women, 7; in U. S., 78, 81, 85-92, 95, 144-145; in West Germany, 58
Abortion reform: American Medical Association and, 145; and Bourne case, 103-108; and Browne, Stella, 103; Buffalo blueprint for, 153, 175; and Catholic heir-

Abortion reform—*Cont.*
archy, 146-147; in Great Britain, 108, 109, 110; and interpretation of laws, 149-154; in New Hampshire, 112-116; newspaper polls on, 144; non-legislative method, 149-154; religious pressures against, 148-149; role of Protestantism and Judaism in, 102; in Sweden, 117-118; in U.S., 145; university forums on, 108; and Women's Co-operative Guilds, 104
"Act for the Suppression of Trade in and Circulation of Obscene Literature and Articles of Immoral Use, An," 91
Adoption. *See* Children, adopted
Alabama, abortion laws in, 3n.
Albania: abortion laws in, 125; birth rate in, 125
ALRA *Newsletter*, 109
American Baptist Convention, 101
American Law Institute, 145, 146, 163; code of, 147, 169
American Medical Association, 145
American Protestant Episcopal Church, 99
Andorra, 70
Andress, Charlotte, 60
Anesthesia: condemned for childbirth, 90; death from overdose of, 65; in hospital abortions, 18
Anglican Church, 110
Anglican Communion, 99
Anson, Margie, 4
Appalachia, 157
Aquinas, Thomas, 78
Aren, Dr. Per, 20
Aristotle, 76, 77
Arizona, 57: abortion laws in, 10, 12
Arizona *Republic*, 11, 12, 13
Arkansas, abortion laws in, 86
Assiniboine Indians, 23
Association for the Study of Abortion (New York), 148, 168, 175
Astor, John Jacob, 85

Ballard, Dr. Francis E., 152, 153
Baptists, attitude of toward abortion, 101
Barnes, Dr. Allan, 39
Barquet, Dr. Luis Bulas (or Dulas), 72-73
Bates, Jerome E., 65
Beilenson, Anthony, 146
Beilenson bill, 147, 163-164
Bellevue Hospital, New York, 16, 66; Infertility Clinic, 7
Berkeley, California, 70
Bertran, Dr. Carlos E., 56
Binder, Dr. Hans, 62
Birkett, Sir Norman, 107
Birth control: and abortifacients, 173-174; and abortion, 130-131, 132-136, 155-156, 157; attitude of U.S. Presidents toward, 92; and Catholic Church, 80, 141; clinics, mobile, 159; education, 135-136, 159; failure and abortion, 153-154, 158; in India, 136-140; and Marxist theory, 124-125; and public opinion polls, 141-142; techniques in Japan, 136; in U.S. and Knowlton case, 90; in Soviet Union, 122, 123-124; and sterilization, 162; and working class, 83-84
Birth Control Association, 133
Birth rate: Albanian, 125; East European, 127-128; Japanese, 133, 135-136; in Latin America, 141; in India, 139; and legal abortion in Soviet Union, 125, in Japan, 2; reduction and birth control, 160

Blackstone, Sir William, 78
Bolter, Dr. Sidney, 4
Boothby, Lord, 104
Boston Watch and Ward Society, 90
Bourne, Dr. Aleck, 103-108
Bourne case, 49, 103-106, 107, 108, 152
Bowler, Dr. John, 114
Brekke, Dr. Bard, 22
Brennan, Justice William Joseph, Jr., 172
British Abortion Law Reform Association, 88
British Humanist Association, 108
British Medical Association, 104
Broun, Heywood, 91
Browne, Stella, 103
Buck, Dr. George H., 152
Buck, Pearl, 61, 62
Buckmaster, Lord, 168
Buddhism, position on abortions of, 94
Bulgaria, abortion laws in, 125

Caesar, Julius, 77
California, 53: abortion case ruling in, 41; abortion laws in, 5-6, 146-148
California Junior Chamber of Commerce, 147
California legislature's committee on the Beilenson bill, 165
California Medical Association, House of Delegates of, 147
California State Assembly, 5
Calvinists, 81
Cambridge University, 88, 108
Canada, abortion laws in, 106-107
Canfield, Cass, 148
Carlisle, Bishop of, 82
Casti connubii (Pope Pius XI), 80, 82, 95
Catholic Church: and abortion committees, 25; and abortion reform, 93, 146-147, 149; and curtailment of hospital abortions, 28; and Finkbine, Sherri, case, 13; and illegitimacy *vs.* abortion, 60; influence of biological research on, 80-82; position on abortion, 2, 47, 77-80, 94-97, 101-102, 128-129; position on birth control, 80, 141, 142; position on fetus, 88; position on sex, 81; position on sin and legislation, 93; position on sterilization, 162; prohibitions against abortion, 75; rulings on ectopic pregnancy, 96; and women's rights, 165-166
Catholics: abortion among, 7-8, 151; and abortionists, 45, 52, 56, 57; and birth control, 133, 141-142; in British Parliament and abortion reform, 109-110; and Church laws, 79; and Finkbine, Sherri, case, 16; as members of abortion committees, 25; and New Hampshire abortion law, 112, 113, 115
Catholic Women's Club of Tokyo, 133
Cernoch, Dr. Anton, 19
Chandrasekhar, Professor S., 137, 138, 140
Children: adopted, 61; rights of, 157, 170; unwanted, 62, 155-156, 159-160
Children's Aid Society, 5
Chile, abortion in, 140
China, abortion in, 75
Chorley, Lord, 108
Christian Science Church, 148, 165
Cohen, Rabbi Armond F., 98
Coke, Sir Edward, 78
Colorado: abortion laws in, 3n., 4-5; location of abortionists in, 54
Colorado State Hospital, 36
Columbia-Presbyterian Medical Center, 148
Columbia University School of Social Work, 155

Commentaries (Blackstone), 78
Commonwealth v. Bangs, 86
Commonwealth v. Wheeler, 50, 152
Community Church, New York, 100
Comstock, Anthony, 90-91
Comstock law, 145
Concord *Monitor*, 113
Connecticut: abortion laws in, 86; sterilization laws in, 162
Contraceptive devices. *See* Abortifacients; Birth control
Copenhagen Mothers' Aid Society, 22
Cost: of abortions, 18, 43-44, 52-53, 55, 56, 57, 58, 64-66, 67, 123, 130, 133; of care for unwanted children, 61, 159-160; of Lippes loop, 138; of police protection for abortionists, 72; of sterilization, 161
Council of Ancyra, 77
Criminal Abortion in America (Storer), 1
Crow Indians, 23
Cushing, Richard Cardinal, 96, 165
Czechoslovakia: abortion laws in, 125; death rate from abortions in, 17; post-abortion study in, 19

Darrow, Clarence, 144
Deaths: from abortions, 3, 17, 47, 64, 65, 66, 70, 74, 121, 134, 140; danger of, and legal abortions, 98, 152; of fetus *vs.* mother, 96, 99, 100-101, 114; infant, 11, 83-84, 141; post-abortion, 19; from pregnancy, 40, 47; from self-induced abortion, 67-69; rates, 132, 140
de Bracton, Henry, 78
Decretum (Gratian), 78
Denmark, abortion in, 22, 117
Deutsch, Rabbi Elizer, 98
Dewey, Thomas E., 145
Diabetes, as ground for abortion, 36
Dickinson, Dr. Robert L., 121
Didache, The, 77
Dhanvanthi, Lady Rama Rau, 137, 139
Doctors. *See* Medical profession
Douglas, Justice William O., 172
Draper report, 80
Dutra, Dr. Frank, 69

Eastern Europe: abortion deaths in, 17; abortion method in, 18-19; birth rate in, 127-128; illegal abortions in, 129-130; legal abortions in, and U.S. citizens, 58
Economic problems and abortion, 139-140, 141, 157
Economist, 108
Edsall, Dr. John T., 160
Effraenatum (Pope Sixtus V), 79
Egypt, abortions in, 75
Eisenhower, President Dwight D., 80, 92
Ekblad, Dr. Martin, 21-22
Ellenborough act, 82
Ellenborough, Lord, 83, 84, 89
Embryo. *See* Fetus
Engels, F., 124
England. *See* Great Britain
Episcopal Church, 13, 114
Episcopal Theological School (Mass.), 97, 148
Episcopalian Church of the Holy Spirit, 95
Episcopalians, abortion and, 99
Ernst, Morris, 149, 154
Essay (Malthus), 83
Eugenic Protection Law, 132
Europe, Eastern. *See* Eastern Europe
Europe, thalidomide in, 11
Evans v. People, 89

Faiman, "Dr." Charles, 69
Family Planning Federation of Japan, 135
Federal Bureau of Investigation, 158
Fertility, post-abortion, 19, 20
Fetus: attitude toward, 164, Catholic, 80-81, 88, 89, 95, 96, in civil law, 88-89, Judaic, 97, 98; chemical destruction of, 174; life of *vs.* mother's life, 96, 99, 100-101, 114; quickening of, and abortion laws, 75, 78, 81, 86, 89, 112, 169
Feuer, Lewis S., 124
Finkbine, Robert, 10-11, 15, 16
Finkbine, Sherri, case of, 1, 10-16
Finland, abortion laws in, 118
Fletcher, Rev. Joseph F., 97, 100, 148
Florida, 53
Foster v. State, 88, 89
France, birth control in, 80, 82
Freehof, Rabbi Solomon B., 98
Fundamentalists, 93

Gaitskell, Baroness, 108
Galdston, Dr. Iago, 32
Gandhi, Mahatma, 137
Genne, Rev. William H., 101
German measles, 6, 30, 36-39, 98, 118, 149, 171
Germany, East, abortions in, 22, 58
Germany, West: abortion laws in, 58; thalidomide in, 11
Goldmark, Dr. Carl, Jr., 6, 26, 27, 144, 148
Coldwater, Barry, 113
Good Samaritan Hospital, Arizona, 16
Government Abortion Committee (Great Britain), 110
Grafton County Medical Society, 111
Grant, President Ulysses S., 91
Gratian, 78
Great Britain: abortion in, 16, 49-50, 75, 82-84, 103-110; thalidomide in, 107-108
Greek city states, abortions in, 76
Griswold v. Connecticut, 172
Grutman, Norman Roy, 170, 171
Guardian, 108
Guttmacher, Dr. Alan F., 5, 20, 40, 74, 178

Hall, Dr. Robert E., 148, 168
Hand, Judge Learned, 94, 144
Hanover *Gazette*, 113, 115
Hardin, Dr. Garrett, 23, 156, 159, 163, 169
Harper & Row, 148
Harper's, 159
Harrington, Rev. Donald S., 100
Hawaii, German measles in, 38
Health, mental, and abortion, 34-35, 98, 105-106, 145
Health, physical: abortion and, 6, 24, 39, 107, 111, 126, 132, 134, 141, 145, 170; and birth control, 153-154; and sterilization, 162
Heer, Dr. David M., 59
Hellman, Dr. Louis M., 28
Henrie, Dr. J. Bryan, 53
Henry Phipps Psychiatric Clinic, 21
Hippocrates, 76
Hippocratic oath, 76
Homiletic and Pastoral Review, The, 96
Hopkins, Dr. Percy, 145
Horder, Lord, 103, 104, 105
Hungary, abortions in, 17, 59, 125-127
Huser, Rev. Roger J., 78

Iceland, abortion laws in, 117
Illegitimacy, 59-62
Illes, Dr. Gyorgy, 126

Illinois, abortion laws in, 86, 146
Illustrations and Proofs of the Principle of Population (Place), 83
Incest, abortion laws and, 5, 6, 146
India: abortions in, 94, 136; birth control in, 136-140
Indiana University Institute of Sex Research, 2, 19
Infants: death of, 83-84, 141; defective, 12, 16, 37, 38, 171; as German measles carriers, 37; illegitimate, 59, 61; premature, and prior abortions, 20; and undetected maternal German measles, 36-38; *see also* Children
Iowa, abortion laws in, 41, 86
Israel, abortion laws in, 58

Japan: abortion in, 2, 23, 57, 94, 132-136; Eugenic Protection Law in, 132; and Finkbine, Sherri, case, 15
Jehovah's Witnesses, 149
Jenkins, Dr. Richard L., 34
Jews. *See* Judaism
Johnson, President Lyndon B., 92
Judaism, position of on abortion, 97-99, 101-102, 116, 147

Kadar, Janos, 126
Karolinksa Hospital, Sweden, 16
Keber, Ferdinand, 81
Kelsey, Dr. Francis, 11
Kentucky, abortion laws in, 86
Kenyon, Dorothy, 9
Khan, Mohammed Ayub, 139
Kheel, Theodore, 148
King George III (England), 82
King George VI (England), 103
Kinsey, Dr. Alfred C., 2
Kinsey report, 19-20, 23, 59, 73
Kinsolving, the Right Rev. Arthur, 13
Kinsolving, the Rev. Lester, 95, 100, 148
Kleegman, Dr. Sophia, 7
Klein, the Rev. Isaac, 98
Klein, Dr. Morton, 150
Knowlton, Dr. Charles, 90
Kolstad, Dr. Per, 19, 20, 120
Kopp, Dr. Marie E., 73
Koya, Dr. Yoshio, 135, 161
Kummer, Dr. Jerome M., 21, 22, 23

Laidlaw, Dr. Robert W., 21, 24
Lambeth Conference, 99
Lancet, 87, 106
Langer, Professor William L., 83, 84
Latin America, abortion and, 140-142
Law, Edward. *See* Ellenborough, Baron
Laws and Customs of England, The (de Bracton), 78
Lecky, William, 75
Lenin, V. I., 121
Leonardis, Frederick, 64
Levine, Dr. Lena, 25
Lex Julia et Papia, 77
Lidz, Dr. Theodore, 35
Lindahl, Dr. Jan, 19, 20
Lion, the Rev. Felix Danford, 163
Lombard, Peter, 81
London, Ephraim, 164, 169
London *Daily Express*, 103, 106
London *Daily Mail*, 108
London *Times*, 82
Los Angeles Obstetrical and Gyneocological Society, 147
Lyle, Dr. John, 111, 114
Lyons, Donald H., 114

McCardie, Justice, 103
Macnaghten, Justice, 105
Maginnis, Patricia A., 147
Maimonides, 97
Malleson, Dr. Joan, 106
Malthus, Thomas, 83
Manchester Ministerial Association, 114
Manchester *Union Leader*, 113
Mandy, Dr. Arthur J., 21, 27, 34
Margaret Sanger Research Bureau, 15, 74
Margolies, Rabbi Israel, 9, 13, 97, 99, 168, 175
Marriage: and abortion rate, 59; adjustment and premarital abortion, 20; Catholic attitude toward, 81; first year, and abortion, 23; privacy rights, and abortion, 173
Marx, Karl, 124
Maryland, abortion laws in, 3n., 49, 54
Masland, Dr. Richard L., 37
Massachusetts, abortion laws in, 3n., 86
Mataco Indians, 23
Means, Cyril, 149, 172
Medical Practice Act, 152
Medical profession: and abortions, 1, 26, 27, 40-42, 64, 92, 144-145, 152; attitude toward Dr. Timanus, 42; and Bourne case, 103; and German measles problem, 38-39; legal rights of, 149-154; and referrals to abortionists, 53-54, 55-56
Mehlan, Dr. K.-H., 20, 22
Mendoza, Dr. Ofelia, 141
Menninger, Dr. Karl, 156
Menninger Clinic (Kansas), 156
Mexico: abortion laws in, 57; unskilled abortionists in, 57
Miller, Elizabeth, 101
Mills v. Commonwealth, 88
Ministry of Welfare, Japan, 134
Mississippi, abortion laws in, 86
Mitchell v. Commissioner, 86
Model Penal Code, 163
Mohammedanism, attitude toward abortions of, 94
Monckton, Viscountess, 108
Montana, 55

National Catholic Welfare Conference, 160
National Catholic Welfare Council, 80
National Committee on Maternal Health, 2
National Council of Churches of Christ, 99, 101
National Council of Women, 108
National Foundation—March of Dimes, 37, 38
National Health Service (Great Britain), 109
National Institute of Neurological Diseases and Blindness, 37
National Institute of Public Health (Japan), 135
National League for Sex Education, 117
National Union of Townswomen's Guilds (Great Britain), 108
Nebraska, abortion laws in, 86-87
Negroes: and abortion, 29, 66; and birth control, 157; self-abortion rates of, 73
Nehru, 137
Neo-Malthusian and Birth Control Conference, 103
New Britain, 23
New Hampshire, abortion laws in, 33, 86, 111, 112-116
New Hampshire Council of Churches, 114
New Hampshire Medical Society, 112
New Jersey, abortion laws in, 3n., 86, 88
New Mexico, 57; abortion laws in, 3n.

New York, 52, 53, 55; abortion convictions, 70; abortion deaths, 3, 66; abortion laws, German measles incidence in, 37, 91; police extortion plot, 72-73
New York Civil Liberties Union, 169, 175
New York County Medical Society, 6, 26
New York Society for the Suppression of Vice, 90
New York Times, The, 64, 106, 142, 145, 157, 170
Niswander, Dr. Kenneth R., 150
Noonan, Professor John T., 78, 79
North Carolina, 55; sterilization laws in, 162
Norway: abortion laws in, 118; post-abortion study in, 19, 20

Ober, Dr. William, 25
Ober-Lader survey, 27, 28, 53, 70
Oettinger, Katherine, 156
Office of Economic Opportunity, 157, 159-160, 161
Ohrenstein, Senator Manfred, 146
O'Malley, Dr. Austin, 96
Oregon, abortion laws in, 3n., 26
Out of Wedlock (Young), 60
Overstreet, Dr. Edmund, 40

Pakistan, 139
Parker, Theodore, 175
Pennsylvania, abortion laws in, 3n., 88
People v. Ballard, 41, 152, 153
Peter, Gyorgy, 126
Phoenix, Arizona. See Finkbine, Sherri
Physicians. See Medical profession
Pilpel, Harriet, 148, 149, 154
Place, Francis, 83
Planned Parenthood Federation, 2, 5, 20, 92, 148, 159
Plato, 76
Plotkin, Rabbi Albert, 99
Poggioreale, Mary, 64
Poland, abortion laws in, 23, 58, 125
Police: and abortionists, 52, 57, 70-71, 72-73; and Bourne case, 105; and Dr. Timanus, 48
Pommerenke, Dr. W. T., 134
Popes: Gregory IX, 78; Gregory XIV, 79; Innocent III, 78; Pius IX, 79, 80, 81; Pius XI, 80, 95; Sixtus V, 79, 80
Population. See Birth control; Birth rate; Death rate
"Post-Abortion Psychiatric Illness—A Myth?" 21
Postgraduate Center for Mental Health, New York, 156
Pregnancy: early, and abortion laws, 75, 112-113; ectopic, 96; extra-marital, 60; false, 73-74; fear of, and morality, 163; and freedom of choice, 8-9; frequent, 134; late, and abortions, 18, 60; and mental health, 34-35; per cent aborted, 59; risk, 17-18, 98, 100; and socio-economic factors, 40; tests, 74, 104; unwanted, 5-7, 144; and undetected German measles, 37, 38
Presbyterian Eye, Ear, Nose and Throat Hospital, Baltimore, 46
Primeau, Bishop Ernest J., 113
Progressive League, 108
Protestantism, position on abortion of, 58, 93, 101-102, 114-116, 147
Puerto Rican Medical Association, 56
Puerto Ricans, abortion and, 29, 61, 66
Puerto Rico: abortions in, 55-57; German measles epidemic in, 38

Quickening. See Fetus, quickening of

Raible, the Rev. Peter S., 90, 100
Rape: and abortion laws, 4, 5-6, 34-35, 36, 147; and constitutional rights, 170, 172; and mental health, 105-106; and Model Penal Code, 146; number of cases of, 158-159; see also Bourne case
Rashbaum, Dr. William, 60
Rashi, 97
Rees, Dr. J. B., 105
Religion. See *under* various denominations, *i.e.,* Catholic Church; Judaism
Restell, Madame, 85, 91
Reston, James, 142
Revelle, Professor Roger, 139
Rex v. Bergmann and Ferguson, 106
Rex v. Bourne, 107
Rex v. Newton and Stungo, 106
Rhode Island, abortion laws in, 86
Ritzman, Dr. Thomas, 115
Roman Catholic Church. See Catholic Church; Catholics
Ronan, Charles N., 13, 14
Rosen, Dr. Harold, 2, 30, 32, 33, 34
Rosenbaum, Dr. Irving, 160
Rozada, Dr. Hector, 141
Rubella. See German measles
Robinson, Kenneth, 109
Robinson, Dr. William J., 70
Robison, Sophia M., 155

Sanders, Marion, 159
San Francisco *Chronicle,* 144, 147
Sanger, Margaret, 91-92, 133, 167
Sanger, William, 92
Scandinavia, abortion in, 17, 21-22
Schiff, Dr. Gilbert M., 37
Schwartz, Dr. Emmanuel K., 156
Scott v. McPheeters, 163
Segal, Dr. Sheldon, 174
Semashko, Professor N. A., 121
Sever, Dr. John L., 38
Severus, Septimius, 77
Sexual morality, 89, 90, 92, 93, 119
Shintoism, position on abortions of, 23, 94
Short, Renee, 109
Silkin, Lord, 109
Smith, Jacqueline, 64
Smith, Sir Sydney, 104
Social class: and abortion, 117, 141, 156, 157; and birth control, 83, 127, 130-131
Society for Humane Abortion, 147, 148
Solomon of Skola, 98
Soranus of Ephesus, 76
South Carolina, 55
Southern Medicine and Surgery, 4, 168
South Korea, 132
Soviet Union: abortions in, 18-19, 58, 59, 120-125; birth control in, 122, 123-124
Spectator, 108
Stalin, J., 122
Stanford University study, 32, 36, 38, 40
State Lutheran Church, Sweden, 100
State v. Buck, 152
State v. Cooper, 87
State v. Dunklebarger, 41, 152
State v. Powers, 151
State v. Siciliano, 88
St. Basil, canons of, 77
St. Bernardine of Siena, 81
St. Gregory, 81
Sterilization, 30-31, 161-162
Stewart v. Long Island College Hospital, 171
Stone, Dr. Abraham, 121, 122

Stone, Dr. Hannah M., 74
Storer, Dr. Horatio R., 1, 85
Suicide, 32-34, 98
Sutton, Percy, 146
Sweden, abortion in, 15-16, 19, 58, 117-120
Switzerland, abortion laws in, 58

Tallin, G. P. R., 107
Taussig, Dr. Frederick J., 7
Taussig, Helen B., 148
Tertullian, 77
Thalidomide, 10-16, 107-108
Therapeutic Abortion (Rosen), 2
Thiersch, Dr. J. B., 174
Third Institute (Coke), 78
Tietze, Dr. Christopher, 2, 17, 19, 123
Timanus, Dr. G. Loutrell, 42-51
Traut, Dr. Herbert F., 40
Trow, Caroline. *See* Restell, Madame
Truman, President Harry S, 92

Unitarian Church, Palo Alto, Calif., 163
Unitarian-Universalists, 100
United Church of Canada, 99
United Presbyterian Church, 99
United States: abortion in, 19, 54-55, 75, 80-84, 88, 94; birth control in, 91-92; German measles in, 37, 38
United States Children's Bureau, 156
U.S. Food and Drug Administration, 11, 69
U.S. Social Security Administration, 61

U.S. v. One Package, 153, 154
Uruguay, abortion rate in, 141
Utah, sterilization laws in, 162
Uziel, Rabbi Ben Zion, 98

Venezuela, birth rate in, 139-140
Vermont, abortion laws in, 86
Virginia, sterilization laws in, 162
Volstead Act, 93

Warren, Chief Justice Earl, 172
Washington, 53, 70
Washington, D.C., abortion in, 3n., 54
Weingand, Alvin, 157
Weiss, Dr. Robert J., 111
Wells, H. G., 104
West Germany. *See* Germany, West
Williams, Glanville, 88, 92, 107, 110
Williams v. State, 170
Willis, Lord, 108
Wilmon, Gyula, 126
Wisconsin, abortion laws in, 88
Women's Co-operative Guilds, 104
World Health Organization, 137, 154
World Telegram and Sun, 73
Wrong, Dennis H., 140

Young, Leontine, 60
Yugoslavia, abortion in, 12, 17

Zawadzki, Edward, 65